THE NEW HUMAN REVOLUTION

VOLUME 1

DAISAKU IKEDA

ILLUSTRATIONS BY
KENICHIRO UCHIDA

World Tribune
—Press—

Published by World Tribune Press
606 Wilshire Boulevard,
Santa Monica, California 90401

Complete Set   ISBN 978-0-915678-32-7
Volume 1   ISBN 978-0-915678-33-4

20 19 18 17 16 15 14 13 12

Contents

Editor's Note

The citation most commonly used in this book has been abbreviated as follows:

◆ WND-1 refers to *The Writings of Nichiren Daishonin*, vol. 1 (Tokyo: Soka Gakkai, 1999).

Introduction

*O*utside, the fog stole silently, gently embracing the green trees and plants. Amid this white veil, I began work on the manuscript of *The New Human Revolution*, as I reminisced about my revered mentor, Josei Toda.

This scene took place on August 6, this year, at the Nagano Training Center in Karuizawa, Japan. Karuizawa is the place where, eight months before my mentor's death, I resolved to write *The Human Revolution* to transmit, without error, a record of President Toda's life and spirit for future generations. It is a place rich with boundless memories of the vow shared by mentor and disciple. This day, August 6, was also the forty-eighth anniversary of the atomic bombing of Hiroshima.

President Toda announced his Declaration for the Abolition of Nuclear Weapons on September 8, 1957, entrusting his youthful disciples with the spread of its ideals throughout the world as part of his legacy.

My mentor strained to hear the faint cries of the silent masses of the world, who suffer endlessly amid warfare and tyranny. Often he would say, "I want to rid the world of misery." This was his dream and his determination.

Mentor and disciple are inseparable. Because they are so united, I, too, embrace my mentor's heart as I travel the world opening the way for a great river of peace and happiness. A river's grandeur attests to the greatness of its source. What inspired me to write *The New Human Revolution* series as a continuation of *The Human Revolution* was my thought that the extent to which kosen-rufu has unfolded since my mentor's passing serves as genuine proof of his greatness. In addition, to transmit my mentor's spirit for eternity, I felt that

I must leave a record of the path his disciples, who inherited his legacy, have followed.

To do so, however, I could not avoid writing about myself, a fact that caused me great hesitation. Moreover, a mountain of issues and problems must be resolved before lasting peace, based upon global kosen-rufu, becomes a reality. With this in mind, I was also concerned whether I could make enough time to write. I cannot deny that my frame of mind at the time was to want to ask someone else, if at all possible, to write the new series.

However, even if there was someone I could ask to document my travels and encounters, that person would be unable to record what was in my heart and mind at the time. There is also a genuine aspect of the Soka Gakkai's history of which only I am aware. In addition, I have received strong requests from the *Seikyo Shimbun* to publish *The New Human Revolution* series. Thus, although I had a number of concerns, I resolved to pick up my pen once again and begin writing.

The New Human Revolution opens on October 2, 1960, the day that Shin'ichi Yamamoto, having succeeded Josei Toda as third president, embarks on a historic journey for peace that will take him to three nations—the United States, Canada and Brazil. The work will go on to portray the Soka Renaissance —the triumph of ordinary people as they illuminate the world with the humanism of Nichiren Daishonin's Buddhism and open a new page in the history of humankind.

Mahatma Gandhi proclaimed that the "power of the spirit" is stronger than any atomic bomb. To transform this century of war into a century of peace, we must cultivate the limitless inherent power of human life. This is the "human revolution," and it will be the theme that flows consistently throughout the series.

Just as before, I will be giving fictitious names to the characters that appear in the story. At times, several real individuals will be combined into a single character and at other times, real individuals will be portrayed as multiple characters. For this reason, each character in the story will not necessarily accord with a single real individual. I hope, therefore, that readers will always view the characters in the narrative as fictional.

I expect *The New Human Revolution* to comprise thirty volumes by the time it is completed. It will certainly be a supreme challenge to finish writing it within my lifetime.

Nevertheless, only by fulfilling our mission in this life do we truly live. Goethe, Hugo and Tolstoy were all still working vigorously in their 80s, continuing to pen their convictions. I am 65 and still young.

I have taken writing *The New Human Revolution* as my life's work. In it, I am determined to continue to record, to the limits of my ability, the diamondlike, genuine path of mentor and disciple, and depict the grand portrait of glory created by the precious children of the Buddha as they have advanced with the dream of worldwide kosen-rufu, just as Nichiren Daishonin taught.

Truth and falsehood, good and evil, winners and losers —all will be rigorously depicted. I cannot help thinking that President Toda is steadfastly watching me. I only ask, from the bottom of my heart, for the warm support of all of you, the readers.

Daisaku Ikeda
November 1993

Sunrise

NOTHING is more precious than peace. Nothing brings more happiness. Peace is the most basic starting point for the advancement of humankind.

October 2, 1960. Shin'ichi Yamamoto was 32 years old. With a passionate resolve for peace burning in his heart, he set out on a worldwide journey. Only five months had passed since he was inaugurated as the third president of the Soka Gakkai.

On this day, Tokyo was blessed with crystal-clear skies and fresh autumn air. Members had been converging on Tokyo's Haneda International Airport since early that morning, and by around 9:30 the observation deck was packed with people. They had come to see their president, Shin'ichi Yamamoto, off on his first visit overseas.

At 10:10, a stir ran through the observation deck as the six travelers, including Shin'ichi, emerged from the terminal building. Besides Shin'ichi, the party included Vice General Director Kiyoshi Jujo, Director Yukio Ishikawa, Study Department Chief Chuhei Yamadaira, Youth Division Chief Eisuke Akizuki and Women's Division Chief Katsu Kiyohara.

Before boarding the plane, the travelers lined up, removed the hats they were wearing and waved them at the crowd. Joyous cheers and applause erupted into the clear sky.

The plane, Japan Airlines Flight 800, dubbed *Fuji*, took off with a thunderous roar at 10:40 A.M. on a direct course for Honolulu, Hawaii. *Fuji* was Japan's first large-scale passenger jet. It had been commissioned to fly only that August 12.

Below them, Shin'ichi could see the ocean off his beloved Omori, the town in which he was born and raised. Countless silver waves sparkled in the sunlight reflecting off the ocean's surface, as if to congratulate Shin'ichi and bid him bon voyage on his journey.

Shin'ichi quietly placed his hand on his chest. In the inner breast pocket of his coat, he carried a photograph of his mentor, Josei Toda. He would never forget the time that Toda, ill in bed at the head temple just prior to his death, told him he had dreamt he had gone to Mexico.

Toda had said to him: "They were all waiting. Everyone was waiting. They were all seeking Nichiren Daishonin's Buddhism. I want to go—to travel the world on a journey for kosen-rufu.

"Shin'ichi, the world is your challenge; it is your true stage. It is a vast world."

ON that day, without speaking, Shin'ichi had firmly grasped the hand Toda extended him from under the covers of his futon. Toda gazed steadily at Shin'ichi's face and then spoke with all the energy he could muster.

"Shin'ichi, you must live! You must live as long as you can and travel the globe!"

Toda's eyes glistened brilliantly.

Shin'ichi had engraved these words in his heart as Toda's will for the future. On behalf of his departed mentor, the disciple was now taking his first step toward world kosen-rufu. When he thought of this, Shin'ichi felt a surge of passionate emotion rise within him.

Shin'ichi had chosen the second day of October as his departure date for this first overseas tour because Toda's passing [on April 2, 1958] is commemorated on the second day of each month. He was acutely aware of the deep import behind Toda's desire that he should travel the globe.

Fifteen years had passed since the end of World War II, yet humanity's hopes for peace still remained in vain. The East and West had become mired in a cold war with no end in sight. At the same time, there was a dramatic escalation in the nuclear arms race among the major nations of the Eastern and Western blocs led, respectively, by the Soviet Union and the United States. Conflict also continued to rage in Africa as struggles for independence against colonial rule erupted in each area, while racial and ethnic strife flared in various parts of the globe.

Everywhere people were quailing under the threat of nuclear holocaust, living in fear amid civil strife or suffering from discrimination, cruelty, poverty and disease. Yet, all surely cherished the hope of witnessing a dawn of peace and happiness.

Toda's words to Shin'ichi had been nothing but an urgent appeal for the happiness of humanity by a Buddhist leader who keenly discerned the state of the world.

Happiness is life's goal. Peace is what all people desire. The course of human history must move toward peace and happiness.

It is the nature of the human being to search for a firm guiding principle that will lead in this direction. Science, politics, society and religion, too, must focus on this crucial point.

Shin'ichi thought to himself: "Nichiren Daishonin regarded the sufferings of humankind as his own and held aloft the banner of *rissho ankoku*—the desire to establish a peaceful society based upon his Buddhism. He clearly revealed the guiding principle that leads humanity to peace and happiness.

"Nichiren Daishonin wrote, 'Can there be any doubt that...the great pure Law of the Lotus Sutra will be spread far and wide throughout Japan and all the other countries of Jambudvipa?' (WND-I, 550. *See also* 976–77). The Daishonin predicted the worldwide spread of his Buddhism and entrusted his disciples of future generations with the realization of this goal."

Thirty-two years after his birth into this world, Shin'ichi had now taken on the accomplishment of global kosen-rufu as his life's mission and was about to open the door to this great task that lay before him. The thought made his heart leap with excitement.

NICHIREN Daishonin's Buddhism reveals that all human beings are endowed equally with the Buddha nature and that each individual is an entity of *ichinen sanzen*. It also elucidates the means by which human beings can cast off the shackles that bind them.

The Daishonin's Buddhism, which espouses the dignity, equality and freedom of human beings, is truly a world religion dedicated to the realization of peace for all humanity. Illuminating the way toward the twenty-first century, it casts a great universal light of happiness over the world.

Nevertheless, this Buddhism of Nichiren Daishonin had yet to cross the ocean to the rest of the world. In fact, no Buddhism from Japan had ever spread widely overseas. With the increase of Japanese emigration that began in Japan's Meiji era (1868–1912), some forms of Japanese Buddhism, such as Jodo Shinshu (True Pure Land school), did undertake propagation activities overseas, spreading in such places as Hawaii, the west coast of the United States, and Brazil. However, these religions were disseminated only among people of Japanese ancestry and never transcended the framework of the ethnic religion called Japanese Buddhism.

The Buddhist scholar Daisetsu (D.T.) Suzuki traveled to America and elsewhere to introduce Buddhist thought to the West, but his efforts created little more than a Zen fad among some intellectuals in Europe and the United States.

It was against this backdrop that Shin'ichi Yamamoto made his first overseas visit—a visit that would open the way for the movement of today's Soka Gakkai International (SGI). Aimed at creating a record of human revitalization, the SGI shines a light of humanism on the world's suffering people. Shin'ichi's trip signaled the start of a new, unprecedented stage in the annals of Buddhism.

Strangely enough, that year, 1960, also marked exactly 700 years since Nichiren Daishonin wrote his treatise the "Rissho Ankoku Ron" (On Establishing the Correct Teaching for the Peace of the Land), thus sparking the initial flame toward the realization of lasting peace. It was a truly mysterious coincidence of timing.

Shin'ichi's trip would take him to nine cities in three countries, beginning with Honolulu, then moving on to San Francisco, Seattle, Chicago, Toronto (Canada), New York, Washington, D.C., São Paulo (Brazil), and finally to Los Angeles. He was scheduled to return to Japan on October 25.

One purpose of the trip was to offer encouragement and guidance in faith to the Soka Gakkai members who were beginning to appear in these areas. Another objective was to purchase building materials for the Grand Reception Hall (Dai-Kyakuden), which the Soka Gakkai would build as a donation to the head temple.

At the Headquarters general meeting in which he was inaugurated as the third president of the Soka Gakkai, Shin'ichi had announced the construction of the Grand Reception Hall as one of the goals he wished to complete before the seventh memorial service for his departed mentor, Josei Toda. The structure was to be built and furnished with the finest materials from around the world.

Yet another aim of the trip was to witness firsthand the conditions overseas, with an eye toward shaping plans for the future realization of kosen-rufu.

*S*HIN'ICHI Yamamoto removed the picture of Josei Toda from the inside pocket of his coat and fixed his eyes upon it. He thought how happy Toda would have been if he could have accompanied him on this journey.

Shin'ichi recalled how Toda had often said:

> Japan lost the war, but it was the abolishment of the Peace Preservation Law [1] under MacArthur's Allied Occupation policy that brought true religious freedom to Japan. This ushered in the time for kosen-rufu. MacArthur functioned as a protective force, a *shoten zenjin*. He functioned as a Bonten or Taishaku. [2] I want to go to America to repay this debt of gratitude.

Toda was surprisingly well versed not only in America's history, but also in that country's politics, economy, literature and philosophy. He often related his view of the lives of such American luminaries as Lincoln, Washington, Emerson and Franklin. His analysis of these and other great people was colorful and vivid, yet penetrating and deep. Listening to him speak, a clear image of the person would emerge, as if he or she were standing before one's very eyes.

Nevertheless, Toda had died at the age of 58 without ever setting foot outside of Japan. Biting his lip, Shin'ichi vowed: "I will stand upon the soil of America on Sensei's behalf. I will definitely make history anew."

Seven hours after taking off from Tokyo's Haneda Airport for Hawaii, the jetliner began its gradual descent. Shin'ichi's watch, which he had set to local Hawaiian time, read 10:30 P.M., October 1. Hawaii was nineteen hours behind Japan. Eventually, the plane entered its final approach for landing. Looking out the window, Shin'ichi saw lights glimmering in the distance like so many jewels scattered beneath the night sky. They were the city lights of Honolulu.

The jetliner *Fuji* landed at Honolulu Airport a little after 11:00 P.M., almost one hour behind schedule. Though it was late at night, the air outside was hot. Hawaii was indeed a land of perpetual summer.

Sweat soon began to appear on the brows of Shin'ichi and his companions, who were dressed for autumn in coats and hats. A long line had formed at the airport immigration counter. As they waited to conclude their immigration procedure, Shin'ichi asked Kiyoshi Jujo, "Mr. Jujo, is your English really okay?"

Before their departure, Jujo had said he was confident about his English.

"Yes," Jujo answered proudly, "I have no problem, so long as it's only daily conversation. English was strictly drilled into me while I was in the Naval Academy."

SHIN'ICHI and his traveling companions had waited about thirty minutes before reaching the immigration counter. As their turn approached, Kiyoshi Jujo said to Shin'ichi: "Sensei, I will go through the immigration procedure ahead of you. After that, I'll interpret for you." Eventually, Jujo's turn arrived. He showed his passport to the official at the counter, who then asked him a question in English. Jujo stood there momentarily with a bewildered look. He then said, "*Wan-su mo-ah pu-ree-zu*" (Once more, please). Jujo repeated the phrase again and again. The official also repeated his question several times but seemed to conclude that the exchange was going nowhere. He turned up his hands and shook his head in a gesture of futility.

A bystander, perhaps a travel agent, who seemed unable to stand by and watch any longer, came over to interpret. Thus the group was somehow freed from their dilemma.

"My gosh, Hawaiian English certainly is hard to follow," said Jujo with a strained smile, scratching his head.

Shin'ichi keenly sensed how important it would be to foster competent interpreters for the full-fledged development of worldwide kosen-rufu.

By the time they got through customs, picked up their bags and headed for the arrival area, it was already after midnight on October 2.

Arrangements had been made for a young men's division member, Nagayasu Masaki, to meet them at the airport. Masaki had come to America to study in May three years before and would be acting as a guide and interpreter for Shin'ichi and the others during their trip.

"The plane was late. Masaki must be tired of waiting," Shin'ichi said to Jujo with some concern.

"Yes, he said he would give us a grand welcome in Hawaii with a large group of fellow members," Jujo replied.

Entering the arrival area, they found it bustling with people, but there was no sign of Masaki. They set their bags down in a corner and waited.

Their first glimpse of Honolulu Airport presented them with many curious and unfamiliar sights. There were young girls dressed in Hawaiian muumuus, carrying brightly colored leis. An older man with gray hair was wearing a red aloha shirt. There was also a group of Japanese men looking neat and proper in neckties.

As the arriving passengers found their waiting friends and loved ones, smiles broke out all around, hugs were exchanged, and one group after another left the airport.

ASAKI'S not here," said Kiyoshi Jujo anxiously to Eisuke Akizuki. "He was supposed to be here to meet us."

"Yes, that's right. It's strange."

The crowd thinned as the other passengers who had arrived with them filtered out of the arrival area.

"It's terrible to be left stranded in a place like this!" the usually confident Katsu Kiyohara said helplessly. "We don't know the first thing about this place."

Just then, a slightly built young man dressed in an aloha shirt, who had been watching them from one corner of the arrival lobby, approached.

"President Yamamoto, of the Soka Gakkai?" He asked somewhat hesitantly.

Shin'ichi Yamamoto recognized the young man's face.

"Yes. Thank you for coming."

With this, the youth relaxed into an open and friendly smile.

"I'm Tony Harada, a member of the young men's division."

"I know you," said Shin'ichi. "We've met once before."

"That's right, I met you at the Soka Gakkai Headquarters before I left for Hawaii," said Harada.

The young Harada placed a lei he had prepared for the occasion around Shin'ichi's neck and shook his hand.

Harada's unexpected welcome brought relieved looks to the travelers' faces. But as soon as he had presented everyone with a lei, Harada said, "Well, I'll be going now."

As Harada was preparing to leave, Shin'ichi said, "Thank you. You're going already?"

"Yes, now that I have welcomed you, I'll be going."

"Are there any others?" Shin'ichi inquired.

"Gee, I don't know. I'm not staying here on Oahu; I live on the island of Hawaii. I received a letter from Japan saying that you would be coming to Honolulu, so I took the plane here."

"I see. Do you have a place to stay?" Shin'ichi asked.

"Thank you, yes. I'm staying with my aunt. Please don't worry about me. Good-bye."

Harada, totally oblivious to the group's predicament, was worried that he would be in the way if he stayed too long.

"Well, in that case, why don't we meet again tomorrow morning?" said Shin'ichi. "I'll be staying at the Kaimana Hotel."

"Yes, sir!" Harada replied cheerfully as he walked off at a brisk pace, the travelers gazing after him in astonishment. With Harada gone, they were again swept by a sense of helplessness.

*T*HE lights in the airport arrival lobby were being gradually dimmed as the area grew steadily quieter and more deserted.

"Where on earth is Masaki?" blurted out the short-tempered Yukio Ishikawa, his voice full of anger.

"Sensei, I'll go out to look for him," Kiyoshi Jujo offered. "Akizuki, I'll have a look outside; why don't you look for him inside?" With this, Jujo headed off with Akizuki to search for Masaki.

Akizuki returned after a short time, reporting that he had not seen Masaki. Jujo followed a few moments later.

"I couldn't find Masaki, Sensei, but there's a car from the Kaimana Hotel waiting outside. It's already very late; why don't we take it to the hotel?" Everyone agreed with Jujo's suggestion and left by car for the hotel.

The Kaimana Hotel was a modest three-story structure right at the end of Waikiki Beach. It was almost 2:00 A.M. by the time they arrived there. After placing their bags in their respective rooms, they all eventually converged on Shin'ichi's room, as if by some unconscious impulse.

It had been quite a while since they had eaten dinner on the plane, and each of them was hungry and looked utterly exhausted.

"I sure am hungry," said Shin'ichi, voicing what was on everyone's mind. But there wasn't a single shop near the hotel, which was quite a distance from the main shopping and business district. Also, perhaps due to the late hour, room service was not available.

Shin'ichi took out some *nori* (dried seaweed) that he had brought from Japan and divided it among them. Everyone looked dejected. With no one to greet them on their first trip overseas, and nothing but dried seaweed to stave off their hunger, they felt forlorn and abandoned.

Sensing this, Shin'ichi smiled cheerfully and said, "Our eating *nori* together like this will be our precious memory in the future. Isn't it exciting to think that this night will remain in the history of our lives as part of the opening act of a grand drama?"

Despite Shin'ichi's words, however, none of them could truly feel any sense of excitement. Nevertheless, just being around Shin'ichi and his confident smile seemed to erase their uneasiness. Outside the hotel window lingered the deep darkness of predawn.

*A*ROUND the time that Shin'ichi and the others were arriving at the Kaimana Hotel, Nagayasu Masaki was at an inn that was run by a Japanese-American family. Having arrived in Honolulu from his home in Washington, D.C., four days earlier, he had been

contacting and encouraging the small number of members who lived scattered throughout the area.

Originally, Masaki had received clear information that Shin'ichi and his party would be arriving at 10:00 P.M. on October 1. This arrival time was also reported in the *Seikyo Shimbun*, which published a schedule of President Yamamoto's planned overseas visit.

From early in the morning of October 1, the day Shin'ichi was to arrive, Masaki set out to visit the homes of about twenty members on the island to reconfirm with them the president's scheduled arrival that evening. Accompanying him were Yumiko Nagata, a young woman who had served as a young women's division unit chief in Japan, and was now playing a central role in contacting the Hawaiian members, and one member of the young men's division.

In the evening, after they had finished their rounds, the two young men escorted Nagata back to her apartment. There she found an airmail letter from Japan. It was from the Overseas Affairs Section of the Soka Gakkai Headquarters. She quickly opened the envelope and found the following message:

"We hasten to inform you of a sudden change in schedule. The originally scheduled arrival in Honolulu at 10:00 P.M. on October 1 has been changed to 7:55 A.M. on October 2. The flight number will be JAL 800, the same as before. Please convey this information to all concerned."

The three were stunned by the news. They hurriedly left the apartment, jumped into the car and began to call on the members at home once again. Besides informing each person of the change in the arrival schedule, they also asked everyone to meet at the airport at 6:00 A.M. the following morning.

It was around 10:00 P.M. by the time they finished making their rounds to the members' homes. On the way back, they stopped the car at Tantalus Hill, overlooking the city of Honolulu. As they stood atop the hill, a beautiful panorama of city lights unfolded beneath their eyes. Off to their right lay the airport.

"Tomorrow, we'll be greeting President Yamamoto at that airport," said Masaki, his voice trembling slightly with excitement.

"Sensei is coming to Hawaii—it's just like a dream!" exclaimed Nagata. "Tomorrow will be a fresh start for Hawaii." There was elation in her voice as well.

The thought of welcoming President Shin'ichi Yamamoto to Hawaii dispelled the fatigue they had accumulated throughout the day while rushing from one member's home to another. The night breeze felt good on their faces, which were moist with perspiration. Just around that very time, however, Shin'ichi's plane was preparing to land at the Honolulu airport.

RETURNING to the inn where he was staying, Masaki immediately began to chant daimoku. "Come morning," he thought, "we will welcome President Yamamoto to the United States. Sensei will take his first step toward worldwide kosen-rufu here in Hawaii. I must do my utmost to ensure that his overseas guidance trip is a success."

Masaki put even more power into his chanting of daimoku. While chanting, he recalled each of the bitter struggles he had been through since coming to America as a foreign student in May three years before.

Five days after leaving Japan and arriving in Los Angeles —in America, the land of his dreams—he had received word that his father had died. He was filled with grief. Four days later, in the morning, he received a letter of encouragement from Shin'ichi, which he read over and over.

Shin'ichi wrote: "My dear Masaki. How sad you must be; how grief-stricken! Yet, I am praying that you will be true to yourself as you live up to your mission, overcome every sadness and difficulty you face, and grow to become a courageous leader."

As Masaki read the letter, his tears flowed. They were not tears of grief, however, but tears of deep passion that brought forth a fresh surge of determination. Masaki arose resolutely from the realm of suffering and embarked boldly on a course of arduous study.

To earn money for tuition, he held down various part-time jobs, including working as an attendant at a bowling alley and as a dishwasher. At the same time, he applied himself earnestly to his studies.

Then, one year later, he heard the news that Josei Toda, the second Soka Gakkai president, had died. To Masaki, who was fighting a lone battle in a foreign country, Toda's death was tantamount to losing his spiritual pillar. On that occasion, too, it was another letter of encouragement from Shin'ichi that roused him from the depths of suffering.

That time, Shin'ichi had written: "Don't forget your true mission. Don't forget to develop into a world leader."

Shin'ichi's fervent appeal enabled him to realize that the time had come for Toda's disciples to stand up and begin to strive in earnest for kosen-rufu.

Two years later, on May 3, 1960, Shin'ichi Yamamoto became the third president of the Soka Gakkai. Masaki and the other members in the United States were overjoyed at the news.

Shortly thereafter, Masaki received an airmail letter from Shin'ichi's wife, Mineko, saying that the new president and a few others were planning to visit America in the near future. The letter also contained a message from Shin'ichi, asking if it would be possible for Masaki to return to Japan for a while to take part in the planning for the visit.

From the way the message was worded, it was obvious that Shin'ichi was concerned over the financial burden such a trip to Japan might impose on Masaki.

Masaki was delighted and, at the same time, grateful.

*I*N early September, Nagayasu Masaki ebulliently set foot upon the soil of his beloved Japan. His heart resounded with anticipation when he thought of meeting again, after so long, President Yamamoto, who had been a constant source of encouragement for him.

Trying to control his excitement, he headed directly for the Soka Gakkai Headquarters from the airport.

"I've just returned," he said in high spirits when he saw Shin'ichi Yamamoto at the Headquarters.

"Hi, welcome back!" said Shin'ichi.

The moment he heard Shin'ichi's warm and familiar voice, Masaki's eyes filled with tears.

To the red-eyed Masaki, Shin'ichi said, "I thought you would grow bigger when you went to America, but instead you seem to have shrunk."

The jacket Masaki was wearing was far too big for him, making his already small frame look even smaller. Masaki looked down at his sleeves, which covered his hands except for his fingers, and said bashfully, "Actually, I borrowed this jacket from my brother-in-law who lives in America. It's a little too big."

With only part-time jobs to sustain him, Masaki could not afford to buy himself a new suit.

"I see," said Shin'ichi. "It must be hard for you to make ends meet. Were you able to buy a gift or souvenir for your mother?"

"Yes, I bought her a suit."

"You don't have a suit for yourself, but you bought clothes for your mother? How admirable! Well, then, I'll buy you a suit."

As a gift, Shin'ichi bought Masaki a new suit. The fit was perfect, and the color, too, became him. Masaki's delight and appreciation soared all the more.

The planning for the first overseas guidance tour began amid an atmosphere of joy. Masaki told everything he knew about conditions in America to Yasushi Muto and the other staff of the newly established Overseas Affairs Section at the Soka Gakkai Headquarters and conferred with them in detail about the schedule.

The majority of the Soka Gakkai members living in America were women, so Masaki proposed that a women's division leader be included in the visiting party.

Masaki stayed in Japan for about ten days and, upon returning to the United States, busied himself preparing to receive the president and his party. Then he went to Honolulu to await the arrival of Shin'ichi and the others.

*A*FTER visiting the members to inform them of the change in schedule, Nagayasu Masaki retired to his room at the inn for the night. Before 5:00 the next morning, he was up again and off to the airport. Around dawn, the members began to arrive at the airport a few at a time. Each carried a lei and wore a shiny, round Soka Gakkai lapel pin in the shape of a flying crane.

More than twenty members had gathered by the agreed-upon time of 6:00 A.M. Most were meeting one another for the first time, and all were heartened to learn that there were so many friends of kosen-rufu living in Hawaii.

As they introduced themselves, conversations sprang up among them. Some took photographs to commemorate the occasion. Though 7:00 A.M. came and went, the lights had still not come on at the airline service counters, and no clerks or airline employees could be seen. Masaki started to grow more and more anxious.

A clerk finally appeared at the Pan American Airlines counter, and Masaki inquired in English about JAL Flight 800, which was scheduled to arrive at 7:55 A.M.

With a puzzled expression, the clerk replied that no flights were scheduled to arrive at that time, but that if Masaki was referring to JAL 800, it had already arrived the night before. Masaki was aghast; he felt the blood drain from his face.

He asked Yumiko Nagata to show him again the airmail letter she had received from Japan the day before. It distinctly stated the arrival time as 7:55 on the morning of October 2.

"How could such a thing happen?" thought Masaki.

If the president and his party had already arrived, all he could do now was phone their hotel. But he realized that he had not been told where they would be staying.

Masaki found a phone book and began to call all the major hotels in the area. Each time, however, he was told that there were no guests registered under the names he mentioned.

Hiroto Hirata, a second-generation Japanese-American who had a thorough knowledge of Hawaii, then spoke up.

"There's a small hotel called the Kaimana, which is frequently used by Japanese visitors," he began. "I really don't think the president would be staying there, but why don't we check just to make sure?"

Hirata looked up the phone number, called the hotel, and learned that the president and his party were indeed staying there.

With that, everyone piled into several cars and headed for the Kaimana Hotel.

When Masaki thought of how President Yamamoto and the others must have felt, arriving in Hawaii with no one to greet them, he wanted to cry, yet more than that, he was numb with shock.

*T*HE emerald ocean glowed through the morning mist that spread across the horizon as silver waves lapped quietly on the white sand.

Early that morning, Shin'ichi Yamamoto stepped outside alone. There was a patio that looked out over the ocean, which was directly behind the hotel.

Shin'ichi had not been able to sleep much that night. He had gone to bed at around 3:00 A.M., but woke up after dozing off for only an hour or two. This was not only because of the time difference. Nagayasu Masaki, who had been scheduled to meet them, had not shown up, and Shin'ichi could not help worrying about his well-being.

With the first light of dawn outside his window, Shin'ichi got up and did gongyo, chanting daimoku for Masaki's safety. Filled also with a heartfelt desire to realize kosen-rufu in Hawaii, Shin'ichi prayed earnestly, as if to permeate the entire island with his daimoku. He then went out to take a walk along the beach. The endless succession of white-crested waves quietly breaking on the shoreline painted a poetic scene.

Turning to look back, he saw a vast expanse of palm trees, beyond which rose the summit of Diamond Head, bathed in the golden light of the morning sun. Shin'ichi recalled the day in the summer of 1954, six years earlier, when he had stood with his mentor, Josei Toda, on the beach of Toda's childhood home of Atsuta Village.

As they watched the brilliant red sun set over the Sea of Japan, Toda had said: "Shin'ichi, I will build a solid foundation for kosen-rufu in Japan, but you will pave the way for kosen-rufu throughout the world. I will create the blueprint; you will make it a reality."

Shin'ichi had engraved these words in the depths of his life. Since that day, he racked his brains over how to open the way for the worldwide spread of Nichiren Daishonin's Buddhism.

Needless to say, the propagation of Buddhism begins with heart-to-heart exchange and mutual understanding among individuals. However, to allow people outside of Japan, who had no relationship to Nichiren Daishonin's Buddhism, to correctly understand it and the Soka Gakkai, Shin'ichi thought that written materials would be necessary to coherently introduce the organization's philosophy and movement.

After his inauguration as president, he immediately set about producing an introductory English-language publication for an overseas audience. Concrete plans toward this end were implemented under the supervision of Youth Division Chief Eisuke Akizuki, who was also the managing editor of the *Seikyo Shimbun*, and Joji Kanda, who taught English at a university.

At first, they had planned to publish translated excerpts from the Soka Gakkai's *Shakubuku Kyoten* (Propagation Handbook), but when they considered the obvious differences between Japan and other countries—in culture and local custom, not to mention in people's ways of thinking—they found it necessary to begin writing suitable material from scratch.

*T*HE book that would introduce the Soka Gakkai to the English-speaking world was being drafted first in Japanese. Upon the completion of that text, an exam was held in mid-July to select translators from among members who had ability in English. The thirty-one people who took the exam ranged from gray-haired senior citizens to young students. From among them eight were selected. However, these eight were still a long way from being experienced translators.

The translation of this introductory book got under way toward the end of July. The most difficult challenge for the translation team was how to render certain Buddhist terminology into English. There were no precedents for terms like *kuon ganjo* (time without beginning, or the infinite past), *ichinen sanzen* (a single life-moment possesses 3,000 realms), or *jikkai gogu* (the mutual possession of the Ten Worlds) in any English dictionary. Yet these terms needed to be translated in a way that would allow those with no prior knowledge of Buddhism to understand them.

Members of the group had given up their summer vacations and thrown themselves feverishly into the task of translation, pondering seriously over which words to use. As a result of their tireless effort, the printing of the introductory book, titled *The Soka Gakkai*, was finished just before Shin'ichi Yamamoto and the others were to depart on their overseas journey.

In mid-July, Shin'ichi had also established the Overseas Affairs Section within the Soka Gakkai Headquarters. Its purpose was to serve as a liaison center to coordinate and facilitate communications among the growing number of members who lived overseas.

Behind the scenes, Shin'ichi had been making steady efforts to open the way for the dawn of worldwide kosen-rufu. Now, as he stood alone on the quiet beach of Waikiki, he ruminated deeply over the fact that he was now taking the first step toward global propagation.

These thoughts, however, were soon replaced by concern. Nagayasu Masaki's whereabouts weighed most heavily on his mind. Because Masaki had not been heard from at all, it was possible that he might have met with an accident.

Or perhaps some grave personal matter had arisen. Yet, why had not only Masaki but also the young women's division member Yumiko Nagata failed to appear?

Shin'ichi was deeply worried. If Masaki remained missing, he would also have to consider what to do about finding a guide and interpreter for the group. Shin'ichi returned to his room and waited for the leaders who were accompanying him to awaken.

At around 8:30, Shin'ichi and his companions had breakfast together on the hotel patio. It was a simple menu of coffee, toast and eggs, but the ocean view made their dining a pleasure.

Just then, they heard a flurry of footsteps. About thirty people were running straight for the patio area.

"Sensei!" a voice cried out from the head of the approaching group. It was Nagayasu Masaki.

NAGAYASU Masaki came running up, out of breath. Close at his side was Yumiko Nagata. "Oh! Masaki," said Shin'ichi.

Masaki stood beside Shin'ichi's table and bowed, his shoulders heaving as he labored to catch his breath.

"Sensei, I'm terribly sorry about yesterday."

"What on earth happened to you? We were all worried."

As soon as Shin'ichi had said this, his fellow travelers each glared stonily at Masaki.

"I'm sorry," Masaki replied. "Actually, we received a message from the Headquarters saying that your arrival had been changed to this morning. Please look at this."

With a tense expression, Masaki showed Shin'ichi the letter sent by the Headquarters Overseas Affairs Section informing them of the change.

After he read it, Shin'ichi laughed and said jovially: "Well, with this, it couldn't be helped. I thought you had gone off somewhere, you know. But I'm glad that you brought this with you. You'd be in trouble if you hadn't, because everyone was pretty upset."

Shin'ichi passed the letter around to the other members of his party.

"But how could such a mistake have happened?" demanded Kiyoshi Jujo angrily. "Unless we investigate the cause, the same thing might happen again. Was it a miscalculation by the Overseas Affairs Section?"

"Someone probably forgot about the time difference," suggested Shin'ichi, "because Japanese people don't often travel outside of Japan!" Laughter arose among his companions.

Shin'ichi's words ended the discussion. Nevertheless, he had understood Jujo's point: When a problem occurs, it is only natural to search thoroughly for the cause and take steps to ensure that it will not happen again.

However, this problem had been resolved for the time being, and they could at last meet with the Hawaiian members. Rather than continue to dwell on the error, Shin'ichi wanted to spend as much time as possible encouraging the members and thanking them for their efforts. Besides, what made him happiest was seeing that Masaki was safe.

Actually, the mistake had been caused by a simple typographical error on the part of the travel agency that had arranged the trip. Several days before the group's departure, the travel agency had sent a schedule—listing the flight number and the name of the hotel where the party was to stay—as a final confirmation. The schedule, however, had contained the error.

The staff of the Overseas Affairs Section, upon noticing the new arrival time, had hurriedly sent off a letter to the Hawaii members to inform them of the change.

*S*HIN'ICHI turned toward the members, who stood crowded into one end of the patio, and beckoned to them, saying: "Thank you so much. Everyone, please come on over." Most appeared nervous, perhaps because they were meeting Shin'ichi, their president, for the first time. But as soon as Shin'ichi spoke to them, their tense expressions relaxed.

"Thank you very much for taking the trouble to come here," Shin'ichi said. "I understand that you went to the airport early this morning to meet us. And so many of you are still here now. Mr. Masaki and Miss Nagata have really worked hard."

A smile finally appeared on Masaki's face. The members all moved toward Shin'ichi and, one after another, placed the leis they had brought around his neck. Soon his face was buried under a mound of leis.

"Not just me," protested Shin'ichi. "Please give them to the others, too!" Lei after lei was placed around the necks of the other leaders who accompanied him.

Shin'ichi passed out to the members some *nori* (dried seaweed) that he had brought to eat with his breakfast.

"It's not much," he said, "but let's eat it together. This *nori* was taken from the sea near Omori, Tokyo, the town where I was born and raised."

Practically all of the members were of Japanese origin, and they nostalgically savored the distinctly Japanese flavor. Through this encounter with Shin'ichi, they received their first real taste of the warmth of the Soka family.

Without resuming his meal, Shin'ichi engaged the members in lively and cheerful conversation, putting his new friends instantly at ease.

He asked one of the leaders accompanying him to bring some *fukusa*[3] from his room. On each was printed the Japanese calligraphy for joy (*kanki*), written in Shin'ichi's hand, in white characters against a purple background.

Even the smallest child present received a *fukusa*. Shin'ichi wanted to encourage every one of the members who had gone to the airport to greet him so early that morning.

Next, a commemorative photo was taken, each person's joy-filled expression caught on film.

Just then, Tony Harada, the young man who had met them at the airport the night before, arrived. Shin'ichi presented him with a medallion that had been cast to commemorate his inauguration as the third Soka Gakkai president.

"Thank you all very much," Shin'ichi said to the members. "I'll see you again at the discussion meeting this afternoon." He saw them off as they walked buoyantly from the hotel.

Taking advantage of the time available to them before the discussion meeting, Shin'ichi and his companions rented a car and took a tour of the island of Oahu. Together, they wanted to get acquainted with this land that was so new to them.

BEFORE leaving the hotel, Shin'ichi Yamamoto asked the member who was acting as their guide, "How should we dress for today's discussion meeting?" In the interests of creating an atmosphere of friendly discussion, Shin'ichi wanted to do all he could to blend in harmoniously with the local members.

"Well, let me see. Here, the women wear muumuus and men wear aloha shirts, so I think it would be best to wear just a shirt without a jacket," their guide said.

"What color shirt would be best?" Shin'ichi asked.

"Since the aloha shirts are a little flashy, I think a light blue shirt would be fine."

"Blue? I didn't bring a blue shirt. Well, I think I'll just wear a white one. Let's all dress casually for the meeting. Miss Kiyohara, why don't you wear a muumuu?" suggested Shin'ichi.

"A muumuu?" echoed Katsu Kiyohara with a dubious look. She turned to their guide and asked in a low tone, "What's a muumuu?"

"They're what the women who were just here were wearing."

"Those loose-fitting outfits? Weren't they some sort of nightgown?"

"No. Women in Hawaii generally wear muumuus wherever they go."

"Oh, really? You know, when they were here, I was thinking about telling them: 'Today is going to be a historic discussion meeting, so you'd certainly better not come dressed like that. Please wear some proper attire.'"

With a laugh, Shin'ichi said: "Miss Kiyohara, this isn't Japan, you know. Hawaii has its own traditions and customs, and we should respect them. The climate and culture here are different from Japan. If Soka Gakkai members overseas had to wear the same kind of clothes and hairstyles as their counterparts in Japan, then no one would want to practice this faith. It would be like the wartime Japanese National Defense Women's Association [which demanded rigid conformity from its members].

"Nothing is written in the Gosho about such matters, and because they are not related to the essential doctrines of Buddhism, they are best left to the common sense and natural taste of the people in each area.

"Especially in a discussion meeting like the one we'll be attending today, our main focus is to listen carefully to everyone's problems, concerns and doubts and to offer them clearcut guidance and encouragement that will leave them feeling confident and reassured.

"To that end, it is essential to create an open and friendly atmosphere in which people can talk about whatever is on their minds. Therefore, everyone should be allowed to dress comfortably, and we, too, should follow suit."

On hearing Shin'ichi's words, Katsu Kiyohara reflected upon how shallow her thinking had been.

YES, I see," said Katsu Kiyohara. "I'm glad I didn't tell them anything foolish. But, Sensei, I didn't bring anything at all like a muumuu."

"I know you didn't. You look fine just as you are." The rest of them laughed.

Jujo then said: "Differences in manners and customs are certainly a big problem. Sensei, I think that the way we sit on our knees to do gongyo would be quite uncomfortable for foreigners, particularly since most American houses have wooden floors. But we can't change the way we do gongyo, can we?"

Shin'ichi responded without hesitation: "Yes, we can. I think that we'll naturally have to consider the possibility that gongyo can be done while sitting in a chair. For people who aren't accustomed to it, sitting on their knees could be as painful as torture. Under such circumstances, it would be impossible to derive any joy from doing gongyo.

"That is why there is a concept in Buddhism known as *zuiho bini*—meaning that so long as one does not deviate from the essential teachings of the Daishonin's Buddhism, that is, faith in the Gohonzon, it is fine to make the formalities of Buddhism conform with the manners and customs of each area and with the conventions of the times."

"I see," said Jujo. "Considering the future, we'll have to become more flexible in our thinking."

"My biggest fear," continued Shin'ichi, "is that leaders might fall into the trap of thinking that the way things are done in Japan is absolute and that members in other parts of the world must do exactly the same. This would be like forcing people in other countries to wear traditional Japanese clothing.

"If leaders come to believe that such ways are what constitute correct faith, they will then be turning Buddhism into something extremely narrow and rigid. Should this happen, then instead of Buddhism, we'll have 'Japanism.' After all, the Daishonin's Buddhism exists not only for the Japanese; it is a religion for all people the world over."

Since the day Josei Toda had entrusted him with the mission of worldwide kosen-rufu, Shin'ichi had considered the various problems he was likely to face overseas and had weighed each one carefully. Naturally, he had delved thoroughly into the question of how to deal with the differences in custom and tradition that existed between Japan and other areas of the world.

Already painted vividly in his heart was a grand and elaborate vision of the future of global kosen-rufu. Yet not one person was aware of this.

ROWS of palm trees could be seen swaying in the breeze through the window of the station wagon that carried Shin'ichi Yamamoto and his companions as they left downtown Honolulu and drove toward the National Cemetery of the Pacific. The air blowing in through the open window was fresh with the scent of greenery.

The National Cemetery is situated in the crater of a small extinct volcanic hill known as the Punchbowl. Brightly colored flowers had been placed upon the grave markers set deep into the lush green lawn, creating a vivid and beautiful contrast.

"Those who lost their lives in World War II are buried in this cemetery," their guide informed them. "During the war, a unit of Japanese-American soldiers from Hawaii was formed. It played a key role on the front lines of the war in Italy. Soldiers from that unit are buried here, too."

After strolling around the cemetery grounds listening to the guide's explanation, Shin'ichi and the others stopped to chant daimoku three times and pray for those who were sacrificed in the war. With only nine participants, it was a tiny memorial service. Yet their offering of daimoku for the deceased was infused with a profound prayer for peace.

The car carrying Shin'ichi and his comrades then headed back to the city. After driving for a while, they saw a stretch of ocean spreading out before them like a giant silver mirror. It was Pearl Harbor.

On the morning of December 7, 1941, a force of 183 Japanese war planes, including both fighters and bombers, launched a surprise attack on the u.s. military facilities in Pearl Harbor and the American warships docked there, thus sparking the beginning of the tragic war in the Pacific. The success of the attack was telegraphed by Japanese forces under the code name "Tora, Tora, Tora." The beginning of the war and this early victory brought a surge of excitement to Japan.

For Hawaiian residents of Japanese heritage, however, it marked the start of a bitter destiny. Since the first Japanese immigrants arrived in Hawaii in 1868, Japanese descendants had labored strenuously to win trust within Hawaiian society. The aerial attack, however, destroyed that trust in a single stroke.

All of the Hawaiian Islands were immediately placed under martial law, and persons of Japanese ancestry were designated as "enemy aliens." A name list of more than 160 individuals who were deemed potentially dangerous had already been prepared by the military in anticipation of war with Japan, and these people were immediately placed under arrest on the day of the attack. Internment camps were set up on the islands for the containment of designated individuals of Japanese ancestry. Later, many were relocated to similar camps on the American mainland.

Many Americans who were enraged by Japan's sneak attack came to view all people of Japanese ancestry as "hostile Japanese." So pervasive was this feeling that some in the military took the uncompromising stance that all persons of Japanese ancestry should be interned.

*B*ECAUSE of the attack on Pearl Harbor, Americans of Japanese heritage had to live under a burden of anxiety and humiliation.

Eventually, the U.S. War Department formed a unit of Japanese-American soldiers from Hawaii who had enlisted before the start of the war and sent them to the mainland for intensive training. That unit was the 100th Infantry Battalion.

Later, a large number of *nisei* (second-generation Japanese-Americans) responded enthusiastically to a call by the army for volunteer recruits of Japanese ancestry. From these new recruits, the 442nd Regimental Combat Team was formed.

These soldiers endured rigorous training, determined to prove their loyalty to the United States of America.

Nevertheless, even within the ranks of the military, they were constantly the target of icy glares of contempt and hatred and subject to prejudice and discrimination.

This was simply because they were of the same race as the enemy, who had resorted to such a detestable surprise attack on their country.

When these Japanese-American soldiers were sent to the front lines in Europe, however, they fought more courageously than anyone. To clear their names of the stigma of "enemy alien," their only recourse was to demonstrate, through their actions, their loyalty as Americans willing to lay down their lives for their country.

They were always first off the mark to charge the enemy's positions, throwing themselves headlong into hostile machine-gun fire without any thought for their own lives. They fought with the hope that, by proving themselves in battle, they could spare their family members and fellow Japanese-Americans back in the United States from prejudice and discrimination and unjust treatment.

As the most highly decorated unit of the war, the 442nd Regimental Combat Team indisputably proved the loyalty of Japanese-Americans to their country. U.S. President Harry S. Truman offered them his unsparing praise, saying that they not only defeated the enemy but also won over prejudice.

It was a bitter, bloodstained victory, however, for which a great many youth paid the ultimate price. According to one account, more than sixty percent of all Hawaiian combatants who lost their lives in World War II were of Japanese descent.

As Shin'ichi Yamamoto gazed out over Pearl Harbor, he reflected deeply on the significance of his taking the first step toward worldwide kosen-rufu from Hawaii.

"No one longs more for peace," he thought, "than those who have known the misery of war. Surely it is those who have wept the bitterest tears that deserve most to become happy. That being the case, then Hawaii—the island where the Pacific War began and a true melting pot of humanity—must lead the world as a model for peace. And it is Buddhism that will make this possible."

Looking out the car window at the vast expanse of the sea, Shin'ichi chanted daimoku in his heart.

After leaving the memorial cemetery, the group visited a number of other well-known sites in the vicinity, including a pineapple plantation and the cliffs of Nuuanu Pali—where the great Hawaiian king, Kamehameha I, fought his fiercest battle in his struggle to unify the islands.

They then headed for the place where the discussion meeting was to be held.

*I*N the car on the way to the discussion meeting, Shin'ichi Yamamoto seemed to be deeply absorbed in thought. After a while, he quietly said, "At today's meeting, I think we should establish a district here in Hawaii."

"A district? Not a group?" asked Kiyoshi Jujo with a look of surprise.

In those days, Soka Gakkai districts usually comprised a membership of several hundred households, and districts with memberships of more than a thousand households were not uncommon. Yet, in Hawaii there were only thirty or forty members in all, children included. This was a small number even for a group.

"Yes, a district," Shin'ichi affirmed. "Hawaii is different from Japan. Kosen-rufu is likely to develop rapidly around the world from here on. For that reason, we need to establish a district, rather than a group, here in Hawaii, which may be thought of as the gateway to America.

"Also, if people's awareness as members of a newly formed district turns into determination, enabling them to carry out activities with renewed vigor, then they will indeed grow into a large district. We must think big.

"By the way, I'd like to hold a question-and-answer session at the discussion meeting today. While I'm doing that, would you mind getting together and coming up with a few suggestions for potential leaders for the new district?"

It was around 1:00 in the afternoon when the group, having lunched on sandwiches in the car on the way, arrived at a member's house on Honolulu's Beretania Street where the meeting was to be held. More than thirty people, most of them of Japanese heritage, had gathered inside.

"Thank you very much for coming; thank you for everything," Shin'ichi said with a smile as he entered the room. "Let's do gongyo together and pray for kosen-rufu in Hawaii as well as for the happiness and prosperity of each of your families."

Shin'ichi began to lead gongyo, his sonorous voice resounding throughout the room. After gongyo, he sat down behind the small table that had been placed at the front. When he had done so, he noticed that a large space had opened up in the middle of the room. The members, looking nervous, had shyly drawn back against the walls on either side, no one venturing to sit directly in front of Shin'ichi.

"Please, come on up to the front," Shin'ichi said with a smile, inviting one person then another to move forward.

At one side of the room was a man in his mid-30s with a sturdy build and gentle eyes. He had been among the members who had come to the hotel that morning. When Shin'ichi's eyes met his, the man smiled.

THE man resembled a professional wrestler who at the time was immensely popular in Japan. Addressing him, Shin'ichi said: "I thought when I saw you this morning that you look just like Rikidozan, the pro wrestler. May I ask your name?"

"My name is Hiroto Hirata."

"I see. Well, I think Rikidozan is an easier name to remember, so do you mind if I call you 'Riki' from now on?" Everyone burst into laughter.

Shin'ichi's good-natured ribbing gradually relaxed the tension that seemed to permeate the room.

"Are you married?" asked Shin'ichi.

"Yes, my wife lives in Sendai, Japan. She'll be joining me in Hawaii in the future."

In Japanese, Hirata had referred to his wife using the word *okusan*, which usually indicates someone else's wife, rather than *tsuma*, meaning one's own wife. This invited laughter from the others. Listening carefully, one could sense that his Japanese was somewhat stiff and awkward.

The path that Hirata had followed in life in a way epitomized the stories of many Japanese-Americans of his generation. He was the son of Japanese immigrants. Soon after the attack on Pearl Harbor, his father was sent to a relocation camp in Hawaii and then on to an internment camp on the U.S. mainland. Hirata and his mother followed his father to the mainland and into the same camp. Then, in 1943, as part of a prisoner-exchange agreement with Japan, Hirata and his parents boarded a ship that left New York and sailed across the Atlantic before rounding Africa's Cape of Good Hope and landing in Singapore.

Singapore was then under Japanese military rule and had been renamed Shonan Island by the Japanese. Hirata disembarked there and, taking advantage of his ability in English, worked for a radio station news team. It was not long, however, before he received a draft notice from the Japanese military.

Hirata was a citizen of both the United States and Japan. Many of his Japanese-American peers from Hawaii were at that time fighting as American soldiers on the front in Italy. But now he would be forced to fight against his compatriots

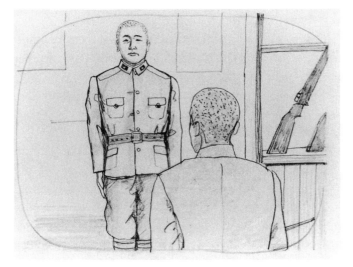

as a soldier in a Japanese military whose enemies were the "demon American and British."

Japan was the homeland of his parents, but his home was America. The war thus tore apart human relationships, and it rent Hirata's heart in two.

Having been born in Hawaii, Hirata could not speak Japanese very well and was scorned by his fellow soldiers on that account. When he became nervous or excited, he would unconsciously revert to English.

When this happened, his superiors would beat him, yelling, "Don't use the enemy language!" Because of his inability to use the correct polite forms of Japanese speech, he was once beaten until his face was no longer recognizable while a senior officer screamed at him, "What kind of Japanese is that?"

*A*FTER enduring the continual beatings and the exhortations to hate his homeland, America, Hiroto Hirata finally witnessed the end of the war. Two years later, he was discharged from the military and took up residence in his father's home in the prefecture of Miyagi, where he eventually married.

His wife, suffering from frail health, had been the first to take faith in the Daishonin's Buddhism. From her and the other Soka Gakkai members who came to visit their home, Hirata had heard about the practice. Moved by the overflowing confidence with which they claimed that "no prayer will go unanswered," he began to practice the religion himself.

Hirata had one wish: to regain his lost American citizenship and return to Hawaii. Though he had grown accustomed to living in Japan and had become fairly fluent in the language, he could not suppress his desire to return home to live in the place where he had been born and raised. He dedicated himself wholeheartedly to the practice of gongyo and daimoku. In the beginning, he would spend almost half the day struggling to master the new routine of gongyo.

Less than one month after beginning his practice, he received a letter from the U.S. government informing him that his application for the restoration of his citizenship had been approved.

Hirata moved back to Hawaii just six months before Shin'ichi's visit. To secure a foundation for his family's livelihood, he had returned to Hawaii alone for the time being.

"Does your wife have a position in the organization in Japan?" Shin'ichi Yamamoto asked him.

"She's a women's division district chief."

"I see. And did you have any sort of position?"

"Before I left Japan, I was appointed as a unit chief."

Shin'ichi then asked each of the other participants how many years it had been since they had taken faith. Most had been practicing for about one year, with the longest having practiced for three or four years.

"Thank you," said Shin'ichi after everyone had answered. "Here with me today are five other leaders from Japan. You might recognize some of them. Now I'd like to ask each of them to introduce themselves. They all speak English fluently." When Shin'ichi said this, the faces of his companions suddenly turned red, while the local members chuckled.

Shin'ichi continued good-naturedly, "Though I know they would much rather speak to you in English, today, in the interest of helping all of you remember your Japanese, they will speak in Japanese."

The leaders got up one after the other to introduce themselves, outlining the organization's activities in Japan and offering guidance and encouragement. Whenever the dialogue became too stiff or formal, Shin'ichi would interject with a humorous explanation. In addition to being the meeting's central figure, Shin'ichi also functioned as the emcee and moderator.

THE participants gradually relaxed and began to feel at home with one another, their laughter and good cheer pervading the meeting place. Until now, they had each been struggling alone, unaware that there were other members practicing in Hawaii. The atmosphere of the discussion meeting thus afforded them a sense of comfort and heartfelt relief. This was what Shin'ichi Yamamoto had been waiting for.

He gazed at everyone, embracing them with his bright smile, and said: "Since coming to Hawaii, all of you must have gone through a variety of hardships and difficulties. And I'm sure many of you have been troubled by the question of how to carry out your faith, given the differences in language, culture and customs. I am well aware of your hardships and concerns. So, today, please feel free to ask me any question you wish; anything at all is okay."

Two or three people immediately raised their hands.

When the question-and-answer session began, the leaders who had come with Shin'ichi quietly rose and left the room to discuss leadership proposals for the soon-to-be-formed district.

The first question was from a young married woman.

"I want to go back to Japan, but I don't know what to do," she said, her voice growing taught and tears flowing from her eyes.

Controlling her sobs, the woman went on to tell her story. She was born in Tohoku, a region in the northeastern part of Japan's main island, and lost her father in the war. Her family was poor, so after graduating from junior high school, she moved to Tokyo and found a job there. A few years later she met her husband, a Hawaiian-born American soldier who was in Japan during the Korean War. Her mother opposed the marriage, but the woman refused to be dissuaded and the two wed.

Around that time, she was introduced to the Daishonin's Buddhism by a friend and joined the Soka Gakkai. That had been two years ago. Soon after, she moved with her husband to Hawaii where they took up residence in his parents' home.

She had cherished hope-filled visions of America as a land of freedom and democracy. She was not alone; many Japanese in those days turned their eyes admiringly to America, imagining it as some sort of dream land. Sadly, however, this woman's dream had been shattered. Life with her in-laws was by no means easy financially. Also, being Japanese, she could not make herself understood well in English, and they treated her coldly.

At the same time, her husband had become physically abusive, and a rift had grown between them. Her sense of regret grew with each passing day. As her feelings of isolation and despair deepened, she would often stand crying on the beach, watching the crimson sun set into the sea beyond the horizon.

"Across that ocean is Japan," she would think. "I want to go home."

The tears that streamed down her cheeks flooded her already wounded heart with an aching, empty coldness, thus intensifying her sorrow.

SHIN'ICHI Yamamoto listened carefully as the woman continued her story: "So I want to leave my husband and go back to Japan. But since I married against my mother's wishes, no one will welcome me even if I do go back. I don't know what to do."

When the woman said this, her shoulders began to heave as she sobbed loudly. Her tears seemed to invite echoing sobs from other women in the room, more than a few of whom found themselves in similar circumstances. Contrary to the attractive image an international marriage had for many Japanese women, life in a foreign country—with its differences in language and customs—turned out to be far more severe than they had anticipated and presented them instead with a multitude of obstacles. There was also lingering prejudice against the Japanese, who had been the wartime enemy. Many of these women, therefore, lived under clouds of misery and despair.

Nodding deeply, Shin'ichi began to speak in a soft tone.

"It must have been really hard for you. You must have really suffered. But you have the Gohonzon, haven't you? Faith is the power to survive." Shin'ichi's voice grew stronger.

"Whether you leave your husband and go back to Japan is something that you must decide for yourself. However, as you already know, happiness will not necessarily be waiting for you there. Unless you change your karma, your problems will follow you wherever you go. The idea that happiness exists somewhere else resembles the thinking of the Nembutsu school of Buddhism, which teaches the existence of a distant Pure Land located billions of Buddha lands to the west.

"Nichiren Daishonin's Buddhism, however, enables us to transform the place where we are now into 'a land of Eternally Tranquil Light' and there construct a palace of happiness. To that end, you have to change the karma that makes you suffer from family discord. There is no other way than to dramatically transform your own life-condition. When you change your state of life, your environment will naturally start changing as well. This is the principle of the oneness of life and its environment (*esho funi*). A grand palace of happiness exists within your own heart. Faith is the key that opens the door to that palace."

Shin'ichi had committed himself to eradicating all forms of unhappiness. Here, at this discussion meeting, he engaged in an earnest, win-or-lose struggle to break through the dark veil of misery that shrouded one woman's heart, to summon forth in her a wellspring of courage and ignite a bright flame of hope. Shin'ichi was keenly aware of her pain, suffering and loneliness. For that very reason, he wanted her to gain the strength to live indomitably.

SHIN'ICHI Yamamoto spoke with powerful conviction. "If you seriously exert yourself in faith, then you will not fail to become happy. Please have confidence in this, first of all. Then, whatever problem you face, laugh it away with a bright smile. It's not pleasant for your husband either if his wife is always moping about or looking sullen.

"If you cannot express yourself clearly in English, then your husband and his family will misunderstand you. Therefore, please make an effort to master the language as soon as possible so that you can communicate what you want to say to anyone. Your efforts in this area are also very important.

"In any event, instead of hating or resenting your husband and his family, strive to become the kind of person who can pray with a generous heart for each person's happiness."

Here, Shin'ichi smiled warmly and said: "I think there are probably many other Japanese women here in Hawaii who are living under similar circumstances. When you become loved and appreciated by your husband's family—shining with sunlike radiance and creating a wonderful home—you will then serve as a symbol of hope and a role model for other women who have come from Japan. Your example will give them courage.

"Your becoming happy affects not only you but will lead to the revitalization of all Japanese women living here in Hawaii. Therefore, you must not be defeated by your suffering. Instead, live strongly and invincibly. Please walk the great path of happiness, always cheerfully, boldly and proudly. Yes! Please wipe away your tears!"

The woman could not help being deeply moved by Shin'ichi's guidance. His deep compassion warmed her heart. Wiping her eyes with a handkerchief, she nodded deeply and said with a bright smile, "I won't be defeated." Tears glistened in her eyes once again, but now they arose from a fresh, passionate resolve that flared in her heart.

Shin'ichi's voyage for world peace thus began by lighting a flame of courage in those who had lost hope and were being crushed under the weight of life's vicissitudes. Though such efforts might seem insignificant and far removed from the goal of world peace, the essential basis for peace lies only within the human being. Shin'ichi was deeply convinced that genuine peace could not be achieved without the revitalization of all individuals and the establishment of true joy and happiness in their lives.

*T*HE next question came from a petite, middle-aged woman who had joined the Soka Gakkai in Japan and moved to Hawaii with her family two years earlier. With a troubled expression, she began in a small, timid voice: "Um, well, my son is going to a Christian school, but I'm wondering if this isn't slandering Buddhism. There's no other school that's suitable, you see."

"That's all right," replied Shin'ichi. "Your son isn't going to school to practice Christianity; he's going there to learn and study. So long as that's the case, there is absolutely no problem."

At Shin'ichi's clear and direct answer, the woman's face brightened with obvious relief.

"Really? I'm so relieved. I was worried that by paying money to a Christian school, I might be making offerings to a non-Buddhist teaching and thereby committing slander."

In Japan, the woman had been taught the importance of making a clear distinction between right and wrong from the standpoint of Buddhism, and now she seemed to be suffering great spiritual anguish at sending her son to a Christian school.

"You may pay money to the school, but that is only for tuition; it is not an offering to Christianity. It is natural to pay a fee if your son is being taught there.

"The basis of our faith is to believe in and pray to the Gohonzon, which was revealed by Nichiren Daishonin. So long as we do not veer from this basic foundation, there is no need to be rigid or intolerant."

Living in American society, which is so strongly influenced by Christianity, many members from Japan no doubt found themselves facing similar dilemmas and agonized over how to come to terms with them. Shin'ichi felt he should delve into the question more deeply.

"Many aspects of our culture and how we live are connected in one way or another to religion. For instance, most companies are closed on Sundays. This is a practice that comes from Christianity, which views Sunday as a day of rest and worship. Yet, anyone who thinks that taking Sundays off is a slander of Buddhism would be unable to live harmoniously in our society.

"Music and art, as well, are often influenced by religion. Yet, there is a difference between appreciating a work of art and believing in the religion that inspired it. Therefore, there is no need to think that you must avoid viewing such artwork or that listening to certain pieces of music constitutes slander. If having faith meant that you could no longer admire fine works of art, then that faith would be denying your humanity."

SOME religions exist for the people, and others exist only for the sake of religion. Religion for the sake of religion descends into dogmatism, ultimately binding and enslaving people in the name of faith. As a result, people are deprived of their spiritual freedom, and common sense and humanity are denied, deepening the rift between the religion and society.

Nichiren Daishonin's Buddhism is a religion that exists for the people, aiming to bring about a flowering of humanity in each person. A religious leader who speaks about the principles of the Daishonin's Buddhism yet declares such humanistic pursuits as art and culture to be slandering the teachings is in fact a pernicious dogmatist who tramples upon the Daishonin's very spirit. The actions of such a person only serve to distort Buddhism and block the way toward worldwide kosen-rufu.

Shin'ichi Yamamoto moved to the next question. One man hesitantly raised his hand. His name was Mitsuru Kawakami, and he had just joined a few days before the meeting.

"Will I be able to save my deceased father through this faith?" he asked.

It was a rather abrupt question. Kawakami, his distinct features expressing his anxiety, gazed intently at Shin'ichi.

"Yes, you definitely can. Proof of this will become apparent in your own life-condition. You, yourself, will become happy."

Shin'ichi's answer was brimming with conviction. The man's expression relaxed and his eyes filled with tears. His concern about helping his deceased father had been weighing on his mind more heavily than his own immediate problems.

Kawakami had been born on the island of Oahu, the second son of a family of nine children. Three of his younger brothers, however, had died of illness one after the other while still very small. He, too, had contracted at the age of 5 an unknown affliction, which doctors had said would require amputation of his right foot.

However, his father wanted him to remain whole of limb by any means. Hoping to find treatment for his son's condition in Japan, the father quit his occupation as a hog farmer and resolved to return to his homeland.

In Japan, Kawakami underwent extensive tests at a hospital in his father's hometown of Hiroshima. He was diagnosed as suffering from a condition known as periostitis and, happily, was spared from having his foot amputated. In a way, he had been delivered from this fate by his father's desire to save his beloved child. His father had died, however, when he was only 13.

When Kawakami turned 15, he left for Hawaii to find work to support his mother and his younger sisters and brothers, who remained in Japan. After many struggles and hardships, he built a financial foothold and eventually established himself in the charcoal manufacturing business. Yet, he regretted never repaying his filial debt to his father. He had seriously begun to wonder whether there wasn't some way to bring happiness to his father in the next world and thereby repay his debt of gratitude to him.

EARCHING for a way to pay back his father's loving concern, Mitsuru Kawakami embarked upon a kind of religious pilgrimage. At the suggestion of one friend or another, he had prayed to a whole assortment of religious objects, including a talisman from the Imperial Shinto Shrine.

He even went to a Christian church and asked the minister there, "Can I save my deceased father through this faith?"

"Yes, you can," the minister assured him.

But when Kawakami pressed him further, saying, "Well then, could you give me some proof?" the man looked offended. After listening to a vague explanation by the minister, Kawakami went home disappointed.

The turning point that led to Kawakami's taking faith in Nichiren Daishonin's Buddhism came when his mother joined the Soka Gakkai in Japan and began sending him its publications. These carried articles that clearly refuted other religions and that stated erroneous beliefs are the cause of unhappiness.

"They dare to make such claims," he thought, "yet if it were not the truth, then they would surely have been sued for libel by now, wouldn't they? Perhaps what the Soka Gakkai says is true."

He invited his mother to come and visit him in Hawaii. When he saw her and listened to her talk at length about her faith, Kawakami began to feel that he, too, would like to join the Soka Gakkai. A few days before the discussion meeting, he had met Nagayasu Masaki and began his practice of faith.

In concluding his explanation, Shin'ichi Yamamoto said: "Nichiren Daishonin writes, 'The Venerable Maudgalyayana put his faith in the Lotus Sutra, which is the greatest good there is, and thus not only did he himself attain Buddhahood, but his father and mother did so as well' (WND-1, 820). Here, the Daishonin makes it clear that both you, the son,

and your departed father will attain Buddhahood and definitely become happy. Therefore, no matter what happens, please persevere boldly in your faith. When you carry out your practice of faith to the point where you can declare confidently how happy you've become, your father will definitely be happy as well."

Hearing Shin'ichi's confident guidance, Mitsuru Kawakami felt as though a thick veil of fog were lifting from his heart.

After answering two or three more questions, Shin'ichi said, "Today we brought some slides showing what Soka Gakkai activities are like in Japan; let's have a look at them now."

Shin'ichi had asked Youth Division Chief Eisuke Akizuki, who also served as managing editor of the *Seikyo Shimbun*, to prepare a slide presentation introducing the Soka Gakkai's fresh rhythm of advancement to these members who lived so far from Japan.

While Akizuki showed the slides and narrated, Shin'ichi joined the other leaders from Japan to discuss the leadership lineup for the new district based on the proposal they had prepared.

VICE General Director Kiyoshi Jujo and the other leaders accompanying Shin'ichi proposed that Yumiko Nagata, who had been acting as a liaison for the Overseas Affairs Section of the Soka Gakkai Headquarters, become the young women's division chief for the new district. They had also agreed on the youth who had served as a driver and guide on their tour of the island as the district young men's division chief. However, they could not decide on anyone to fill the positions of district chief and district women's division chief.

On hearing this, Shin'ichi responded immediately: "Let's ask Riki to be the district chief. He's fluent in English. Since it's likely that more and more non-Japanese people will begin practicing this faith from now on, the ability to speak English will be an important requisite.

"Also, Riki's painful struggles—torn between conflicting loyalties to Japan and the United States during the war —make him ideally suited to take the lead here in Hawaii, which is a true ethnic melting pot. He also has a likable personality."

The others seemed somewhat uncertain about Shin'ichi's proposal but could offer no better alternative.

"What shall we do about a district women's division chief?" asked Soka Gakkai Women's Division Chief Katsu Kiyohara.

"Riki said that his wife is a district women's division chief in Japan and that he will be asking her to join him in Hawaii some time soon, didn't he?" Shin'ichi said. "In that case, we should ask her to be the district women's division chief when she comes. I don't think there will be any problem if the position remains vacant until then. There's absolutely no need to rush."

After the slide show, Shin'ichi announced the establishment of the new district.

"Today, I would like to form a district here in Hawaii. Would that be all right with all of you?"

For a moment, everyone was dumbstruck. With the small number of members living in Hawaii, no one had even imagined that a district could be established.

"Hawaii is a place of geographic importance for the worldwide propagation of Nichiren Daishonin's Buddhism," Shin'ichi continued. "It will also shine forever in the annals of kosen-rufu as the place from which the first step in the Soka Gakkai's global journey for world peace was taken. For this reason and for the sake of the future, I especially wish to create a district here in Hawaii."

When Shin'ichi said this, the members cheered joyously.

"I would like to ask Riki here to be your new district chief; how is that with all of you?"

The room filled with approving applause. Yet, nobody was more surprised that Hiroto Hirata himself.

"I'm going to be the district chief?" he asked. "I don't know if I can fulfill such a big responsibility. I really don't know anything about faith."

YES, I'd like to ask you to be the district chief," Shin'ichi said to Hiroto Hirata, who was clearly perplexed. "You may not know what to do yet, but you can learn as you go. What you'll need, first and foremost, is a strong determination to help each person in the district become happy. You should also try to become someone whom everyone can talk to, always thinking about how to enable each person to bring forth his or her potential. From now on, the organization in Hawaii will develop to the extent that you pray sincerely and take action. All your efforts will turn into your own benefit and good fortune.

"Your namesake, Rikidozan, is the world's strongest wrestler. I hope that you, Riki, will be no less of a champion in building the world's strongest and finest district. I'm looking forward to your success."

"Yes!" Hiroto Hirata replied.

Hirata shuddered at the weight of his new responsibility, but Shin'ichi's words brought forth a surge of courage, allowing him to conquer his fears. His eyes blazed with a fighting spirit.

Just then, a young man stood up. It was Tony Harada.

"Sensei," he said, "I'm very sorry, but I'm running late. Please excuse me, I have to be going."

"Harada, you're leaving us again?" said Shin'ichi, smiling warmly.

"Yes, I have to catch the plane back to the island of Hawaii."

"I see," said Shin'ichi. "I'll never forget you as long as I live. By the way, I was thinking of asking you to be a young men's division group chief; is that all right with you?"

"Yes, sir."

"In Japan, a group chief is usually responsible for about 100 members. You won't have any members to begin with, but you'll be a group chief nonetheless. Based on this awareness, it will be up to you to build a group through your own efforts. This is the true way of the Soka Gakkai organization.

"President Toda once said: 'Youth, stand alone! Another will definitely appear and a third will soon follow!' To strive with this spirit is to be a true youth of the Soka Gakkai. I will be watching closely to see how you live and fight from here on—ten, twenty and thirty years into the future. Let's win in life! I hope you will join me. Please never be defeated by your own weaknesses."

"Yes! I'll do my best!" Harada's face was flushed with determination.

"All right then, please take care. Thank you very much—and I'll see you again!" said Shin'ichi as Harada took his leave.

*A*FTER Shin'ichi Yamamoto had finished outlining the new district leadership appointments, he began to speak with powerful conviction.

"Though you may think Hawaii and Japan are separated by a great distance, they are really just a stone's throw away from each other. They are right next door. These days, you can board a jet in Japan and arrive here just seven hours later.

"So instead of feeling sad and lonely, please accumulate good fortune quickly so that your circumstances will allow you to visit Japan any time you want. I, too, will definitely come back. I will visit Hawaii again and again.

"This is a paradise, a land of perpetual summer. The sea and flowers are beautiful. People the world over dream of Hawaii.

"But Hawaii's past is by no means steeped in happiness. Those of Japanese ancestry, in particular, have had a sad and painful history. All of you, though, are here to change that destiny. As children of the Buddha, you each have a mission of boundless proportions. With that mission and pride in your hearts, please become excellent citizens who are trusted by all. To win the love and respect of others leads to the propagation of Buddhism; kosen-rufu exists in developing such trust.

"I am praying that you will bring a great flower of happiness splendidly to bloom here in this beautiful paradise. Next time, I'll see you in Japan!"

For most of the members, coming to Hawaii had meant a weeklong journey by boat. As a result, they had a strong sense of living in a faraway place, separated from Japan by a vast ocean. Many had been homesick and unable to forget about Japan. But Shin'ichi's encouragement that they were "just a stone's throw away" completely transformed their outlook.

Those who are aware of their mission are strong. Those who live for a mission are beautiful.

The members felt as if a blindfold had been removed from their eyes. They even felt it strange that they had suffered so much from feelings of loneliness and isolation until then. The mountains and sea of Hawaii, which just moments ago had seemed to be tinged with gloom and despair, now appeared to glow with hope.

The members' situations and circumstances changed not in the least. But something intangible had most certainly changed. This invisible transformation in the innermost depths of their lives would ultimately effect a change in each of their circumstances.

Shin'ichi shook everyone's hand and left the meeting place, praying in his heart that each of his treasured friends—all of whom were children of the Buddha—would lead a life of happiness. From the car window, he could see the ocean bathed in crimson hues by a blazing sunset—a scene too beautiful for words.

*T*ONY Harada watched the brilliant red sunset from the window of the plane as it took him back to the island of Hawaii. Burning in his heart, as well, was a red-hot flame of determination. "I won't let my weakness get the better of me anymore," he thought. "I am a young leader of Buddhism—a leader of the Soka Gakkai young men's division!"

As he contemplated his mission to live for kosen-rufu in Hawaii, he reflected on the tortuous path he had followed during his twenty-or-so years.

Tony Harada spent his early childhood in Yokohama, Japan. His father, a second-generation Japanese-American from Hawaii, died of tuberculosis when Tony was just 4. The death of his father plunged the family into the depths of poverty, and when Tony was in the second grade, he was placed in a foster home. For the rest of his family, it was one less mouth to feed.

From then on he was shifted frequently from one foster family to the next. The families he lived with always used him as an extra pair of hands, forcing him to carry out such tasks as baby-sitting, drawing water and chopping wood. He was made to slave and toil, though he was forever feeling hungry and sleepy.

Even harder on him, however, was the bullying he received from the other children, who, because of his English first name, called him the "orphan American." On more than a few occasions, he was pelted with stones. He deplored his own name and resented his mother who had sent him away.

After Harada graduated from junior high school, he took a job on a fishing boat—work that was always fraught with danger. In autumn 1954, when he was 17, Harada and his fellow crew members encountered extremely rough seas spawned by Typhoon No. 15. This was the storm that sank the *Toyamaru* ferry, which ran between Japan's main island of Honshu and the northernmost island of Hokkaido, leaving more than 1,100 people drowned or missing.

Harada's fishing boat was tossed like a leaf upon the billowing waters, and the entire crew was sure that they were going to die. While gripped by his own fear of death, a thought occurred to him: Should he return home safely, he would quit the fishing boat and try to find his mother.

Having narrowly escaped death, Harada resigned as a fisherman and was reunited with his mother whom he had not seen for almost ten years. Though unable to sense any parental love or warmth on her part, he decided to live with her for a while. After staying with his mother for about a year, he went to visit the house in Yokohama where he had lived as a child. In addition to seeing the house, he wanted to try to revitalize any faint images of his father that might still be dwelling deep within his memory.

When he got to the house, a woman came out to greet him. She clearly remembered back to when she had bought the house and also recalled Tony when he was a small child.

*T*HE woman gave Tony Harada a friendly smile. "So, you're little Tony," she said, warmly welcoming him inside. The woman turned out to be a Soka Gakkai member, and it was from her that Harada first heard about Nichiren Daishonin's Buddhism. He was particularly struck by the concept of changing one's karma or destiny. The woman's genuine warmth and the sincere and unpatronizing way she spoke to him deeply penetrated his troubled heart. He decided to take faith and began to participate in activities as a member of the young men's division.

One day he found among his mother's belongings a postcard that appeared to be from his father's older brother. He thus learned that he had an uncle who lived in Hawaii. He wrote a letter and received a reply. In it, his uncle invited him to come to work in Hawaii. Harada could not have wished for anything better. There was nothing to keep him in Japan.

When he eventually obtained a passport and the date of his departure for Hawaii was set, he went with his young men's division leader to visit the Soka Gakkai Headquarters. That was two years ago. There he met the youth division chief of staff, Shin'ichi Yamamoto, who congratulated him on his move abroad.

Once in Hawaii, Harada went to work for his uncle's food wholesale business. It was a demanding job that required him to work from morning until night with almost no time off. The determination he had made to carry on with his Buddhist practice in Hawaii began to fade quickly.

The woman who had introduced him to the Soka Gakkai faithfully mailed him every issue of its newspaper, the

Seikyo Shimbun, and he also received letters from his young men's division leader in Japan. These were the only things that sustained his faith.

It was through the newspaper and a letter from his leader that he learned that the Soka Gakkai president and other leaders would be visiting Hawaii. In the letter, his leader had written that Harada should definitely go to meet the president and his party, as it would no doubt prove to be an important encounter that would have a strong bearing on the rest of his life.

Harada had received encouragement from Shin'ichi in Japan, yet here he was in Hawaii having trouble doing gongyo regularly. He thought it would be inexcusable if he did not, at the very least, go to greet Shin'ichi. He pressed his uncle to give him some time off and flew from the island of Hawaii to welcome Shin'ichi at Honolulu Airport.

Now, as Harada reflected on his practice of faith since coming to Hawaii, he felt ashamed.

He thought, "Sensei gave a medallion commemorating his inauguration to someone like me." A powerful sense of joy surged up from deep within him.

"Youth must stand alone! I will fight!"

A fresh determination filled his heart. He was not alone. It was a feeling shared by all who had been appointed as new leaders that day.

*T*HAT evening, the new district leaders came to Shin'ichi's hotel. After the earlier meeting, Shin'ichi Yamamoto had felt extremely fatigued, but now he exerted himself even more strenuously to give guidance and encouragement to the new leaders.

A freshly planted seedling will wither and die unless it is given water and fertilizer. Thus Shin'ichi spared no effort, pouring his heart and soul into providing the nourishment necessary for the "seedling" of the new Hawaii District to flourish. He especially took time to give guidance to the new district chief, Hiroto Hirata, late into the night.

He and Hirata went out onto the hotel patio, which was mostly deserted. Shin'ichi offered him advice from a number of perspectives on everything from personal matters to the management of the organization.

"Riki, to gain trust in society, it is first important to succeed on your job. That is the foundation for everything. To do so, you will naturally have to work twice as hard as those around you. You will also need to activate your wisdom by consistently chanting daimoku.

"Kosen-rufu means to pray and take action for the happiness of others and thereby create a supreme path of good fortune. When you make kosen-rufu your life's objective and pray to excel at your work in order to show proof of that goal's validity, you will be opening the way for your own victory and good fortune."

Hiroto Hirata's eyes sparkled as he listened intently to Shin'ichi's guidance. Shin'ichi clearly sensed that his words were getting through to Hirata. He then began to talk about the proper attitude a leader should have toward faith.

As he spoke, the full moon cast a dim white reflection on the water, and waves could be heard lapping quietly upon the beach.

"I ask you to please spend your life from now on as a district chief who, together with me, lives for the members' happiness. Most people find it is all they can do to worry about their own happiness and that of their immediate family. It is, therefore, no easy feat to live for the happiness of your friends and fellow members, for the sake of the Law and for kosen-rufu, while at the same time grappling with your own personal problems.

"The fact is, however, that when you worry, pray and struggle for the sake of others, you are proving by your very actions that you have transcended the bounds of your own individual concerns and are opening the way for your own splendid human revolution.

"The organization will change and develop in any number of ways depending on the *ichinen*, or deep-seated determination, of the central figure. People will follow a leader who always fights for them. But they will eventually perceive the real nature of someone interested only in personal fame or fortune and will stop supporting that person."

*I*N his pure seeking spirit toward Buddhism, Hiroto Hirata was like dry sand soaking up water. Shin'ichi Yamamoto grasped Hirata's hand and said: "I am the one who appointed you as district chief. If you fail, then I, too, will have failed. I will take full responsibility. Please fight to your heart's content and to the best of your ability."

"Yes! I'll fight. I'll fight to the end," Hiroto Hirata said, firmly clasping Shin'ichi's hand in return. The eyes of the two men gleamed in the moonlight. Shin'ichi felt that with Hirata in charge, the organization in Hawaii was secure.

The moon was reflected as a silver strand of light across the sea.

One cannot foster capable people without investing full energy and effort. Only with passion and sincerity that wells forth from the depths of life can one inspire people and help them grow.

Their conversation in the moonlight continued until late in the evening. As Shin'ichi returned to his room, the other leaders who had come with him were still speaking with different Hawaiian members. It was after midnight when the members left. The leaders then discussed with Shin'ichi various requests and matters requiring attention that had come to light during their conversations. The following morning, October 3, they were scheduled to fly to San Francisco.

Shin'ichi and his party left the hotel at 7:00 A.M. When they arrived at the airport, nearly twenty members were waiting to see them off. Shin'ichi took advantage of the time before his flight to send a postcard to the Soka Gakkai Headquarters in Japan.

On it he wrote: "We are now about to leave for San Francisco to continue our guidance trip. Please take care of everything while we're away." The organization in Japan never left Shin'ichi's thoughts.

As he wrote the postcard, Shin'ichi found himself surrounded by Hawaiian members who were holding books and cards of their own.

"Sensei, could you please write something to commemorate this occasion?" they asked. Though hesitant for a moment, when he saw the members' faces, he felt he wanted to do whatever they asked of him.

"I'll do it if it will make you happy," he said. And, with a heartfelt prayer for each member's growth, he took up his pen and wrote something for one person after another. He continued to use every moment right up until he had to board the plane to offer them encouragement.

The plane carrying Shin'ichi and the others was United Airlines Flight 98, which departed from Honolulu Airport at 9:00 A.M. Their visit to Hawaii, which had opened the first page in the drama of worldwide kosen-rufu, had lasted only a little more than thirty hours. Yet, during that time, the sun of peace had risen in Hawaii, heralding a new dawn in the history of humankind.

"Sunrise" Notes:

1. Peace Preservation Law: A 1925 law enacted by the Japanese government to check the spread of communism and anarchism. With the strengthening of wartime government regulations, application of the law was broadened to adherents of religion and liberal ideals. It was brandished flagrantly as a weapon to suppress free thought and speech. This was the law under which the first and second Soka Gakkai presidents, Tsunesaburo Makiguchi and Josei Toda, respectively, were imprisoned for upholding their belief in the Daishonin's Buddhism.

2. Bonten, Taishaku: Brahma and Indra in Sanskrit. The two major tutelary gods of Buddhism, adopted from Indian mythology, who are sworn to protect Buddhism and its practitioners. They represent, with the other *shoten zenjin*, the protective functions called forth by the emergence of one's Buddha nature.

3. *Fukusa*: Squares of cloth for wrapping precious items, such as prayer beads.

A New World

A NEW arena unfolded before them. Beyond the silver waves lay a vast world poised in anticipation of an era of dynamic progress, an era of unlimited possibilities.

Five-and-a-half hours after leaving Honolulu, Shin'ichi Yamamoto could see the North American continent stretching out beneath him from the plane window. The land extended as far as the eye could see, blending with the sky in the faint haze of the horizon.

In the foreground was a city situated around a bay. From its northernmost extremity rose the towering red structure of the Golden Gate Bridge, bathed in the light of the setting sun. They had reached San Francisco.

It was here, Shin'ichi recalled, that the first Japanese mission to the United States had set foot on American soil exactly 100 years earlier.

On February 13, 1860, a contingent of seventy-seven Japanese representatives left the port of Yokohama on the American warship *Powhattan* to exchange ratifications of the United States–Japan Treaty of Amity and Commerce. The ship encountered violent storms along the way and passengers were forced to endure a difficult crossing. However, after stopping in Hawaii, they finally arrived in San Francisco on March 29.

The Japanese vessel *Kanrinmaru* had arrived in San Francisco ahead of them. The purpose of its voyage had been to provide its crew with hands-on training and experience in seamanship and to deliver provisions and supplies for the Japanese mission. The captain of the *Kanrinmaru* was Katsu Rintaro,[1] and also on board was Fukuzawa Yukichi.[2]

After long years of national seclusion, Japan had finally opened its doors to international exchange. Fukuzawa and his compatriots were thus deeply affected by what they saw during their first real encounter with Western culture.

The *Kanrinmaru* and its passengers soon sailed back to Japan, but what Fukuzawa and his fellow travelers had witnessed during their short stay in San Francisco helped to trigger Japan's drive toward modernization.

The members of the Japanese mission to the United States, meanwhile, boarded the *Powhattan* again and sailed on southward to Panama. After crossing the Isthmus of Panama by train, they then boarded another ship and sailed up the Atlantic Ocean to Washington, D.C. It was here that representatives of both countries finally exchanged ratifications of the United States–Japan Treaty of Amity and Commerce.

From that point on, however, relations between Japan and the United States encountered many twists and turns, until the two countries were eventually forced to confront each other as enemies during World War II. The war finally ended with the United States dropping the world's first atomic bombs on the cities of Hiroshima and Nagasaki, leaving a tragic scar upon human history.

A defeated Japan was placed under U.S. occupation. Six years later, on September 8, 1951, a peace treaty was signed in San Francisco together with the United States–Japan Security Treaty [which was implemented in 1952]. Though these treaties released Japan from its status as an occupied nation, the security treaty itself was, for Japan, an extremely unequal and nonreciprocal agreement.

In 1960, the year in which Shin'ichi made his first step toward worldwide kosen-rufu, Japan was being violently rocked by an internal debate over whether to amend the security treaty.

THE United States–Japan Security Treaty of 1952 was signed together with, and was inseparable from, the Treaty of Peace with Japan [also known as The San Francisco Peace Treaty]. The gist of the security treaty was as follows: Though Japan would regain its independence and sovereignty as a result of the peace treaty, since it had been completely disarmed, the country possessed no viable means of self-defense. American forces would therefore stay on to guarantee Japan's security.

But this brought with it many problems. To begin with, the peace treaty signed in San Francisco was incomplete in that it was not ratified by all of the Allied powers. It was a partial treaty, agreed upon only by the United States and the other Western powers, and thus aligned Japan from the very beginning with the United States and the other anti-communist nations of the Western bloc.

The provision in the security treaty that Japan rely on the United States for its defense only served to solidify Japan's military and political subordination to that country. Moreover, while the treaty clearly stipulated the rights of the United States, it did not define any of its obligations.

For example, it stated that American forces in Japan could be mobilized to preserve the peace and security of the Far East, to suppress internal riots and disturbances when requested to do so by the Japanese government, or in the case of an armed attack on Japan from without. None of these provisions, however, set forth any obligation on the part of the United States to mobilize its forces to protect Japan. Furthermore, the treaty prohibited Japan from granting bases or other military privileges, such as the right of passage, to any third power without prior consent of the United States, thus severely limiting Japan's sovereignty.

While the security treaty was described in its own preamble as a "temporary measure," its term of implementation was left undefined. Moreover, in the text of the treaty, the United States expressed its expectation that Japan would increasingly assume responsibility for its own defense. Despite the mild wording, this was ultimately a demand for Japan to rearm itself. American forces would stay until Japan could maintain the military power for its own defense. For the United States to withdraw, Japan would have to expand and strengthen its military capability.

Japan did in fact respond to this expectation of the United States. It did so by reorganizing and strengthening its National Police Reserve, which had been established in 1950, into a national security force. This was eventually expanded in 1954 into the Self Defense Forces.

The San Francisco Peace Treaty and the United States–Japan Security Treaty were both ratified by Japan's Lower House on October 26, 1951. There was, in one sense, no other option for a defeated and occupied Japan.

*T*HE inequity of the United States–Japan Security Treaty was apparent to all, and it was Japan's Prime Minister Nobusuke Kishi[3] and his cabinet who were strongly intent upon revising it.

When Prime Minister Kishi formed his cabinet in February 1957, he immediately set about amending two laws—the Self Defense Forces Law and the law establishing Japan's Defense Agency. As a result, he expanded the Self Defense Forces by approximately 10,000 troops and generally bolstered Japan's military strength.

By then, Japan was entering a period of rapid growth. The 1956 White Paper on the Economy stated that Japan's "postwar" period was already over and that the country was approaching the nations of the West in terms of economic strength.

Against this background of military and economic development, Prime Minister Kishi embarked on securing a revision to the security treaty with the United States. By turning Japan into an anti-communist military force in Asia, Kishi's intention was to put the relationship with the United States on a more equal footing, while at the same time establishing a strong position for its foreign relations with the Soviet Union and China.

This path diverged greatly from that of former Japanese Prime Minister Shigeru Yoshida,[4] who signed The San Francisco Peace Treaty. Yoshida had sought to rely on the United States for military power while Japan channeled its energies into economic development and worked to earn a place as a member of the family of free nations through its economic strength.

The United States had insisted up to this point that any revision of the security treaty would be premature. But various developments around this time caused the United States to reassess its military strategy in the Far East.

Soviet technology had advanced to the point of developing ICBMs (Inter-Continental Ballistic Missile) capable of making a direct strike on Washington, D.C., from Moscow.

America lagged behind the Soviet Union in missile technology. As it poured energy into developing its own ICBMs to counter the Soviet threat, the United States also focused effort on promoting an accord with the nations of NATO (North Atlantic Treaty Organization) to establish a network of missile bases in order to encircle the Soviet Union with IRBMs (Intermediate-Range Ballistic Missiles).

In its military strategy in the Far East as well, the United States began placing high priority on nuclear missiles. Therefore, as America's need for missile bases increased, the importance of stationing and maintaining ground forces in Japan steadily diminished. It was against this setting that the United States agreed to revise its security treaty with Japan, and the first U.S.-Japan conference for this purpose was held on October 4, 1958.

As if to stay apace with these developments, the Kishi cabinet, four days later, on October 8, suddenly submitted a bill to amend Japan's Police Duties Execution Law for deliberation by the Lower House.

*T*HE proposed amendment to the Police Duties Execution Law initiated by the Kishi administration was aimed at strengthening police authority. It sought to grant broad discretionary powers to police in matters such as the questioning and search of suspects and the right to enter buildings or property.

As soon as the amendment was submitted to the Lower House, however, the Socialist Party—then the largest opposition party—sought its immediate withdrawal and assumed an intractable stance by refusing to participate in any deliberation on the issue.

The media also strongly opposed the measure, charging that it would invite violations of basic human rights. Even popular news and gossip magazines featured the issue, while one weekly warned of the dangers of the proposed legislation under the disparaging headline, "Police Law will interfere with dating."

It was said that the ruling Liberal Democratic Party's motivation in proposing the amendment lay in its desire to suppress certain activities. These would have included the labor dispute then taking place at the Oji Paper Company, LTD., and the Japan Teachers' Union campaign against the government's teacher-performance rating system, which had been fully implemented that year and was arousing powerful opposition. Another view held that it was a preemptive measure to thwart an anticipated movement against the new revision of the security treaty.

Not only did the Socialist Party maintain its vehement opposition to the Police Law amendment in the National Diet, but it organized a "Citizen's Conference Against the Wrongful Amendment of the Police Law," which was joined by an array of groups transcending political philosophy or ideology.

On November 5, 1957, a mass demonstration took place with participants including celebrities, scholars and women's groups; in all, some 4.6 million workers are said to have walked off their jobs in protest. Then, on November 15, mass rallies were held throughout the nation, as the protest movement unfolded on an unprecedented scale. The government of Prime Minister Kishi found itself with no choice but to try to gain control of the situation, and at last abandoned the proposed amendment.

Nothing is stronger than the people. The power of the people is similar to the power of the earth. Once the magma of the people's anger arises, tremors will follow with an energy that can even move mountains. One must never forget that the people are always the driving force for transforming society and the times.

The success of the public's opposition in forcing the withdrawal of the Police Law amendment had a powerful impact on many spheres of society, underscoring eloquently the great potential contained in a movement led by the people. This experience no doubt bolstered the confidence of the Socialist Party. For although it did not have a majority in the National Diet, it could block the passage of key legislation through the momentum of a popular movement. There was a latent danger, however, that such thinking could foster contempt for the parliamentary system of democracy.

In any event, the debacle over the Police Law amendment caused Prime Minister Kishi to lose the public's trust in a single stroke, incurring such suspicion toward his administration that its future was thrown into grave doubt.

*O*N November 27, 1959, as the Kishi government found itself immersed in a quagmire of public displeasure, it was announced that Japan's Crown Prince Akihito [who became emperor in 1989] was to be formally engaged to Michiko Shoda, the future crown princess [who became empress that same year].

The media, which had been restricted from speculative reporting on the marriage of the crown prince, was now free to give extensive coverage and issued daily reports about the royal love story.

Michiko would be the first commoner to wed a crown prince in Japan, and public attention suddenly turned away from politics to focus on the future princess. News stories emphasized the couple's romance, which had blossomed freely on the tennis courts of the resort city Karuizawa (in Nagano Prefecture). Dubbed the "Cinderella of the Showa Era,"[5] Michiko found herself suddenly bathed in the media spotlight as what came to be known as a "Michi boom" swept the country.

As a result, the harsh criticism directed toward Prime Minister Kishi and his government soon subsided, and the adverse winds that had buffeted them gradually eased. Some reportedly believed that the maneuvering of the Kishi administration lay behind this seemingly fortuitous timing of the royal marriage announcement. If that was indeed the case, it would have to be called a typical example of the public being manipulated by the powers that be.

Its crisis now past, the Kishi cabinet proceeded steadily to lay the groundwork for the revision of the United States–Japan Security Treaty, engaging in preparations within its party ranks, while furthering its treaty-related negotiations within the United States–Japan Joint Committee.

The Socialist Party, meanwhile, based on a political platform of unarmed neutrality for Japan, opposed revision of the security treaty. The public's interest in the treaty, however, remained low. The Socialist Party agreed with the ruling Liberal Democratic Party (LDP) that the current security treaty was unequal. Yet, because the Socialists also sought to maintain Japan's military neutrality, aligning it neither with East nor West, they held that the current treaty should be abolished and that a new security arrangement be formed among Japan, the United States, the Soviet Union and China.

This contrasted completely with the LDP's position, which recognized the necessity of a security treaty with the United States, but insisted that the inequity and one-sidedness of the current treaty must be revised to form a truly reciprocal agreement.

The opposition parties began preparing campaigns against the revision of the security treaty around the end of March 1959. Mobilizing the same basic structure they had used for the National Citizens' Conference Against the Wrongful Revision of the Police Law, the Socialist Party, together with the General Council of Trade Unions and other organizations, eventually succeeded in establishing a group called the National Citizens' Conference To Halt the Revision of the Security Treaty. However, the movement to block the revision of the treaty tended to lack cohesive unity.

In October 1959, thirty-three representatives broke away from the Socialist Party under the name of the Socialist Club. The following January, they formed the Democratic Socialist Party based upon a platform of anti-communism and parliamentary democracy.

*L*ACK of unity in the movement against the security treaty revision was not limited to groups formed by the Japan Socialist Party (JSP), but could also be seen in those organized by the labor unions. In addition, the Zengakuren (All-Japan Federation of Student Self-Governing Associations), the national organization of Japan's left-wing student movement, had split into mainstream and anti-mainstream factions, with a deep rift separating the two.

The Zengakuren originally fell under the leadership of the Japan Communist Party (JCP). Toward the end of 1958, however, student members opposed to central control by the JCP formed an alliance called the Communist League, also nicknamed the "Bunto" (after the German word *Bund*, meaning an alliance or federation). The students in the league composed the mainstream of the Zengakuren and dominated its executive leadership, while the pro-JCP students formed the anti-mainstream faction.

On November 27, 1959, as negotiations for revising the U.S.-Japan Security Treaty were entering the final stage, the National Citizens' Conference To Halt the Revision of the Security Treaty planned its eighth nationwide mass protest and held a demonstration outside the National Diet compound to petition for termination of the revision negotiations. It was a peaceful and orderly demonstration.

At the same time, however, a group of students from the Zengakuren mainstream (the Bunto), together with a small core of labor unionists, gained entry to the National Diet complex. When they opened the main gates, some 20,000 protesters then stormed the compound.

The storming of the parliament building had been planned by the Bunto leadership, which not only denounced "American imperialism" but also claimed that Japan and even the Soviet Union had become corrupted by imperialism as well. They called for the destruction of imperialism in all forms. As a first step toward this in Japan, the Bunto advocated blocking the security treaty revision and, to that end, began to advance a radical agenda that did not rule out violent protest.

The following morning, headlines like "Demonstrators Storm Diet Compound" appeared in the newspapers with articles extremely critical of the incident. The ruling LDP issued a statement saying that the storming of the Diet showed a blatant contempt for that body's authority and called the incident "a deliberate and destructive act of revolution arising from a conspiracy [between the Socialist and Communist parties]." The JSP, for its part, announced that it would take a strict stance toward this faction of individuals from the Zengakuren and other bodies and demand that they reflect seriously upon their actions. The Communist Party, meanwhile, criticized the mainstream faction of the Zengakuren, calling them "Trotskyites."[6]

Nevertheless, the incident ultimately heightened public interest in the proposed security treaty revision. This had a strong impact on those students who had wondered whether conventional protest methods would be enough to stop the revision. Despite the condemnation from the established political parties, the Zengakuren rallied many students to its cause, thus increasing its momentum.

Spurred by the student's storming of the Diet, the LDP immediately sponsored a Guarantee of Parliamentary

Deliberation Rights Act, which was intended to restrict demonstrations and other group activities in the vicinity of the National Diet building. Though it was approved by the Lower House following deliberation by the ruling party alone, the bill was ultimately abandoned.

O N January 16, 1960, a fully empowered Japanese delegation, headed by Prime Minister Kishi, left Japan's Haneda Airport for the United States to sign the new U.S.-Japan Security Treaty.

The night before, approximately 700 students from the mainstream faction of the Zengakuren attempted to block the delegation's departure by staging a sit-in at Haneda, only to be dispersed by police.

The delegations of both countries, headed respectively by U.S. Secretary of State Christian Herter and Japanese Prime Minister Kishi, signed the new security treaty at 2:30 P.M. on January 19. The signing, which was also attended by U.S. President Dwight Eisenhower, took place in the East Room of the White House—the same room where, 100 years before, the first Japanese mission to the United States had concluded the U.S.-Japan Treaty of Amity and Commerce. In tandem with the conclusion of the new treaty, the representatives of both countries also signed the Status of Forces Agreement, designating the status of the United States armed forces in Japan, and exchanged related notes and minutes.

The new security treaty, formally called the "Treaty of Mutual Cooperation and Security Between Japan and the United States of America," consists of a preamble and ten articles, with a term of effectiveness initially set at ten years. In addition, the new treaty rectified the inequality and lack of reciprocity in the original treaty by clarifying America's defense obligations to Japan. At the same time, however, it bound Japan to expanding and strengthening its military and thereby shouldering part of the U.S. military commitment in the Far East.

In this connection, Article 3 of the treaty states that both Japan and the United States will "maintain and develop, subject to their constitutional provisions, their capacities to resist armed attack." As witnessed in the Second Defense Plan subsequently enacted by the Japanese government and other policy measures, this article was a virtual mandate for Japan to strengthen its military.

Further, Article 5 of the security treaty stipulates that "Each party recognizes that an armed attack against either party in territories under the administration of Japan would be dangerous to its own peace and safety and declares that it would act to meet the common danger." In other words, if American military bases in Japan were attacked, Japan would be obliged to help protect them, a provision that exposed Japan to the risk of being embroiled in war.

Article 6, meanwhile, clarifies Japan's recognition of the right of American forces in that country to use their bases for the purpose of contributing not only to the security of Japan but also "to the maintenance of international peace and security in the Far East." This meant that Japan was now incorporated as an integral part of U.S. Far East strategy.

*A*FTER the new security treaty was signed, it was presented before the Diet for ratification. A Special Security Committee was formed in the House of Representatives (Lower House) and deliberations commenced in earnest on February 19, 1960. The committee began by wrangling over whether the Diet in fact had the authority to modify the treaty. Turbulent debate also ensued over such questions as the scope and perimeter of what the treaty refers to as the "Far East" and the meaning of the term *prior conferral* as a condition for mobilizing American troops.

Then, suddenly, a new incident took center stage. It came to be known as the "Black Jet" issue. In September of the previous year, a jet aircraft of unknown national origin, which had been painted entirely black with no visible insignia, made an unscheduled landing at a commercial airport in the city of Fujisawa in Japan's Kanagawa Prefecture. While many details concerning the U-2 jet remained unexplained, the United States dismissed it as an American weather-observation plane.

Eight months later, on May 5, 1960, Soviet Premier Nikita Khrushchev[7] reported in a speech before the Politburo that the Soviet Union had shot down an American plane that had violated Soviet airspace. On that occasion, the United States announced that the jet in question was an unarmed weather-observation plane.

On May 7, however, Khrushchev made a shocking counterclaim, calling the American statement a lie. In fact, he said, the plane's pilot was alive and had confessed under interrogation that the purpose of his intrusion into Soviet airspace was to conduct photo reconnaissance for purposes of espionage.

The United States' response to the Soviet charges was defiant as well. All nations gather intelligence, it said. In 1955, the United States had proposed to the Soviets a joint agreement to monitor each other's airspace in order to forestall the possibility of a surprise attack with weapons of mass destruction. The Soviet Union, however, had rejected the proposal. The unarmed u-2 aircraft had, for the past four years, been patrolling the borders of free nations as an unavoidable preventive measure against such a surprise attack. This was the stance taken by America.

On May 9, the Special Security Committee of the Diet took up the issue at once. That day, Premier Khrushchev had issued a stern warning to any Western nation permitting its air bases to be used for the purpose of violating Soviet airspace, threatening that "those bases will become targets for Soviet rockets." Khrushchev's warning also heightened the sense of danger felt by the Japanese that the conclusion of the new security treaty might entangle Japan in a conflict between the United States and the Soviet Union, thus leading it back down the path to war.

T HE u-2 spy plane incident brought home to the world just how deep-rooted the Cold War between East and West had been.

The year 1960 had opened with hopes of a thaw in East-West relations. Premier Khrushchev had visited the United States the previous September, attending a session of the u.n. General Assembly and holding meetings with President Eisenhower at the White House and at Camp David, Maryland. It was the first time in the fourteen years of the Cold War that a springlike ray of sunlight had emerged, easing the tensions between the two camps.

This warming in relations was prompted in part by the threat Soviet progress in nuclear missile development posed to the United States, which still lagged behind in such technology. Dialogue between the leaders of the two nations was also essential to resolve disputes over the partitioning of Berlin [as a result of Germany's defeat in World War II].

Undoubtedly the greatest factor of all, however, was that the leaders of both nations had begun to understand the dangers inherent in a cold war where both sides were engaged in heated competition to develop and stockpile nuclear weapons. According to American scientist Linus Pauling, the United States at that time possessed a stockpile of nuclear weapons twenty times larger than that necessary to wipe out the entire population of the earth, while the Soviet Union had an arsenal about half that size.

At the U.N. General Assembly, Khrushchev outlined a plan where each nation of the world would do away with its armaments in four years, and he submitted it as a proposal before the assembly. His talks with Eisenhower also resulted in the two leaders pledging to each other and the world to settle international problems not by military force but through peaceful dialogue. It certainly seemed that a momentous turning point had arrived.

In addition, that year the people of the world were placing their hopes for peaceful coexistence in the East-West Summit. Slated for May 16 in Paris, it would be the first such meeting in five years. However, revelations concerning the U-2 spy plane incident derailed the Paris summit and caused Soviet leaders to effectively reject Eisenhower's scheduled June visit to the Soviet Union. The Cold War instead intensified, and relations that had shown signs of a thaw were plunged once again into the depths of winter.

The people of both the Soviet Union and the United States yearned for peace. However, the hearts of their respective leaders were separated by an unbridgeable gulf of mutual distrust. It was such distrust that gave rise to the U-2 spy plane affair, the discovery of which fueled the atmosphere of suspicion and recrimination on both sides, reversing what progress had been made thus far toward peace.

*S*HIN'ICHI Yamamoto had kept a sharp eye on the news each day. The tense situation deeply stirred his interest as he turned the details over in his mind again and again. On May 19, 1960, as opposition to the new security treaty mounted following the U-2 spy plane incident, the Kishi administration embarked on a brash course of action that was to leave a great blemish upon Japan's parliamentary system of democracy.

That evening, the Diet Committee on Rules and Administration—which had recessed after becoming dead-locked in a debate over extending the then-current thirty-fourth session of parliament—suddenly reconvened on the one-sided decision of the committee's ruling-party member-ship. The ruling-party majority then voted to place a motion for a fifty-day extension before the full Diet.

Outraged at the unilateral action, Diet members of the Japan Socialist Party staged a sit-in in a hall outside the office of the Speaker of the House. Their intent was to block com-mencement of a plenary session of the House of Representa-tives [which required the Speaker's presence]. Unable to leave his office, House Speaker Ichiro Kiyose then requested a unit of 500 police officers be dispatched to the Diet compound. It was truly an unprecedented scene in postwar Japanese politics.

Some 30,000 demonstrators responded to a call from such organizations as the mainstream Zengakuren and the National Citizens' Conference To Halt the Revision of the Security Treaty and jammed the area outside the Diet com-pound in the pouring rain.

At 10:25 P.M., the opening bell rang for the plenary ses-sion of the Diet. As if in response to a prearranged signal, it was suddenly announced that the Special Security Committee, which had been in recess, would now reconvene. The majority of the JSP members on that committee were still engaged in the sit-down in front of the Speaker's office. Pandemonium ensued as the remaining JSP committee members rushed the Special Security Committee chairman, and pushing and shoving broke out among opposing party members. As the uproar continued, the Security Committee passed a motion to submit the new security treaty to the National Diet. The entire episode took only three minutes. However, the continued shouting and jostling prevented any transcript of the proceedings from being recorded.

Just after 11:00 P.M., police arrived and began to bodily remove the JSP members lodged in front of the Speaker's room. Finally, at around 11:50 P.M., House Speaker Kiyose entered the main assembly hall, escorted by Diet guards. Under these highly irregular circumstances, the Diet was declared open with only members of the ruling Liberal Democratic Party present. The fifty-day extension was immediately approved. Then, just after midnight on the morning of May 20, after a report from the chairman of the Special Security Committee, approval of the new security treaty was rammed through the Diet without deliberation or discussion.

It was truly a delinquent course of action, subverting the very process of parliamentary democracy. Even some members of the LDP opposed the move. Nearly thirty representatives had been absent during the proceedings, excluding those missing due to illness.

Why had the LDP decided to employ such strong-arm tactics to force passage of the new security treaty? On June 19, President Eisenhower was scheduled to visit Japan to commemorate the centennial of the first United States–Japan Treaty of Amity and Commerce.

Since thirty days was required for the new security treaty
to take effect once it was passed by the House of Representatives, May 20 was the final chance to have the treaty
approved and in force by the time of Eisenhower's visit.

*T*HE people's indignation flared at the outrageous tactics of the LDP in forcing passage of the new security
treaty. From this point on, the anti-security treaty
movement grew to a scale and intensity unprecedented in
Japan's postwar history. However, more than the actual content of the security treaty itself, it was the people's anger at
the Kishi administration's disregard for the process of parliamentary democracy that rallied them to action.

Many scholars and intellectuals who had previously been
undecided about the security treaty now expressed their
opposition to it out of their desire to protect the democratic
process. People joined the demonstrations in growing numbers, carrying placards with slogans like "Kishi Resign!" and
"Dissolve the Diet!"

Shin'ichi Yamamoto, meanwhile, had just been inaugurated as the third president of the Soka Gakkai earlier that
month, on May 3, and was devoting himself energetically to
creating a fresh surge of progress toward kosen-rufu. He was
also deeply concerned about the tenor of events that had
unfolded in the Diet concerning the security treaty.

Shin'ichi, like many others, was pained by what he per-
ceived as a threat to Japan's system of democracy.

Needless to say, the question of what to do about the
security treaty was one of profound importance to Japan.
The old security treaty clearly was an unequal agreement
that limited Japanese sovereignty. Yet, there were many
points about the new treaty as well that begged for improvement. But if the new treaty was abandoned completely, as
the JSP proposed, it would leave Japan facing the major

problem of how to mend the inevitable rift in Japan-u.s. relations such a move would cause.

This only underscored the vital need for conducting thorough deliberation with the aim of finding better solutions and reaching a consensus, while making a conscious effort to clarify problem areas by focusing squarely on the realities involved.

Although quite a long time had been spent discussing the new security treaty, there had been no deliberation in the true sense of the word. Representatives of both the LDP and JSP had taken a stubborn and inflexible stand, their minds already made up before the talks even began. While the LDP ran impetuously toward passage of the new treaty, the JSP obstinately pursued its rejection.

The arbitrary way in which the LDP had rammed the treaty through the Diet, by relying on its strength in numbers, symbolized a destructive act toward Japan's parliamentary system of government. It must be said, however, that a great portion of the responsibility for what happened also lay with the JSP, which failed to respond with any effective countermeasures in the Diet.

Though one cannot deny the importance of citizens' movements, it is the responsibility of the nation's elected representatives to carry out thorough discussion and thereby arrive at a solution. It should never be forgotten that the very life of the democratic system lies in tenacious dialogue and debate aimed at reaching a consensus.

*F*ROM the day the ruling Liberal Democratic Party forced the vote on the new security treaty, the area around the National Diet compound was packed with more than 10,000 protesters daily. The demonstrators ranged from intellectuals to lantern-carrying housewives, attesting to the breadth and scope of the anti-security treaty movement. It was only natural that the issue became a topic of great interest among the Soka Gakkai youth division members as well.

One day, toward the end of May, Shin'ichi Yamamoto was engaged in a conversation with some representatives of the young men's division. One of them said to him, "With the new security treaty now such a big issue, I was wondering whether the Soka Gakkai shouldn't also express a consolidated position on the matter."

With a smile, the youthful president responded, "Well then, let me ask you this: Are you against the treaty, or are you for it?"

"I'm solidly against it. I think we should do away with the security treaty and take a neutral stand in international relations."

At this, another youth spoke up: "I can't say that I completely approve of the treaty, but I think that it's an unavoidable necessity for the time being. Right now, Japan is incapable of standing on its own militarily or economically without U.S. cooperation. If we abolish the treaty now, Japan will create ill feelings with the United States. Therefore, to talk about scrapping the security treaty at this stage is to ignore reality."

Other young men expressed their opinions, too, but their responses divided them into two camps. Shin'ichi looked at them warmly and said with a smile:

"Do you see how much the opinions vary just among yourselves, the members of the youth division? Though you are all Soka Gakkai members, you have many different ideas about the security treaty. Some of you are for it and some against it. And no matter which side you choose, each has its pros and cons. The Soka Gakkai cannot tell people what to do with regard to the security treaty. I want as much as possible to respect all of your opinions.

"The Daishonin's teachings, of course, say nothing about the security treaty, so isn't it permissible for various thoughts on the matter to exist within the Soka Gakkai? Politics and religion occupy different spheres. The foremost mission of religion is to cultivate and nurture human life, which forms the basis for everything else. The Soka Gakkai is a religious organization and, as such, will not be declaring its views on each political issue that arises. I think we should trust our fellow members who have been elected to sit as representatives on the House of Councilors and leave what needs to be done politically to them.

"Nevertheless, even if it be in the sphere of politics, should a fundamental problem arise that, if ignored, will definitely cause unhappiness for the people and lead to the destruction of peace for humanity, then I will speak out. Better yet, I will take the lead and fight in the forefront."

The youths' eyes sparkled.

*O*N June 10, amid rising anti-security treaty protests, President Eisenhower's press secretary, James C. Hagerty, arrived in Japan to coordinate final plans for the president's scheduled visit later that month. As Hagerty's car prepared to depart for the American Embassy via Haneda Airport's main exit, it was surrounded by a sea of demonstrators—members of the anti-mainstream (pro-Communist Party) faction of the militant Zengakuren student federation and labor unionists opposed to the security treaty. With demonstrators rocking the vehicle and climbing onto its roof, Hagerty and his party were held under siege for more than an hour until a U.S. Marine Corps helicopter came to rescue them.

The incident caused a stir not only in Japan but internationally as well. Hubert Humphrey, U.S. senator and chair of the Senate Foreign Relations Committee, lodged a stern protest, calling the episode "a direct insult to the American people."

It was five days later, however, on June 15, that the most tragic and painful page in the history of the 1960 movement against the security treaty was recorded. That evening, groups of demonstrators from the radical mainstream faction of the Zengakuren, as well as from the labor unions and the "new theater" alliance of anti-traditional dramatists and actors, began marching toward the National Diet compound.

Suddenly, scores of ultra-rightists, arriving on trucks emblazoned with banners, surged into the crowd and began attacking the protesters. In the ensuing melee, it was the members of the "new theater" alliance, many of whom were women, who sustained the greatest injuries. Armed with wooden clubs, the rightists randomly struck the fleeing demonstrators. The authorities were slow in responding to the sudden outbreak of violence, a fact some viewed as evidence of the police officials' tacit approval of the extremists' outrageous actions.

The vicinity around the Diet was filled with close to 20,000 demonstrators who had been summoned there by the mainstream Zengakuren faction and other groups. When the students heard about the violence and the delay in police intervention, they assumed that the rightist attack had been instigated by the Kishi administration.

Implementing their plan to storm the Diet, the Zengakuren leaders shouted "Charge!" Enraged students then broke down the gate to the south entrance and set to work removing a barricade of police trucks that had been set up just inside, finally managing to gain entry.

Police turned powerful water cannons onto the crowd, while the students responded by throwing stones. The air between the two sides bristled with a menacing intensity. Baton-wielding police, who had been waiting in the shadows of the Diet building, launched themselves on the students

entering the compound. There was a thunderous roar of angry shouts intermingled with screams of agony. Students were even clubbed from behind by police as they attempted to escape.

Some slipped and fell in the pools of water caused by the water cannons and then were trampled by scores of other students. The water became tinged with blood.

Tragically, one student died in the turmoil. Her name was Michiko Kamba, a literature major at the University of Tokyo.

*S*HIN'ICHI Yamamoto was at the Soka Gakkai Head-quarters when he heard the news of Michiko Kamba's death. The tragic loss of the young student, who had participated in the demonstration out of her hopes for democracy and peace and her concern about Japan's future, weighed heavily on Shin'ichi's mind. It also deeply pained him that the student demonstrators and the police who had been dispatched to disperse them—all fellow youth—had had to spill one another's blood.

Prospects for repealing the security treaty, now that it had been passed by the House of Representatives (Lower House), were almost nil. Through the process of automatic ratification, it seemed inevitable that the treaty would become law thirty days after its passage by the Lower House, just as Prime Minister Kishi had planned.

When that happened, it would also signal an end to the battle against the security treaty. Where would the students direct their energies then? Shin'ichi wondered. Though he had been concerned about their movement getting out of hand, he was also keenly aware of the purity of spirit that motivated them. For this very reason, he hoped that each youth would continue to live for peace and democracy. If, with the passage of time, they were to forget their original purpose, then the death of that one young woman would have been in vain.

Filled with pain and grief at the events that had come to pass, he firmly resolved to create an era of genuine democracy and peace, hoping that in doing so the young woman's sacrifice might also be vindicated.

The day after the incident, the Japanese government decided that it would be inadvisable to have President Eisenhower come to Japan under the present circumstances and requested that his visit be postponed. Prime Minister Kishi then held a press conference, at which he stated: "It is extremely alarming to behold the situation now facing Japan, where destructive forces of violence threaten to subvert democracy and our parliamentary system. The government is determined to stand up against such communist anarchy and assiduously protect democracy, which safeguards the dignity of human freedom. To do so, it is a matter of the utmost urgency that we take the necessary measures to maintain public order."

Kishi's words displayed the arrogance of a politician unwilling to reflect upon his own responsibility. Wasn't it the LDP's forced passage of the security treaty—an action of blatant contempt for democracy and the parliamentary process— that served more than anything to fuel the flames of the people's anger?

At midnight on June 18, the new security treaty, without being put to a vote before the Upper House, automatically passed into legislation. As that time arrived, a hush fell over the crowd of demonstrators that had gathered outside the National Diet compound.

"We declare the treaty void!" a voice rang out over a loudspeaker, followed by echoing shouts from some of the students. But most just listened, their faces blank and lifeless. Some dropped to their haunches, as if their legs had crumbled beneath them, while some of the female students sobbed. All shared the bitter taste of defeat.

*T*HE exchange of ratification documents for the new U.S.-Japan Security Treaty took place on June 23, 1960, upon which the treaty went fully into effect.

As soon as the treaty was in place, Prime Minister Kishi announced his resignation,[8] and a new cabinet was formed under his successor, Hayato Ikeda, on July 19. For Japan, this marked the end of what some called an "age of politics" and heralded the arrival of a new "age of economics." The people's energy, which had been directed against the security treaty, could increasingly come to be channeled toward the pursuit of a more prosperous lifestyle.

Recalling these events of some three months before, Shin'ichi stepped off the plane at San Francisco Airport. The clock in the terminal indicated 4:35 P.M. They were two hours ahead of Honolulu time.

Several members had turned out to meet them.

"President Yamamoto, welcome!" a woman said. This greeting, however, was directed at Vice General Director Kiyoshi Jujo.

Though the woman had seen Shin'ichi's picture in the Soka Gakkai's newspaper, the *Seikyo Shimbun*, she had never met him in person and could not immediately tell who was whom. She had mistaken Jujo, who had a more imposing presence than Shin'ichi, for the Soka Gakkai president.

Jujo's face turned red as he pointed toward Shin'ichi, saying, "That's President Yamamoto." The other leaders traveling with Shin'ichi could not help being amused by Jujo's diffident manner.

"I…I'm sorry," the woman stammered, embarrassed at her mistake and repeatedly bowing her head in apology.

"It couldn't be helped; we've never met," said a smiling Shin'ichi. "Thank you for troubling to come and meet us."

After offering these warm words of appreciation, he accompanied the others to the airport lounge. There, Nagayasu Masaki introduced the party from Japan to the San Francisco members, beginning with Yukiko Gilmore, a woman who had been playing a leading role in promoting propagation activities in that West Coast city.

Mrs. Gilmore had taken faith five years earlier in Yokohama, Japan, and came to the United States with her American husband a year after that. Through her faith, during the short time she practiced in Japan, she transformed a condition of chronic illness, which had necessitated endless hospital visits, into one of robust health. Arriving in San Francisco with this experience under her belt, she devoted herself wholeheartedly to sharing the teachings of Nichiren Daishonin's Buddhism with anyone of Japanese ancestry she encountered.

She did not understand a word of complex or difficult theory. She simply possessed powerful confidence in faith—confidence that she had gained through her own experience. More than ten people had begun to practice after listening to her talk about Buddhism. They also held discussion meetings, gathering together three or four members at a time.

THOUGH discussion meetings had indeed been held in San Francisco, they were far from resounding with the joy of faith. If anything, they had become a kind of "commiseration gathering" in which the participants consoled one another about their problems.

The members who attended these meetings were having a hard time coming to terms with life in a foreign country and were desperately homesick for Japan. Whenever they met, they would naturally voice their dissatisfaction. Sharing their complaints, however, only served to deepen their misery, and inevitably the meetings would end with everyone in tears.

After exchanging only a few words with Yukiko Gilmore, Shin'ichi Yamamoto could discern the great struggle she had mounted in conducting activities. He wanted to offer his wholehearted praise and encouragement to this woman who had, with all her might, been waging a solitary battle.

"It must have been very difficult for you. Thank you for all you have done. Please don't worry, everything will be fine from now on!" Hearing his words, the woman's eyes grew moist with tears.

Next, Shin'ichi addressed another woman from Japan who had been standing shyly behind Mrs. Gilmore. He was concerned because she looked unhappy, as if worn out by her daily existence.

"May I ask your name?" he said.

"Ai Lin," the woman replied.

"Please, come on over and have a seat."

Shin'ichi offered the woman a chair. Ai Lin was extremely tense. Her husband worked for the American military and had developed a severe gambling problem. He had run up an enormous debt and they were now virtually destitute. She had become physically and mentally exhausted and had even begun to contemplate suicide when, in June of the previous year, she had learned of the Daishonin's Buddhism. Like a drowning person clutching at straws, she had decided to join.

"Are you practicing this faith wholeheartedly?" Shin'ichi asked her.

"Yes. I'm carrying out faith like fire,'" she answered without hesitation.

Although the woman had been taught that "faith like flowing water" was the model for strong faith and that "faith like fire" instead meant faith that flared temporarily like a flame and died out quickly, in her nervousness she had inadvertently confused "faith like fire" as meaning a strong and passionate belief.

"Oh, no! It's just the opposite!" protested Yukiko Gilmore, tugging at Ai Lin's sleeve. "I never taught you that."

Shin'ichi smiled warmly.

"It won't do for you to have faith like fire," he said. "But if you persevere with faith like flowing water, then you will definitely become happy."

Shin'ichi's words were charged with confidence. With this single statement, Ai Lin felt the thick cloud of sorrow lift from her heart.

*S*HIN'ICHI then spoke to the woman standing next to Yukiko Gilmore. "And may I ask you your name, too?"

"Yes, my name is Chiyoko Taylor. In Japan, I was a unit chief in Kamata Chapter."

"Kamata Chapter? I have many fond memories of Kamata. Do you perhaps know my wife?" Shin'ichi queried.

"Yes, your wife came to discussion meetings at my parents' house several times with your children. Also, the first discussion meeting I attended was at the home of your wife's parents, Mr. and Mrs. Haruki."

"Really? It's a small world, isn't it!" exclaimed Shin'ichi. "And your husband?"

"This is my husband," she answered, pointing to the big man standing beside her. "His name is Paul. He works as an auditor for the federal government." She then added, somewhat apologetically, "But he doesn't practice yet; he does support my practice, though."

"That's enough, isn't it?" Shin'ichi replied instantly. "He happily came with you to welcome us. Doesn't that make him an excellent member already?"

At that moment, a beaming Paul Taylor offered a greeting in broken Japanese: "*Konnichi-wa* (Good afternoon)!"

"Oh! How do you do," Shin'ichi responded in labored English, gesturing broadly. Shaking Paul's hand, he continued in his native tongue: "I'm so glad you came here with your wife to meet us. That's very kind of you!"

Yukiko Gilmore's husband, who stood beside Taylor, also reached out to shake Shin'ichi's hand. He had a dignified look.

"Oh! Thank you very much!" Shin'ichi said in English. "Thank you for all your support."

Genuinely pleased, Mr. Gilmore then responded in heavily accented Japanese, "Yamamoto Sensei, *o-machi-shitemashita* (President Yamamoto, I've been waiting to meet you)."

"Thank you very much. I'd like to ask that you continue to support your wife and the Soka Gakkai."

The two Americans seemed very amiable and good-natured. Shin'ichi presented Paul Taylor, who had yet to take faith, with a pin commemorating his own inauguration as president. Paul quickly put it on and displayed it proudly. He then held up a camera and said again in broken Japanese, "*Minna de, shashin, torimasho* (Everyone, let's take a picture together)."

It was a bright and cheerful welcome, in complete contrast to their lonely arrival at Honolulu Airport.

SHIN'ICHI and the leaders accompanying him left the airport for the Sir Francis Drake Hotel, which was located on a steeply sloping street near Union Square. The twenty-one-story building of classic architecture looked out over a typical San Francisco scene, complete with passing cable cars.

After resting at the hotel for a while, Shin'ichi and his companions went out for dinner with the Gilmores and the Taylors. They were taken to a tempura restaurant where menu items were written in Japanese on worn-out sheets of paper pasted to the walls. There was something modest and homey about it—a dining place for ordinary folks. The Taylors assumed that the visitors would have grown tired of Western-style cuisine by now and had chosen this restaurant to give them a chance to eat some Japanese food.

Not usually able to afford the luxury of dining out on Japanese cuisine, the Taylors probably knew very little about the Japanese restaurants in the area. Although his traveling companions frankly thought the restaurant was a little too spartan, Shin'ichi himself was touched more than anything by the Taylors' sincerity and deeply appreciated their gesture.

The greatest treat for Shin'ichi was to meet these two ordinary yet brave and noble women who had been striving to lay down the roots of kosen-rufu in America. In turn, the supreme treat for the women was to hear President Shin'ichi Yamamoto's heartfelt words of appreciation for their efforts and to see his encouraging smile. Though the meal was an extremely simple one, it was the first dinner meeting for kosen-rufu to be held on the American continent.

Shin'ichi also repeatedly expressed his gratitude to the two husbands. Though neither seemed to understand Japanese that well, when their wives interpreted what Shin'ichi had said, they nodded and smiled back, their eyes sparkling.

During the meal, Yukiko Gilmore received a phone call. Several members had gone to the airport to meet the Soka Gakkai president and his party but had arrived too late; now they had assembled at the Gilmores' home.

As he listened to Mrs. Gilmore explain the situation, Shin'ichi thought: "The circumstances of these members must not be easy. It must have been a real challenge for them to find the time and means to travel to the airport to meet us. They probably worried the whole way whether they would make it on time. How sad they must have been when they arrived only to find that we had already gone; they must have been filled with disappointment as they made their way to the Gilmores. They are the ones who need my encouragement more than anyone now. It is my responsibility to encourage them."

SHIN'ICHI Yamamoto wanted to go right away to meet the members but felt that leaving in the middle of dinner would be very discourteous to the Taylors and the Gilmores, who were escorting him. He saw no choice but to ask the women's division chief, Katsu Kiyohara, and Nagayasu Masaki to accompany Yukiko Gilmore to meet with the waiting members in his stead. He sent a message and some gifts with them as encouragement.

Shin'ichi was always aware of the importance of each moment. Victory or defeat in battle hinges upon whether one seizes the initiative at a key moment. When it comes to encouraging friends, as well, there are crucial times when one must act. Shin'ichi was always quick to respond, taking prompt and timely action. His swiftness of response could perhaps be attributed in part to a keen sensitivity that had been honed by an intense determination to fulfill his responsibilities as Soka Gakkai president. He was driven by the thought that failing to seize the moment might result in a chance being lost forever. The importance of acting quickly was also something that he had engraved deeply in his life as a youth, when he had poured all of his energies into serving his mentor, Josei Toda, while undergoing strict training as a disciple who would shoulder the future.

After Kiyohara and the others had left, Shin'ichi said to Paul Taylor: "I apologize for the commotion. I really want to do my best to respond to the sincerity of those who went all the way to the airport to meet us. Buddhism is nothing out of the ordinary. It teaches the true way for people to live and behave as human beings."

As Chiyoko Taylor interpreted what had been said, her husband, Paul, listened intently with a serious expression. Then, his eyes shining, he smiled and extended his hands in a gesture of understanding, exclaiming in a mixture of English and Japanese, "Oh, *Buppo* (Buddhism), wonderful!"

Tears welled in his wife's eyes. She had clearly been agonizing over how to get her husband to understand Buddhism, even if only a little. Her face showed deep emotion as she said to Shin'ichi: "Sensei! Thank you. This is the first time I have seen my husband so happy listening to someone talk about Buddhism. To think that you will be coming to our discussion meeting tomorrow seems like a dream. I'm just sorry to say there aren't many members here in San Francisco."

"That's fine," Shin'ichi said. "I've come to plant seeds. Tomorrow will be a new beginning."

Chiyoko Taylor etched Shin'ichi's words into her heart.

A NEW day dawned in San Francisco. On this day, October 4, a discussion meeting was to be held with Shin'ichi Yamamoto attending.

Shin'ichi and the other leaders spent the morning sightseeing around the city, while in the afternoon they paid a visit to the Japanese Consulate. They then made their way to the Gilmores' house, where the discussion meeting was scheduled for 6:30 that evening. The house was located on Cole Street, set among a row of classic San Francisco–style residences with their distinctive bay windows.

Shin'ichi and his party arrived at the Gilmores' shortly after 5:00 P.M. In a room that had been set aside for their use, they immediately began discussing the leadership appointments for a new district.

The night before, Shin'ichi had informed his colleagues that he intended to establish a district here in San Francisco as well. He had then asked Vice General Director Kiyoshi Jujo and the others to come up with a blueprint for the leadership of the new district.

Jujo now showed Shin'ichi their proposal.

"Yes, that's the only possible choice," said Shin'ichi quietly. "Let's go with it."

He continued, "On this trip, I also plan to set up chapters and general chapters in North and South America, because in the future, the sphere of our endeavors to propagate the Law will encompass the entire world."

The others could not believe their ears.

Yet, since the district in Hawaii was established, they had come to realize that Shin'ichi possessed a monumental vision for kosen-rufu that far surpassed anything they could imagine. Thus, although they were stunned by his words, the idea didn't seem all that preposterous. In fact, they were exhilarated at the thought that something new was again about to emerge.

Shin'ichi then invited several of the key local members into the room. "The reason I asked you in here," he began, "is that today, I intend to form a district in San Francisco. I therefore would like to ask Yukiko Gilmore to be the district chief and Chiyoko Taylor the women's division district chief."

Both women nodded, their expressions tense.

"Mrs. Gilmore will be the district leader, a position that is usually assigned to a man. However, I think it is perfectly

acceptable for her to fulfill this position. Not only are there many women among the members here, but America is a country that stresses the equality of the sexes. Moreover, there is no discrimination in Buddhism. As Nichiren Daishonin states, 'There should be no discrimination among those who propagate the five characters of Myoho-renge-kyo in the Latter Day of the Law, be they men or women' (WND-1, 385). Therefore, it's not at all strange to have a woman in the position of district chief. If the two of you combine your energies and work together, you can create a wonderful district."

"I'll do my best!"

"I'll fight with all my might!"

Each woman replied with firm resolve. The seed of kosen-rufu had just been planted in their hearts.

TO the husbands of Yukiko Gilmore and Chiyoko Taylor, Shin'ichi then said: "I would also like to ask you, Daniel and Paul, to become advisors to the district. In addition to supporting your wives as you've been doing, I'd really appreciate it if you could warmly watch over the members of the district and, if need be, make yourselves available for advice and assistance. Would you mind doing this?"

Nagayasu Masaki, who was standing at Shin'ichi's side, translated this for them. Smiling, the two men nodded their agreement.

Shin'ichi's companions, however, could not hide their astonishment. Daniel Gilmore seemed to have almost no knowledge of profound Buddhist doctrines, while Paul Taylor was not even a member. The idea of appointing the two as district advisors would never have entered the leaders' minds.

Sensing the others' thoughts, Shin'ichi said promptly: "I treasure people like Paul—people who, though not practicing faith themselves, have a good understanding of the Soka Gakkai and lend their support to our activities. Nothing is more gratifying. I want to show my utmost appreciation and respect for their contribution.

"Many members tend to look at people simply in terms of whether they are practicing: if a person is a member, they feel reassured; if not, they feel uneasy. But this kind of thinking is wrong; it is not Buddhism. There are many fine people of upstanding character who don't practice. When we look at how these people live, we see much that accords with the Buddhist way of life.

"On the other hand, there are people who practice this faith yet cause trouble for their fellow members or society, or end up betraying the Soka Gakkai. Therefore, to think that those who practice are good and those who do not are bad is to make a terrible mistake. Indeed, I would even say it violates the principles of human rights."

In Shin'ichi's mind there was no wall separating the Soka Gakkai from society. In accord with the principle that "Buddhism manifests itself in society," those who practice Buddhism should naturally yearn for the happiness of all people and peace throughout the world.

Moreover, a great mountain that rises from a broad base is not easily destroyed, whereas a sheer cliff is fragile and easily crumbles. To firmly establish kosen-rufu, the Soka Gakkai also needed to possess a solid base like that of a majestic mountain.

Thus, the support of people outside the organization—people from every walk of life—has been important. Shin'ichi was also keenly aware that the very presence of such friends would clearly attest to the validity of the Daishonin's Buddhism as a religion that exists for the people.

*A*FTER he finished discussing the new organizational arrangements, Shin'ichi chatted with those who were there. It was then that he heard the rhythmic sound of gongyo emanating from the main meeting room.

Shin'ichi went to have a look. Two or three members were doing gongyo, led by an American man of around 30. It was a truly sonorous gongyo; the American's enunciation of the liturgy was extremely clear.

Shin'ichi returned to the other room. A little while later, he invited the man who had led gongyo, along with his wife, to join him for a chat.

"What is your name?' asked Shin'ichi.

Smiling, the man shook his head, indicating that he didn't understand. His wife answered on his behalf.

"I'm sorry. My husband doesn't speak Japanese. His name is George Oliver, and I'm Yasuko, his wife."

George Oliver had taken faith in Japan six years earlier and had returned to the United States with his wife three years after that. In Japan, he had been taken under the wing of Joji Kanda, the chief of Tokyo's Nakano Chapter and a teacher of English literature at a university. With Kanda's guidance and support, George participated in Soka Gakkai activities and steadily exerted himself in faith. He and his wife continued their practice after returning to the United States, and had succeeded in leading a number of others to embrace the Daishonin's Buddhism.

"Where did you come from today?" asked Shin'ichi.

"From Reno, Nevada."

"Thank you for coming such a long way. How many hours did it take you to get here?"

"Five hours by car."

"Is that so? It must have been a strenuous trip. Please be sure to leave right after the discussion meeting, so that you don't get back too late."

Yasuko translated these words for her husband.

"*Domo arigato gozaimasu* (thank you very much)," responded George in Japanese.

He then continued in English, with Nagayasu Masaki interpreting for him:

"It is a great honor to welcome you to America, President Yamamoto. When my wife and I were living in Japan, we were in a dilemma over whether to stay in Japan or go back to the United States. At that time, we had a chance to receive guidance from President Toda. He told us, 'Buddhism must be propagated widely throughout the world; therefore, I want you to go back to America and do your best!'

"When I heard this, I keenly sensed the depth of his desire to achieve worldwide kosen-rufu.

"Now, here you are in America, only five months after your inauguration. This clearly shows that you are putting into practice President Toda's spirit to spread the Daishonin's Buddhism throughout the world."

GEORGE Oliver's words riveted the attention of the leaders accompanying Shin'ichi. "After President Toda's death," Oliver continued, "I worried about what would become of the Soka Gakkai. But meeting President Yamamoto like this, I can sense that the Soka Gakkai has made a fresh start with its youthful president toward a limitless future.

"I also deeply appreciate your concern about our journey back home. Meeting you today, President Yamamoto, will remain a precious memory for the rest of my life."

Hearing Oliver's words, Shin'ichi's companions exchanged looks of surprise. Somewhere in their hearts they had felt that perhaps only a Japanese could comprehend and appreciate faith in the Daishonin's Buddhism and the Soka Gakkai spirit. But seeing this American member firsthand, they were struck by how wrong their thinking had been.

The principle of the mutual possession of the Ten Worlds is universal to all human beings. Therefore, faith in the Daishonin's Buddhism is open to all people, transcending ethnic or national differences.

As Shin'ichi Yamamoto listened to George Oliver speak, he considered whether he should establish a district in Nevada as well and appoint the Olivers as the district chief and district women's division chief. He had already learned that there were almost no other members in the region of Nevada. Certainly, it would be a first to appoint an American of non-Japanese descent to the position of district chief.

But without planting a seed, no fresh new shoots would emerge. Unless non-Japanese leaders eventually appeared in each country, the full-fledged development of kosen-rufu could not be realized. Moreover, an organization is determined by its leaders. If the central figure resolves to stand up alone, then everything will develop from there.

Shin'ichi's mind moved with lightning swiftness. In a moment, he announced, "I will establish a district in Nevada, too."

The decision was clearly beyond the comprehension of his companions. This was because of the disparity in determination between them and Shin'ichi. Having made worldwide kosen-rufu his life's mission, Shin'ichi was now forging ahead with the single-minded purpose to realize that goal. None of his decisions or responses was made on a mere impulse or whim. Even split-second decisions contained his concentrated thought for kosen-rufu that came from exerting infinitely painstaking effort in each moment of life.

The entire world beat vibrantly within Shin'ichi's heart.

*A*S the time for the discussion meeting approached, Yukiko Gilmore wondered anxiously how many members would turn up. In preparation for Shin'ichi's visit to San Francisco, the Overseas Affairs Section of the Soka Gakkai Headquarters had sent her a list with the names of some twenty members living in and around the San Francisco area. She had either gone to visit them at their homes or contacted them by letter, but she didn't think that many of them would come to the meeting.

By the time the discussion meeting was about to begin, however, the room was packed with about thirty people. Not surprisingly, the majority were Japanese women now living in America. All were amazed to see how many fellow members had gathered. Members in Japan had also contacted those they knew who had gone to live in the San Francisco area, informing them of the planned discussion meeting with President Yamamoto.

Ai Lin whispered to Yukiko Gilmore: "Wow! There are so many people. Talk about Bodhisattvas of the Earth! I wonder if they don't actually pop up out of the ground after all."

"Don't talk such nonsense!" replied Yukiko. "It was bad enough when you proudly told President Yamamoto yesterday that you practice 'faith like fire.' People will think I'm always teaching you strange things."

Shin'ichi happened to overhear this frank yet innocent exchange and smiled.

When the meeting began, Shin'ichi's companions stood up one by one to speak. They were all top leaders of the Soka Gakkai whom the members had seen only in the *Seikyo Shimbun*: the vice general director and the chiefs of the study department, women's division and youth division. It felt like a dream to the participants to be listening to their encouragement firsthand.

Finally, it was time for guidance from President Shin'ichi Yamamoto. Here, as in Hawaii, he decided to field questions. The members' questions were colored by the heartache of living in a foreign land where they were unable to speak the language. Here, too, the words "I want to go back to Japan" were heard. It was apparent that many of the members had been living from one day to the next under a cloud of anguish.

Shin'ichi had to pour every ounce of his energy and passion into giving courage to those held captive by sadness and despair so that they could regain the strength to live vibrantly. This required strenuous effort, like that needed to produce fire from damp wood. Cherishing each person, Shin'ichi spoke of the greatness of Buddhism, offering advice and direction with painstaking care, his words at times blazing with conviction.

*B*Y the time the question–and–answer session drew to a close, the room was filled with cheerful smiles and glowing expressions.

Shin'ichi took a moment to wipe the perspiration from his brow, then stressed powerfully: "All of you have come to San Francisco because you have a mission. Each day may be a great struggle for you right now as you grapple with a host of trying problems. But all of these exist so you can prove the great beneficial power of Buddhism.

"You are the great pioneers of kosen-rufu in America. I want you to understand that America's future rests entirely on your shoulders. For that reason, I ask three things of you today.

"The first is that you acquire citizenship and become good American citizens. Accomplishing kosen-rufu will ultimately hinge on the trust and respect those who promote it earn from those around them. Though you live here, you cannot win society's trust by leading a rootless existence, feeling no love for America and constantly thinking about returning to Japan. Acquiring citizenship means taking on certain obligations and responsibilities for this country while also gaining certain rights. This is the first step toward laying down roots of trust in society.

"The second thing I ask is that each of you obtain a driver's license. Unlike Japan, America is vast. You need a car to go anywhere. Given that kosen-rufu will develop to the extent you are mobile, a driver's license is indispensable as you begin your struggle to spread the Daishonin's teachings in earnest.

"Third, I would like you to master English. If you become proficient in English, you will gain more American friends and can communicate and exchange opinions with many people. Propagation begins from our interactions with others, and dialogue forms the basis for such interaction.

"The Daishonin's Buddhism exists not only for those of Japanese descent. If kosen-rufu is to be achieved in America, discussion meetings and guidance eventually will have to be conducted in English. It will fall on those of you here to take the lead in this task.

"Therefore, at least for a start, I would like you to become proficient enough to where you can recount something like, say, a Japanese fairy tale in English—for instance, *Kaguyahime* (The Shining Princess)."

SHIN'ICHI looked around the room. Some people nodded in agreement, while others looked doubtful. A few of the women exchanged glances with their neighbors. None could imagine the other behind a steering wheel or speaking English fluently.

Sensing their thoughts, Shin'ichi continued: "You may think I'm asking a lot, but it will be up to you and no one else to accomplish kosen-rufu in America. Some of you, particularly the women, may think that you couldn't possibly speak English fluently or drive a car. But I would like you to challenge yourselves first and try. Determine to yourselves: 'I can do it! I definitely will!' I know you can do it."

"Many women drive in the United States; it is perfectly normal. It will be the same in Japan in another ten years or so. In that respect, too, I would like you to be pioneers among Japanese women.

"Also, there is no reason why you cannot master English. Even 5 year olds here can speak English, can't they? Japanese, with all its Chinese characters, is supposed to be far more difficult to learn. Yet haven't you all mastered that language splendidly?"

Laughter rang out in response to Shin'ichi's humorous observation, replacing the heaviness in the members' hearts with a burgeoning sense of hope.

"Yes!" they began to feel. "There isn't anything we can't do if we try!"

At each subsequent meeting on this first overseas trip, Shin'ichi was to set forth these three guidelines and eloquently stress their importance to the members in that area. They were eventually to become a solemn vow for the Japanese members living in America.

A slide presentation on the Soka Gakkai's activities in Japan followed Shin'ichi's guidance. Finally, he announced the formation of the new districts.

"Today, I would like to establish a district here in San Francisco to make a fresh start for America's future. Two days ago, a district was formed in Hawaii, but this district will be the first on the American continent."

The members burst into loud applause.

Shin'ichi went on to introduce the leaders of the new district, which was to comprise three groups encompassing the San Francisco, Suisun and Sacramento areas, respectively.

*A*FTER introducing the leaders of San Francisco District, Shin'ichi Yamamoto then announced that a district would also be established in Nevada. "I would like to appoint George Oliver as the chief of Nevada District and Yasuko Oliver as the women's division district chief. Although there are only two or three other members in that region—all of whom were introduced to the practice by Mr. and Mrs. Oliver—I have nevertheless decided to form a district there."

The Olivers stood up. Murmurs of surprise arose from the participants. As if to forestall their speculation, Shin'ichi continued: "You may be wondering why I've decided to establish a district in Nevada where there are so few members. It is a step I am taking to prepare for the future.

"The district lies on the forefront of our movement and has a direct connection with each individual. At the same time, it is endowed with all of the functions necessary to support our daily activities. You might say that all our struggles in the realm of faith have centered on the district and that it is within the district that each of us has grown.

"If we liken the Soka Gakkai to an orchard, each district corresponds to a single fruit tree, while the fruit represents each of you. Without the tree, there will be no fruit. Everything depends on the tree. Similarly, the real basis of the Soka Gakkai is each district that composes it. One could even say that the district itself is the Soka Gakkai.

"When a district is formed and becomes fully functional, kosen-rufu in that area will progress by leaps and bounds. Nevada is a large state. It is a land rich with unlimited possibilities for the future. Therefore, though there are now scarcely any members besides the two district leaders now, I have established this district with a view toward the future—three, five or ten years from now.

"While I am certain that Mr. and Mrs. Oliver have a formidable task ahead of them, President Toda, too, stood up alone to accomplish kosen-rufu after his release from prison. As a result, the Soka Gakkai's membership grew to more than 1.5 million households in the space of only fifteen years. I ask Mr. and Mrs. Oliver to please stand up resolutely in the vast land of Nevada, holding aloft the banner of the Law.

"Moreover, George Oliver will be the first person of non-Japanese descent to be appointed as a district chief in our organization. His appointment will attest to the fact that the Soka Gakkai is a religious organization for the entire world. I ask you to strive hard so that your efforts may become a model for the kosen-rufu movement in America."

"*Hai* (Yes)!" George responded energetically. His voice resounded with a fresh and vibrant determination.

Another seed of kosen-rufu had been planted, this time in Nevada. Everybody sensed that a new era had arrived.

*E*VEN after the discussion meeting ended, hardly anyone made a move to leave. Everyone was overjoyed. Refreshments of tea, cakes and colorful rice rolls were served and joyous conversations unfolded around the room.

Some members sought guidance from the visiting leaders, while others could be seen exchanging addresses.

Shin'ichi Yamamoto had just gone into the other room when Katsu Kiyohara, the Soka Gakkai women's division chief, entered.

"Sensei," she began hesitantly, as if wondering how to broach a difficult subject. "It seems that Yukiko Gilmore and some of the others have collected a dollar from each member because they want to treat us to dinner."

Shin'ichi's face clouded when he heard Kiyohara's words. "That won't do," he said.

He sent for Yukiko Gilmore and proceeded to give her careful and detailed instruction on this point.

"I am touched and gratified by your thought. But surely everyone here is having a hard time making ends meet. You mustn't do anything that will put an additional burden on them, nor is there any need to do so.

"By announcing that you have decided to collect money to buy me dinner, you end up creating an atmosphere where everyone will feel they should comply even if they don't really want to. Therefore, though you may say it's everyone's wish, in effect it will be half-compulsory. This may actually cause some people to harbor mistrust toward the Soka Gakkai.

"Even though the original intent may have been sincere, it could quite easily throw the members' faith into confusion. Therefore, leaders must take great care never to irresponsibly collect money from members. In the Soka Gakkai, we are very strict about money matters — if anything, tending toward over-cautiousness.

"Although it may seem like I'm being very harsh, I want you to take the money you have collected and respectfully return it to each person, carefully explaining to each the reason why."

Mrs. Gilmore seemed perplexed by Shin'ichi's words at first but soon said apologetically, "I understand," and left the room.

Shin'ichi was fully aware that her actions had been well intentioned. Thus the thought of her having to apologize and return the money to each member pained him.

However, if she was to lead the organization as district chief, she had to learn the Soka Gakkai's strict attitude toward money matters. Otherwise, there was a possible danger that some major problem over money might erupt in the future.

Shin'ichi's guidance had been based on his concern and compassion for his fellow member.

A LITTLE while later, Shin'ichi looked in again on the main meeting room. Ai Lin was busily weaving her way among members, engaging in conversation and serving tea. She moved about as if she were in her own home, even going freely in and out of the Gilmores' bedroom. Shin'ichi saw this and stopped her.

"Mrs. Lin, you may be Mrs. Gilmore's friend, but you really should refrain from going in and out of people's bedrooms when you visit their homes. Respecting each other's privacy is an important rule in American society. Buddhism teaches how we should conduct ourselves as human beings. Buddhism also manifests itself in society. To win people's trust, it is vital to pay attention to the smallest detail."

The members who gathered would all one day become key figures in America's kosen-rufu movement. For that very reason, Shin'ichi felt compelled to give detailed advice on even the most seemingly innocent and casual actions. Starting from scratch, he engaged himself firsthand in the fostering of able individuals.

Just then, Director Yukio Ishikawa came over and sat down beside Shin'ichi.

"We may have created a district, but the way things look, I'm worried, aren't you? None of them has an iota of common sense, including the newly appointed leaders; they're just too naive. Can they really do it, I wonder? There's not one capable person among them."

Shin'ichi replied indignantly to the director's derisive tone: "I completely disagree. They are all capable people. They will begin to shine from here on. If they persevere with pure-hearted faith, their names will all go down in the annals of kosen-rufu as pioneers. I'm looking to their future with high hopes."

"Oh, really," Ishikawa grunted and left the room.

Certainly, there was no doubt that the members who had been appointed that day had little experience or training as leaders. Their status or position in society was also far from prestigious.

However, they were all exerting themselves in faith, undergoing one painful struggle after another in America—a land that for many of them was strange and new. They, more than anyone, could empathize with other people's sorrow and pain. In that respect, they surely possessed a most suitable and respectable mission as leaders who would write the great human epic of kosen-rufu.

Shin'ichi couldn't help thinking of them as diamonds in the rough that would one day sparkle with dazzling brilliance.

*A*FTER breakfast the next day, Shin'ichi Yamamoto and the other leaders from Japan, with the Gilmores and Taylors as their guides, set off to visit the Muir Woods National Monument, a natural reserve noted for its giant coastal redwood trees. One of their aims was to ascertain whether redwood timber would be suitable as construction material for the Grand Reception Hall, which the Soka Gakkai was planning to build for the Head Temple Taiseki-ji.

As they headed away from the city, San Francisco Bay unfolded off to their right. Soon, the Golden Gate Bridge with its magnificent red towers came into view. As they approached, its soaring structure seemed to loom above them.

The group decided to stop for a short break at a small park near the bridge. Stepping out of their cars, they saw on display a section of the suspension cable used in the bridge. A sign explained that the cable was thirty-seven inches in diameter and comprised 27,572 separate strands of wire. Shin'ichi and the others stood in a circle around the display.

"The cable is thick, but each wire is quite thin. How amazing that it can hold up the bridge!" exclaimed Katsu Kiyohara.

Nodding in agreement, Shin'ichi then spoke to Yukiko Gilmore and Chiyoko Taylor, who had been appointed respectively as the San Francisco District chief and women's division chief the day before.

"It's true that the individual wires are not very thick, but when bunched together in great numbers, they display incredible strength. This resembles the unity of *itai doshin* (many in body, one in mind). In the Soka Gakkai, too, though each person's strength may be small, when that strength is combined and the members are firmly united, they can display unimaginable power. Unity is strength.

"From now on, you must play a central role in unifying the members' efforts to support the kosen-rufu movement and the happiness of the people of San Francisco."

"Yes!" the two women replied in unison.

The immensity of this lofty mission with which they were entrusted filled them with a sobering sense of responsibility.

Following their short break, the group climbed back into their cars, crossed the Golden Gate Bridge and drove steadily up into the mountains. The steep and interminably winding road hugged the mountain's edge as it continued to climb before them.

*T*HE group parked in front of a densely wooded forest. They had arrived at the entrance to the Muir Woods National Monument.

Immediately inside the national reserve entrance was a cross section of a giant coast redwood about six-and-a-half feet in diameter. The tree's growth rings were clearly discernible, forming a series of closely packed concentric circles.

Display markers indicating 500 and 1,000 years were attached at intervals, tracking the course of the tree's growth. The members of Shin'ichi's group tapped on the giant cross section, examining its hardness and closely inspecting the cracks formed in the wood due to drying.

The group then lunched on rice balls in the shade of the trees. Just as their cheerful meal was drawing to a close, a park official came along and addressed them in heated tones.

Paul Taylor stood up to offer a confident reply.

Nagayasu Masaki informed Shin'ichi of the gist of their exchange: "The official is asking us to move because eating and drinking are prohibited here. Mr. Taylor said: 'Okay. We didn't know. We'll move right away.' He then spoke about you, saying: 'By the way, do you know Mr. Shin'ichi Yamamoto, the president of the Soka Gakkai in Japan? That's him over there. He's a great Buddhist leader. You should consider yourself quite honored to meet him.' That's what he said."

Everyone smiled wryly.

"That's our district advisor!" proclaimed Chuhei Yamadaira. "Trust him to be on the ball. He's more dependable than a Gakkai member. It's great!" Everyone burst out laughing.

After their meal, the group strolled through the park, following a trail that weaved among the giant trees. Even though it was daytime, the forest lay dark and hushed all around them.

If the cross section of tree near the entrance was any guide, most of the redwoods in the forest would have been far older than 1,000 years. That would mean they had been standing here since before the time of Nichiren Daishonin.

Shin'ichi couldn't help thinking that these trees had been waiting patiently through all this vast space of time for the day when the sun of the Mystic Law would rise over the American continent.

A breeze rustled through the giant redwoods.

The lush green foliage seemed to tremble with joy at the arrival of the dawn of worldwide kosen-rufu.

*O*N their way back from the Muir Woods National Monument, Shin'ichi and the members accompanying him that day stopped off at Telegraph Hill with its sweeping views of San Francisco Bay. The usual mist that descended upon San Francisco toward evening was nowhere in sight, and off in the distance the ocean shimmered in the light of the setting sun. They also had an unobstructed view of both the Golden Gate and the San Francisco–Oakland Bay bridges. Fanned by a gentle autumn breeze, the members soaked up the breathtaking panorama.

Crowning the top of the hill was the Coit Memorial Tower. Resembling the nozzle of a fire hose, the structure had been built by Lillie Hitchcock Coit, a well-known philanthropist who had an abiding love for San Francisco.

In the middle of the square immediately below the tower was a bronze statue of a man wearing a long cape and a cross around his neck.

"Whose statue is that, I wonder?" said Shin'ichi.

Nagayasu Masaki went to have a look at the inscription on the plaque at its base.

"It's Christopher Columbus—Columbus is known for 'discovering' the Americas," he informed Shin'ichi.

The statue had been erected by San Francisco citizens of Italian descent on October 12, 1957, in recognition of the fact that Christopher Columbus was a native of Genoa, Italy.

Columbus first set foot upon the shores of the New World on October 12, 1492, landing on an island in the Bahamas, which he renamed San Salvador. This statue had been erected on the 465th anniversary of that occasion.

"October 12—that's the date Nichiren Daishonin inscribed the Dai-Gohonzon," murmured Shin'ichi, his voice filled with deep emotion.

Columbus had originally set out on this voyage in search of Japan, which had been described by Marco Polo in a record of his travels as the fabulous golden island of Zipangu located 1,500 miles to the east of the Asian continent.

Marco Polo, who first introduced Japan to the people of Europe, was actually living in Asia when, in 1279, the Daishonin inscribed the Dai-Gohonzon for the happiness of all humankind.

In reality, Japan at that time was far from the golden land of fabled treasures Marco Polo extolled it to be.

With the Daishonin's inscription of the Dai-Gohonzon, however, the brilliant light of the great Buddhist Law that would bring peace and happiness to all people began to shine out to the world from this island on the eastern rim of Asia.

COLUMBUS, his imagination captivated by tales of Zipangu, left the Spanish port of Palos just before sunrise on August 3, 1492, with three ships—the *Niña*, the *Pinta* and the *Santa Maria*. Crossing the Atlantic via the Canary Islands (off the coast of Africa), he sighted the island he was to name San Salvador on October 12, his seventy-first day at sea.

This was the date 213 years earlier on which the Daishonin inscribed the Dai-Gohonzon. Shin'ichi sensed an unfathomably profound connection.

This island that Columbus found was neither Zipangu nor the East that had been his destination. It was part of what the Europeans would come to call the New World of the Americas. The discovery was to open a new epoch of great ocean voyages.

More than four centuries had passed since Columbus had set foot in the Americas. His quest had been for gold and land to colonize. But for the indigenous peoples, his arrival marked only the start of an invasion of their lands.

Shin'ichi's journey, in contrast, was one of peace—a quest to illuminate the world with the golden light of humanism. It marked the beginning of an "age of great voyages" for global kosen-rufu.

After the group had come together for a photo in front of the statue, Shin'ichi looked up at the bronze figure of Columbus and said: "Like Columbus, we have now taken our first step on American soil. But we are engaged in a far nobler undertaking—for we are striving to create here on earth a new world where indestructible happiness and eternal peace reign supreme. With the passage of time—in twenty, fifty or a hundred years from now—today will without a doubt be remembered as a day of profound significance in the history of our movement."

Although everyone listened solemnly as Shin'ichi spoke, it would be many years before they could really grasp with their lives the full import of what he had said.

Shin'ichi gazed steadily out over the sea toward the distant horizon, his form a dark silhouette against the crimson glow of sunset, the breeze ruffling his hair.

He stood motionless for a long time, holding a conversation in his heart with his mentor, Josei Toda.

"Sensei!" he reported silently, "I have opened the door of kosen-rufu for the creation of a new world, just as you instructed."

His face, bathed in the sun's streaming rays, shone the color of burnished gold.

"A New World" Notes:

1. Katsu Rintaro (1823–1899): Also known as Katsu Kaishu. Statesman active during the period of transition from Japan's Tokugawa shogunate to the new Meiji government. He was instrumental in forming what eventually became the modern Japanese navy. At the time of the Meiji Restoration in 1868, he acted as the chief negotiator for the Tokugawa shogunate, supervising its demise and ensuring that the transfer of power took place in an orderly, peaceful fashion.

2. Fukuzawa Yukichi (1835–1901): Prominent educator, writer and propagator of Western knowledge during Japan's Meiji period (1868–1912); founder of the Keio Gijuku (now Keio University). He strove to inculcate the spirit of individual and national independence and pride he found in the West into Japanese society, and called for a revolution of the spirit through such works as *Gakumon no Susume* (Proposals on Learning).

3. Nobusuke Kishi (1896–1987): Japanese bureaucrat, politician and prime minister (February 1957–July 1960). Kishi served as vice minister of commerce and industry before World War II, overseeing the conversion of peacetime industries into wartime industries. During the war, he was in charge of Japan's economic mobilization as a member of Prime Minister Hideki Tojo's cabinet. Imprisoned by the Occupation authorities as a class-A war criminal following Japan's defeat, he escaped prosecution. After his return to public office, Kishi served as a representative in Japan's Lower House and became prime minister in 1957, a position he held until his resignation in 1960 after the passage of the new United States–Japan Security Treaty.

4. Shigeru Yoshida (1878–1967): Japanese diplomat and politician. After retiring from diplomatic service in 1938, Yoshida become prime minister in 1946, serving in that post until 1954, reforming his cabinet a total of five times during that period. As the Japanese signatory of the 1952 peace and security treaties with the United States, he helped to establish the foundation for Japan's postwar reform and reconstruction.

5. Showa Era: The name of the era during which the Japanese Emperor Showa (formerly, Hirohito) reigned, from 1925–1989.

6. Trotskyite: Refers to an adherent of the political, economic and social principles of Leon Trotsky (1879–1940), Russian theoretician and organizer, along with Vladimir Lenin, of the Bolshevik phase of the Russian Revolution of 1917. After Lenin's death, Trotsky, who advocated the concept of worldwide revolution as opposed to socialism in one country, waged an unsuccessful struggle for power with Joseph Stalin. He was subsequently exiled and assassinated. The term *Trotskyite* was used in Japan in those days to refer derogatorily to ultra-leftists and other extreme elements.

7. Khrushchev, Nikita Sergeyevich (1894–1971): Russian politician and premier of the Soviet Union. After Stalin's death, Khrushchev became the first secretary of the Soviet Communist Party (1953–1964) and effective leader of the Soviet Union (1956–1964), serving as premier from 1958. He was critical of Joseph Stalin's rule and worked to ease tensions between East and West.

8. Under intense public pressure over the security treaty fiasco, Kishi's party could no longer support him as prime minister, thus forcing his resignation.

Golden Autumn

S OWING innumerable seeds of happiness along his way, Shin'ichi continued his travels for peace in this new realm of America. Wherever he went, he brought with him a light of hope and sent forth waves of joy and delight.

On the morning of October 6, Shin'ichi and the other leaders from Japan left San Francisco for Seattle, which by plane was about two hours further north along the west coast of the United States.

According to information received from the Overseas Affairs Section at the Soka Gakkai Headquarters, there were about twenty members living in Seattle, but they had not yet even begun to hold discussion meetings. In addition, the

Overseas Affairs Section had been able to contact the local members only by mail and therefore did not know whether anyone would be available to welcome Shin'ichi and his party on their arrival. Thus the group embarked for Seattle with some sense of apprehension.

The plane landed in Seattle shortly after 10:00 A.M.

Contrary to their fears, however, a group of more than a dozen members was there to greet them.

"Sensei! Welcome!" several voices called. Having spotted Shin'ichi Yamamoto and his party, the members hurried over to greet them.

Shin'ichi waved to them and said with a smile: "Hello, there. Thank you for coming."

"Um, I don't know if you remember me," began one of the women, blushing, "but you were kind enough to meet with me in March last year, just before I left Japan."

"Yes, I do remember you," Shin'ichi assured her.

On that previous occasion, Shin'ichi had sensed during their conversation that there was some discord between the woman and her husband, a member of the American armed forces. He remembered stressing to her that family harmony was a foundation for happiness, and to encourage her, he had given her a medal commemorating a youth division athletic meet.

Now, beside her, clinging shyly to her skirt, stood a small boy, who appeared to have just started walking, and a little girl of about 3. The boy would have been born since his mother's arrival in the United States. Shin'ichi could sense from the woman's bright expression that she was now happy in her family life, and he felt delighted for her.

With a few words of encouragement, it is possible to help someone open his or her life to a profound extent. Consequently, Shin'ichi always strove earnestly to cherish each momentary encounter and offer heartfelt encouragement to his fellow members.

"What a cute little fellow!" Shin'ichi said as he bent down and scooped the boy up in his arms.

With his free hand, he reached into his coat pocket, brought out a copper penny and gave it to the boy.

"I'm sorry. I don't have any gifts," Shin'ichi said apologetically.

Snug in Shin'ichi's arms, the boy clutched the coin, gurgling and laughing contentedly.

*T*HE women had been somewhat nervous at the thought of meeting the Soka Gakkai president in person, but when they saw the warm and unaffected manner in which Shin'ichi picked up and played with the toddler, their tense expressions visibly relaxed.

A young woman brought out a camera and said, "Sensei, please join us for a photo!"

"All right, since you're all here, let's take a picture together," Shin'ichi agreed.

As the members began to line up with Shin'ichi in the center, he suddenly slipped to the back of the group. Everyone turned around and gave him a puzzled look.

"All of you please stand in front. I'm fine back here. I want to watch over you from behind."

This was Shin'ichi's honest, heartfelt sentiment.

Although he naturally took leadership for the kosen-rufu movement in his capacity as Soka Gakkai president, Shin'ichi's real wish was to always support his fellow members from behind the scenes.

The members could not hide their surprise at Shin'ichi's words, which contrasted with their image of a president of a large organization. Shin'ichi's entire attitude was completely different from the authoritarian behavior displayed by many leaders in society. Not only did he shun formality, but warmth and sincerity emanated from his very being.

After they had finished taking photos, Shin'ichi asked, "Why don't all of you come with us to our hotel?"

The members cried out with delight; all of them were overjoyed at the suggestion. But the leaders accompanying Shin'ichi were somewhat apprehensive; they wondered whether it would be all right to bring so many people en masse to their hotel.

The group then split up and piled into several cars to make their way to the hotel.

Seattle, which is surrounded by water and mountains, is renowned for its great scenic beauty. Elliot Bay, the city's harbor, opens out onto Puget Sound and, ultimately, the Pacific Ocean. The bay is fringed by gentle slopes descending almost to the water's edge. Beyond the thickly wooded hills glistens the silvery, snowcapped summit of Mount Rainier, which bears a striking resemblance to Mount Fuji in Japan.

Although latitudinally Seattle is situated further north than the northernmost tip of the Japanese island of Hokkaido (known for its cold and snowy weather), its climate is only slightly cooler than that of the more temperate, southerly city of Tokyo. Seattle is shielded from cold winter winds blowing in from both the Pacific Ocean and the continent by the Olympic Peninsula to the west and the Cascade Range to the east. Even in January, the coldest month of the year, Seattle's average temperature is around forty-one degrees.

Nevertheless, having just been in Hawaii, a land of perpetual summer, Shin'ichi found the weather somewhat chilly.

The hotel where the Japanese party was staying was located in the center of the city and commanded a clear view of Elliot Bay, bustling with marine traffic.

As soon as the members had assembled in Shin'ichi's room, the atmosphere became like a discussion meeting.

*T*HE members introduced themselves to Shin'ichi one by one, reporting to him on their current situations. They had been eagerly awaiting Shin'ichi's visit, and some were so overcome by emotion that tears flowed as they spoke.

After the introductions, Shin'ichi said, "Since we have this opportunity to talk together, please feel free to ask me anything you like."

As if they had been longing for the chance to do just that, the members bombarded Shin'ichi with questions—some concerning problems at work, some about illness. A middle-aged American man requested that the Soka Gakkai produce a sutra book for English speakers containing an English transliteration of the liturgy. Since there was no English sutra book available, members who did not understand Japanese had been forced to learn gongyo by ear.

"Yes, I can see that this must be a great problem. I'll look into the matter right away."

Upon his return to Japan, Shin'ichi immediately set the wheels into motion for the production of an English sutra book.

Wherever he was, Shin'ichi took pains to hold frank discussions with the members. From such dialogue, he would grasp what was in people's hearts, drawing out their hopes and wishes to spot any problem areas that might stand in the way of their advancement. Moreover, when a problem did exist, he acted quickly to resolve it.

When presented with a particularly difficult problem, it was not at all unusual for him to ponder and agonize over it for days on end, going through many a sleepless night as a result.

Genuine dialogue is characterized by empathy, joy and understanding. Leaders who neglect dialogue invariably become authoritarian and bureaucratic.

Shin'ichi's thoughts were always with the members who were struggling valiantly on the forefront of the kosen-rufu movement. If anything, he was a young general constantly moving from one site to another on the front lines.

Shin'ichi noticed that one of the members who had come to welcome him and the other leaders at the airport had so far failed to show up at the hotel. Concern over her absence nagged at him as he strove to respond to the members' questions.

"We're missing one person," he remarked. "I wonder what happened to her?" He repeated the question again and again during the discussion.

The members had just about exhausted their store of questions when the door swung open with a loud thud.

Everyone turned around, startled.

There, standing barefoot, a pair of high heels in one hand and a large, heavy-looking tape recorder in the other, was a rather tall woman of Japanese descent.

Gasping for breath and perspiration streaming down her face, she placed the machine on the floor.

"What happened?" asked Shin'ichi.

I'M sorry," the woman replied, breathing heavily. "On the way from the airport, I got separated from the other cars, and I lost my way."

"Oh, so that's what happened. You must be exhausted. I was worried about you, you know," Shin'ichi said, smiling.

The woman, whose name was Taeko Goodman, had come from Montana. Leaving by car the previous day, she had driven through the night, crossing the snow-covered Rocky Mountains. It was shortly after dawn when she finally arrived at the airport in Seattle to welcome Shin'ichi and the other leaders from Japan. On the way from the airport to the hotel, however, she had lost sight of the other members' cars.

Unfamiliar with the layout of Seattle, she had spent quite some time driving around in search of the hotel. When she finally managed to find it after much trouble and distress, she made the mistake of parking her car in a lot some distance away. She then set off on foot toward the hotel, lugging with her a huge tape recorder—a piece of equipment she had bought specially to record President Yamamoto's guidance and play it for the people she had introduced to the Daishonin's Buddhism back in Montana.

The bulky recorder was excruciatingly heavy; her arm ached after walking only a few yards. And to make matters worse, she was wearing a new pair of high heels that didn't fit properly and chafed at her heels as she walked. Time after time, the combined pain from the heavy weight of the recorder and her ill-fitting shoes forced the woman to stop walking.

Meanwhile, time was slipping away.

The thought that perhaps President Yamamoto had already left the hotel made her grow more frantic, but her progress remained painfully slow. Tears of frustration welled helplessly in her eyes.

By the time she arrived in the hotel lobby, she was barefoot, the offending shoes in her hands. The intense pain of walking with the heavy recorder while wearing shoes that rubbed her heels raw had made her forget all sense of shame or concern for what others might think.

Shin'ichi looked at the tape recorder and said: "Thank you. I'm so touched that you would think of your fellow members. There is nothing more praiseworthy than a person who strives earnestly for others."

These words pierced Taeko Goodman's heart. Returning to her senses, she looked at Shin'ichi.

"Sensei," she attempted in response, but she was so moved that no words would come.

She felt her spirits suddenly lifting, the despondent feeling in her heart swept away like the clearing of a heavy mist.

Shin'ichi's words were to change the course of her life.

AEKO Goodman had taken faith three years earlier in Japan when her mother developed cancer and doctors had given her just six months to live. Taeko had heard about the Daishonin's Buddhism in the midst of her despair and immediately started exerting herself earnestly in faith, exactly as her sponsor instructed. When her mother went back into the hospital for tests two months later, all signs of cancer had completely disappeared.

Shortly thereafter, Taeko married an American she had become acquainted with at work and returned with him to the United States. But her new life in a strange and unfamiliar land only made her increasingly homesick for Japan.

Taeko's intense longing to return to her homeland prompted her to strive diligently in faith. She persuaded first one, then another, to embrace the practice until she had introduced more than ten people. It was then that her resolve began to waver.

"If I go home, who will look after the members I leave behind?" she thought.

Thus all her diligent practice and energetic efforts at propagation—undertaken solely for the purpose of returning to Japan—had instead given her second thoughts about leaving America.

Taeko was torn. It could be said that this marked an awakening to her mission.

In the midst of this dilemma, she learned of the scheduled visit to America by President Shin'ichi Yamamoto and other leaders from Japan. She had driven all night to Seattle with the fervent wish to meet the Soka Gakkai president.

"There is nothing more praiseworthy than a person who strives earnestly for others." The moment she heard Shin'ichi say this, emotion and determination welled up inside her.

"I will fight here, in America," she vowed in her heart, "for those who have placed their trust in me and started practicing Nichiren Daishonin's Buddhism."

Human brilliance derives from the light of altruistic action. It is not an exaggeration to say that people are truly human only when they endeavor to dedicate their lives for their friends and fellow human beings. Here, too, lies the way to break through the shell of the small ego and develop and expand one's spiritual capacity to a profound degree.

Shin'ichi was overjoyed to see the pure-hearted seeking spirit of this woman who had traveled all the way from Montana for the sake of the Law. He sensed that, scattered throughout this vast land of America, friends were beginning to "emerge from the earth"—friends who would lead lives dedicated to the mission of propagating the True Law far and wide. The time of worldwide kosen-rufu had truly arrived.

Shin'ichi presented the members who had come to his room with copies of *The Soka Gakkai*, the English-language publication introducing the organization's activities, as well as *fukusa* inscribed with the word *joy* in Japanese, which he had brought along as gifts.

It was after 1:00 in the afternoon when the members' encounter and dialogue with Shin'ichi drew to an end, and they all finally left the hotel.

Shin'ichi had wholeheartedly thrown himself into the task of giving guidance and encouragement to the members without even taking a short rest after his plane trip. He now felt deeply fatigued.

SHIN'ICHI decided to accompany the other leaders for a look around the streets of Seattle and then lunch. As they drove through the city, Nagayasu Masaki pointed to a steak-house's sign.

"Sensei, that restaurant has steaks for $1.15. It's a bargain too good to miss. How about having lunch there?"

The party from Japan had made frugality their motto on this trip, an idea that had come from Shin'ichi, who proposed that they keep their personal expenditures to a minimum. That way they could use their funds more effectively to bring joy to the local members—for example, treating them to refreshments.

Strict foreign exchange regulations in Japan in those days limited to $35.00 per day the amount of foreign currency its citizens traveling abroad could purchase (at an exchange rate of 360 yen to the dollar).

Given this situation, the only way for the group to keep their expenses down was to cut back on spending for meals.

Throughout the entire trip, Shin'ichi and his party, when they were alone together, never once ate a full-fledged meal at any restaurant, whether in the hotels where they stayed or elsewhere. They usually contented themselves with coffee and toast, bought a hot dog or went to a self-service cafeteria. Occasionally, in search of something nutritious to eat, they would look for an inexpensive Chinese restaurant.

Therefore, a steak for $1.15 was a most welcome find. Cheerfully, the group entered the restaurant and ordered. The steaks that were brought out, however, were as tough as shoe leather and thoroughly unappetizing.

"So these are real American steaks. Not much, are they?" remarked Katsu Kiyohara dryly to Chuhei Yamadaira.

"Well, for the price, you can't really expect them to taste all that great. The meat's tough all right, but if we had a little soy sauce, it probably wouldn't be that bad, I suppose."

Listening to their casual exchange, Shin'ichi wished that he could give them a trip where they could at least enjoy satisfying meals. However, when he thought of the local members, many of whom were struggling to make ends meet, it was natural that he and the other leaders maintain a spirit of prudence in their own affairs and exert their utmost efforts to serve the members. This is the spirit of a true leader of kosen-rufu. And it is the conduct and sincerity of such a leader that inspire people's trust.

With a bright smile, Shin'ichi said: "I'm so sorry you have to eat steak like this. But let's always uphold the spirit of 'desiring little and contenting ourselves with what we have'[1] in the Gakkai—especially remembering that leaders begin to grow corrupt when they forget about frugality and purity of intention."

*A*FTER lunch, the group strolled through the streets of Seattle. Noticing an elderly man polishing shoes on the sidewalk, Shin'ichi said to him genially in Japanese, "Hello, how's business?"

Masaki translated this for the man, who asked, "Are you from Japan?"

When Shin'ichi nodded that he was, the man gave him a friendly smile and said, "I saw the Japanese prince and princess yesterday."

Until the day before, Crown Prince Akihito and his wife, Princess Michiko, had been visiting the United States at the invitation of President Eisenhower to commemorate 100 years of U.S.-Japan friendship. The royal couple had left Japan for the United States on September 22, their itinerary including stops in Honolulu, San Francisco, Washington, D.C., New York and Chicago before finally making their way to Seattle.

On October 5, the previous day, they had attended a reception in their honor hosted by Japanese-American citizens at the Japanese Garden located on the grounds of Seattle's University of Washington. The prince and princess then departed for their final stop in Portland, Oregon, before flying back to Japan that evening.

This visit to the United States marked the royal couple's first visit overseas since their wedding in April of the previous year. From the shoeshine man's account, the entire city of Seattle had turned out to welcome the Japanese royalty.

Earlier in June that year, President Eisenhower's scheduled visit to Japan had been postponed at the request of the Japanese government, with internal instability stemming from opposition to the ratification of the new U.S.-Japan Security Treaty cited as the prime reason. Ever since then there had been growing reports in Japan that the visit's suspension had exacerbated anti-Japanese sentiment in America. Consequently, the Japanese government was concerned with how the American people would react to a visit by Japanese royalty.

The tour by the shy young royal couple, however, seemed to leave many Americans with a favorable impression, promoting a greater sense of affinity with Japan.

Shin'ichi was relieved to hear that their trip had been a success.

The group then did some more sightseeing around the city by car. Upon returning to the hotel, Shin'ichi began to feel strange. The area from his neck down to his chest began to itch with a burning intensity. Looking in the mirror, he saw that not only his neck and chest but also his face was covered with red welts; it was a rash that soon covered his entire body.

But that was only the start. Within moments, he felt the onset of spasms and pain in his stomach and began to have diarrhea. He also seemed to be running a high fever.

Thinking he would feel better if he rested for a short while, Shin'ichi lay down on the bed. No doubt because of the fever, however, suddenly he felt deathly cold and started shivering so badly that his whole body shook.

He lay on the bed, his lips pressed together in a painful grimace.

*T*HE steak Shin'ichi had eaten at lunch apparently had not agreed with him. In addition, fatigue resulting from jet lag and lack of sleep, and the temperature

difference between the year-round summer weather of Hawaii and the cooler climate of Seattle, had all combined to severely undermine his already frail health.

Shin'ichi took some of the medicine he had brought along for just such a contingency, but it seemed to do little to relieve the itching, diarrhea or chills.

Yet he could not remain in bed forever. There was a discussion meeting to attend that evening. As he got out of bed, there was a knock at the door.

It was Kiyoshi Jujo. When he saw the rash on Shin'ichi's face, he said in alarm, "Sensei, what's the matter?"

"It seems to be some kind of rash," Shin'ichi said. "I've also had a touch of diarrhea."

"Shall I call a doctor?" Jujo inquired.

"No, I'll be fine. I took some medicine. I'll feel better after a short rest."

"Sensei," began Jujo adamantly, "please don't go to the discussion meeting this evening. After all, you met quite a few of the members earlier. And besides, you still have a long journey ahead of you. Please try to regain your health."

"But everyone has been looking forward to today's meeting," Shin'ichi said. "They'll be so disappointed if I don't go."

"If you push yourself unreasonably now and collapse later, it'll be too late. The other leaders and I will take care of the discussion meeting as well as the formation of the new district. Please get some rest—at least for today," urged Jujo.

It was painfully hard for Shin'ichi to miss the meeting when he thought how disappointed the members would be, but Jujo was right. They had only just begun their overseas trip, and they had yet to visit Canada and Brazil. If he were to fall ill now and be unable to carry out his objectives, far more members would end up being disappointed later. Besides, if he went to the meeting looking like he did—his face all red and swollen with a rash—it would only worry the members needlessly. Reluctantly, he took Jujo's advice.

Shortly after 5:00 P.M., Jujo and the other leaders left the hotel for the discussion meeting. Outside, it had started to rain.

After they left, Shin'ichi kneeled on the bed and chanted daimoku for a while. He prayed fervently, fighting a desperate life-and-death struggle to conquer this devil of illness that was sapping his health.

*A*FTER he finished chanting, Shin'ichi lay in bed and rested. He felt bitterly frustrated to be plagued by such ill health when he had so long a road yet to travel for the goal of kosen-rufu.

He thought back to the conversation he had had with his wife, Mineko, on the evening of May 3 earlier that year —the day that signaled the beginning of a grand journey for the widespread propagation of the Daishonin's Buddhism throughout the world.

Mineko had been waiting with a meal prepared for him when he returned home late that evening. The table was set with the usual modest fare.

"I thought there'd be *sekihan* (rice mixed with red beans and served on festive occasions) to celebrate my inauguration, but I see it's the same as always," commented Shin'ichi.

Mineko smiled and replied resolutely: "As of this day, I no longer consider this house to have a husband. So since today is a funeral for the Yamamoto family, I haven't prepared any *sekihan*."

"Yes, you have a point." Shin'ichi smiled too.

At her stouthearted words, he felt a momentary twinge of remorse, but more than anything he was gladdened by her invincible spirit. Her words had given him immense courage.

From now on there would probably be almost no time for him to play with his children or to enjoy quiet moments at home with his family. It would be unbearably lonely for his wife. However, Shin'ichi had vowed to dedicate his life to kosen-rufu, and Mineko, as his wife, boldly showed her resolute determination to support him.

Shin'ichi did not desire ordinary, mundane happiness for himself. In some respects, he gladly chose to sacrifice himself for kosen-rufu. Thus he was deeply touched and gratified to learn that his wife was of the same mind.

Nevertheless, Shin'ichi thought it enough that the sacrifice stop with his own family, praying fervently that his fellow members would realize a flowering of harmony and tranquillity in their own families and that each person would savor true happiness. He had resolved to dedicate his life to that goal.

Mineko said to Shin'ichi, "I didn't prepare any *sekihan*, but I'd like to buy you a present to celebrate your inauguration. Is there anything you'd like?"

"Well, a travel bag would be nice—the biggest, sturdiest one you can find!"

"A travel bag? May I ask where you plan to go with such a big bag?" inquired Mineko.

"I'm going to travel around the world on President Toda's behalf," Shin'ichi responded.

Mineko smiled, her eyes sparkling. "So the journey for worldwide kosen-rufu is about to begin at last."

Shin'ichi smiled back and nodded.

*F*ROM the beginning, Shin'ichi was prepared to lay down his life for the cause of propagating the Daishonin's Buddhism. He had not the slightest fear nor regret about fighting on the battlefields of kosen-rufu and one day falling there.

The doctors had told him that he would not live to the age of 30; he could collapse at any moment and it would come as no surprise. But he had inherited the dream of his mentor, Josei Toda, and had just taken the first step for world kosen-rufu; he could not afford to succumb to illness now.

As he lay in bed, Shin'ichi lamented over his poor health. "I want to live," he prayed as the fever wracked his body, "so that I may fulfill my vow to Sensei." All the while, he recalled the Gosho passage: "Nam-myoho-renge-kyo is like the roar of a lion. What sickness can therefore be an obstacle?" (WND-I, 412).

The rain outside intensified, lashing against the window.

Meanwhile, Vice General Director Kiyoshi Jujo and the other leaders had left the hotel and gone to the home of a member who had taken on the central role for activities in the Seattle area. After discussing the details for the planned formation of a district in that city, the leaders then headed for the hall where the discussion meeting was to be held.

About forty members had assembled when they arrived. It was quite a large turnout for this, the very first discussion meeting in Seattle. This time, the meeting was not held at a private home but at a medium-sized hall. Consequently, there was something forlorn about their small gathering.

At the start of the meeting, Vice General Director Jujo explained that Shin'ichi would be unable to attend the meeting. The members were clearly crestfallen at the news.

The leaders from Japan then got up one by one to address the gathering, trying with all their might to change the somber atmosphere that hung heavily in the room. But all their efforts were in vain.

Many of the Japanese women had brought along their American husbands, who were non-members. This made Jujo and the others exert themselves all the more strenuously. However, the more they raised their voices and spoke with excited and energetic fervor, the gloomier the expressions of the members grew.

The happy, smiling faces and the warm, friendly atmosphere always evident at the meetings Shin'ichi attended were nowhere to be seen.

"This is terrible," thought Jujo to himself, a wave of panic washing over him. "Something's wrong. What is it?"

His mind raced back over the meetings Shin'ichi had participated in and how the Soka Gakkai president had given guidance on those occasions.

The members then split up into Japanese- and English-speaking groups for informal discussions.

*J*UST before the meeting ended, everyone reassembled. Vice General Director Kiyoshi Jujo then announced the formation of Seattle District. There was applause, but it lacked real enthusiasm. After the meeting, a woman told Jujo that she would soon be going to live in Ethiopia because her husband had been transferred there. Entrusted by Shin'ichi with full responsibility for the formation of a new district, Jujo appointed this woman as chief of the Ethiopia Group under the umbrella of the Seattle District. That was the only time during the entire meeting that there was a heartfelt burst of applause.

On returning to the hotel that evening, Jujo went to Shin'ichi's room to report on the meeting. Shin'ichi's rash was starting to clear up, but he still suffered from diarrhea and a high fever. Nevertheless, he got out of bed to listen to Jujo's report.

After Jujo had given him a detailed summary of the meeting, he said to Shin'ichi: "Although I honestly did the best I could, somehow the atmosphere was different from the discussion meetings you attend. Where's the difference?"

Shin'ichi nodded silently and then spoke with powerful conviction: "I'm not doing anything special. I just always exert myself with the burning resolve that 'I must not let any of the precious children of the Buddha become unhappy' and a keen awareness that 'now is my only chance to lead these people to happiness.' This unwavering determination is the power that opens people's hearts.

"A mother who loves her children and thinks constantly of their welfare knows what they want merely from their cries. Children, too, feel content and reassured when they hear their mother's voice. Similarly, a leader who has a strong determination to cherish the members can understand their worries and desires, and the members will in turn respond to such a leader.

"Leaders must also carefully consider what they are going to speak about, and how to present it, so that the members will readily understand and accept what they have to say. It is important to continue making such efforts. When I have a meeting to attend, I always make sure that I am thoroughly prepared. I rack my brains and try to come up with creative ideas.

"This is a leader's duty. If a leader just talks about the same old thing and never offers anything fresh or new, it is discourteous to the listeners. It is a sign of an irresponsible leader who has fallen into force of habit."

Listening to Shin'ichi's words, Jujo was deeply ashamed of his own attitude.

*S*HIN'ICHI'S condition still had not improved by the next morning. His fever remained high, and when he tried to walk, his legs were shaky. Nevertheless, he dressed and prepared to go out. A trading company representative was coming to take him and the others to tour a sawmill to see about buying Canadian cedar lumber for the planned Grand Reception Hall at the head temple.

At the sawmill, there was a large pond stacked with giant Canadian cedar logs, some of which were ten feet in diameter. It was awesome to behold the mechanical saws slicing through the logs as easily as if they were bread and turning them into lengths of timber. After carefully inspecting the wood for quality, Shin'ichi decided to purchase some for the construction project.

On their way back, Shin'ichi and his companions stopped by Lake Washington, one of the famed scenic sites of Seattle. A canal connected the lake to Puget Sound, and a lock had been built to regulate the difference in elevation between the canal and the lake [enabling boats and ships to go from one water level to another]. As they watched the lock being closed and the ships making their way into the canal, a gentle rain started to fall.

The group decided to go down onto the pontoon bridge that spanned the lake. Far off beyond the lake's edge, they could see mountains covered with trees aflame with red and golden hues and veiled in a fine mist of rain. It looked like a watercolor canvas.

"How beautiful! It's just like a painting," exclaimed Katsu Kiyohara. She then added in a soft, reflective tone, "But when I think that these beautiful leaves will soon fall, I'm reminded of life's impermanence."

Shin'ichi smiled and said quietly: "Perhaps the vivid autumn colors are the leaves' attempt to express their fullest brilliance in the limited span of their lives. Everything is impermanent. None of us can escape the cycle of birth, aging, sickness and death. All we can do is base ourselves on the eternal Law and dedicate ourselves to our respective missions, while striving to burn strongly and brightly at each moment. Life is a struggle against a finite length of time. Hence, the Daishonin writes: 'Life is limited; we must not begrudge it. What we should ultimately aspire to is the Buddha land' (WND-1, 214). What I desire most right now is enough time to fulfill my mission."

There was a sense of urgency in Shin'ichi's last words, but none of the others could grasp the depth of their meaning. Even more vivid than the golden autumn colors that spread among the trees was the vow to achieve kosen-rufu that blazed like a brilliant red flame in Shin'ichi's heart.

*I*T was already dark when the group returned to their hotel. That evening, the newly appointed district leaders came by to discuss with Shin'ichi how to go about building their district. Though Shin'ichi's fever had still not subsided and his body felt as heavy as lead, his manner gave none of this away. The members took his fever-flushed face to be a sign of robust health.

Overflowing with strong conviction for the realization of kosen-rufu, he spoke passionately of the hope-filled future he visualized for Seattle. Missing the discussion meeting the night before made him exert himself all the more in offering guidance to the new leaders. As a result, their hearts leapt with excitement, and dreams for the future unfolded before them.

Their discussion with Shin'ichi continued late into the night. By the time they had all gone, Shin'ichi didn't even have the energy to take a shower.

The party from Japan left the hotel before 5:30 the next morning to embark for their next destination, Chicago. Despite the early hour, about a dozen people were waiting at the airport to see them off. Even in the short time left before his departure, Shin'ichi applied himself wholeheartedly to talking with his fellow members.

Still running a high fever, Shin'ichi needed more than anything to rest. But all he could think of was giving everything he had to encourage the members for the sake of forging an eternal path to kosen-rufu.

Their flight to Chicago was scheduled to depart at 7:00 A.M., and Shin'ichi continued to advise members right up to the very last minute before boarding. He had been sitting on a sofa in the waiting area, and when he tried to stand, he swayed dizzily. Everyone caught their breath in concern.

"Thank you all for coming to see us off," said a smiling Shin'ichi, as if nothing untoward had happened. "See you soon, and take care." He then hurried through the boarding gate with the other leaders.

"Don't tell me Sensei was ill?" murmured one of the women. Everyone paled at the thought.

The realization that Shin'ichi had been waging a desperate battle with the devil of illness the entire time he had been encouraging them moved the members to the core. From then on, the movement to propagate the Daishonin's Buddhism accelerated rapidly in the Seattle area.

Two-and-a-half years later, in March 1963, the first overseas conferral of Gohonzon was conducted in several cities in the United States, including Seattle. Dispatched by the head temple to oversee the conferral was Shinno Abe, the Study Department chief and subsequent sixty-seventh high priest of Nichiren Shoshu.

History would later testify to the exact nature of his actions in Seattle on that occasion.

*S*OME time had passed since the group boarded the plane, but their flight to Chicago still had not taken off. An announcement over the P.A. system informed the passengers that their departure would be substantially delayed due to a problem found in the plane's navigational system.

It wasn't until after 8:30 A.M. that the flight finally left Seattle. As a result, the group arrived at Midway Airport in Chicago shortly after 5:00 P.M. local time, an hour-and-a-half later than scheduled.

As they set off toward the lobby, Shin'ichi and the others could hear voices raised in spirited song—a song that seemed strangely familiar to them. As they drew nearer, they realized that it was "Ifu Dodo no Uta" (Song of Indomitable Dignity). When they finally came out into the lobby, they found a dozen or so people lined up, singing passionately:

Into this defiled and evil world go we of the Gakkai.
Whatever obstacles stand in our way....

The group from Japan was deeply touched to hear such a well-loved Soka Gakkai song here in America. "Ifu Dodo" had originally been the chapter song of Japan's Kyoto Chapter and was a great favorite among the Kyoto members.

Shin'ichi had heard the song during a visit to the city and, on his proposal, it had been adopted as a Soka Gakkai song nationwide.

A figure in a white shirt and tie stood in front of the small group of members and was energetically conducting their performance. It was Susumu Aota, a young men's division leader from Japan.

"Oh, it's Aota!" exclaimed Jujo, when he recognized who it was. "Wasn't he supposed to meet us in New York?"

While a student, Aota had been a member of the University of Tokyo Lotus Sutra Study Group formed by the second Soka Gakkai president, Josei Toda, for members attending the prestigious Japanese national university. As a result, he had received personal instruction from Mr. Toda on many occasions. After graduating, Aota had joined a petrochemical company and at the end of July, he had been sent to America for three months to work on the design of a petrochemical plant.

He was filled with joy and excitement when he realized that President Yamamoto's historic guidance tour of America would coincide with his own stay. Acting as though he were part of an advance party for the trip, Aota tirelessly went about visiting and encouraging the members. A disciple of Shin'ichi Yamamoto, the leader of the kosen-rufu movement, Aota had resolved to work together with the local members to create a surge of propagation to prepare for the visit by the Soka Gakkai president and his party.

Stationed in New Jersey, Aota had originally planned to meet Shin'ichi and the others in New York. However, when he discovered that the group would be arriving in Chicago on October 8, a Saturday and a day off from work, he gladly flew there to welcome them.

*I*MMEDIATELY after his arrival in Chicago shortly before noon, Aota set off to visit the home of Miyako Coleman, who was acting as the central contact for members in the Chicago area. Several Japanese women were already there when he arrived. They had traveled eleven hours by bus all the way from Kentucky.

Wherever members met, discussion naturally blossomed. Gathering around Aota, the women began sharing stories of the hardships they had gone through to prepare for this day. One told how overjoyed she was to be in Chicago. Although her family was leading a meager existence, as a result of her steadfast prayers, her husband had finally agreed to let her come and had given her thirty dollars for the bus fare—an amount that was enough to feed the family for a whole month.

"I'm just so thrilled when I think that I can meet President Yamamoto at last," said the woman, her voice choked with emotion.

Listening to their stories, it was apparent that all the women had endured much difficulty and suffering. Many were facing misunderstanding from family members regarding their faith or living in difficult financial circumstances. The thought of this day had been all that kept them going. Aota was deeply moved by their tenacity.

Soon the time neared for them to leave for the airport to welcome Shin'ichi and the others. Aota called the airline to reconfirm the arrival time but found that the flight was running an hour and a half behind schedule.

"Why don't we use this time to learn a Gakkai song and welcome Sensei with a chorus to express our determination!" Aota proposed. The song he taught them was "Ifu Dodo," because he thought it a fitting one to convey their determination to undertake the task of kosen-rufu in America.

When Aota and the others arrived, about ten members were already waiting. Together, they rehearsed the song once again. Midway Airport resounded with the members' joy-filled chorus—a melody that embodied a solemn pledge.

Shin'ichi approached and stood before them as they sang with all their might. With clenched fist, he began to move his arm up and down in rhythm to the music. The members responded by singing even more powerfully.

Today and tomorrow,
as the march for propagation advances,
our ardor surges....

While they may have presented a peculiar spectacle to passersby, Shin'ichi wanted above all to respond to the members' sincerity. He was a leader who empathized, perhaps better than anyone else, with those who had experienced great hardship and suffering.

S HIN'ICHI was profoundly moved by the members' passionate chorus. He sensed that each of them had been striving alone to keep the flame of faith alive, without anyone to depend on. As they waged their solitary struggles against loneliness and financial hardship, all had been looking forward eagerly to this day.

"Thank you for your heartwarming chorus," said Shin'ichi when they had finished, expressing his praise.

At these words, many of the members, who had been trying not to cry, started sobbing openly. Though they now wept hot tears of emotion, how many cold, bitter ones must they have shed while enduring countless difficulties!

"It's all right; everything's fine," Shin'ichi reassured them. "You've won. All of you have made it to Chicago. I'm here now, so there's no need to worry. Let's go then, toward brilliant, hope-filled lives!" These words deeply penetrated their hearts, kindling their courage.

With this emotional encounter still resonating in the members' hearts, Shin'ichi and the others made their way by car to their hotel.

Unfortunately, they got caught in evening rush-hour traffic on the way, so it was almost 7:00 when they arrived at the hotel. A discussion meeting had been scheduled to begin at 7:00 that same evening. The group rushed to check in but encountered an unexpected hitch: They were told that the hotel had no reservations for them. Whether the error had been made by the travel agent or the hotel was unclear, but the front desk clerk insisted that he couldn't let the party stay without reservations.

Nagayasu Masaki began arguing heatedly with the clerk. By now it was already after 7:00. The leaders quickly decided to send Katsu Kiyohara, the women's division chief, Chuhei Yamadaira, the study department chief, and Susumu Aota to attend the discussion meeting. More than an hour passed before rooms were found for all of them.

Shin'ichi finally decided to forego that evening's meeting. If he were to attend at this late hour, the meeting would run substantially overtime. Besides, another discussion meeting was scheduled for the following day.

After Kiyohara and Yamadaira returned from the meeting, the leaders gathered to discuss the formation of a district in Chicago. The scope of the discussion, however, did not stop at this one city.

Not only did Shin'ichi outline his concept for establishing an American general chapter, he also went on to speak of plans for visiting India and Europe. In his mind, a vision for the worldwide kosen-rufu movement was already taking shape.

THE next day, October 9, was a Sunday. Shin'ichi did not want to disturb the local members on the morning of their day off, so he hadn't scheduled any activities before the afternoon. He and the other leaders took a morning walk in Lincoln Park, which ran along the shore of Lake Michigan. Set against a backdrop of skyscrapers, the park itself was a haven of lush trees, frolicking squirrels and wide stretches of green grass.

In one of the park's open areas, several children were playing, kicking a ball between them. They were all boys of around 7 or 8. Seated on a bench to one side and with a smile watching over the children's happy antics was an elderly, white-haired man. It was a heartwarming scene—a leisurely Sunday in the park. The elderly man would laugh and call

out encouragingly to the boys whenever their attempts to kick the ball failed. Whenever another child approached, the others would call out and invite him to join in, and their ranks grew by ones and twos.

Then a boy in a jumper came along, but no one asked him to join in. Unlike the others, this boy was African American. He stood in the shade of a nearby tree, his gaze riveted on the children playing with the ball. The old gentleman also ignored him. Another child then came along and, at everyone's beckoning, joined the game. Nobody, however, called out to the boy who was standing in the shadows of the tree.

When one of the children missed the ball and fell down, the boy laughed out loud and cheered. The elderly man rose from the bench, red-faced, and started to scream at him. The boy glared back at the man, his eyes burning with anger and hurt. He shot a retort at the man, then abruptly turned and ran away, his shoulders quivering with painful humiliation.

Shin'ichi's face clouded over. He wanted to run after the boy, but the boy had disappeared from sight. Powerful indignation seized Shin'ichi. His hands, unconsciously clenched into fists, trembled. He felt a helpless sense of anger toward a society where such unjust treatment of a young boy passed unchallenged.

This incident happened as the centennial of Abraham Lincoln's Emancipation Proclamation abolishing slavery in America was approaching, and in a park that bore this American president's name. It may have been a small, insignificant episode, but Shin'ichi felt that he had caught a glimpse of the dark abyss of prejudice that lay behind it.

*W*HAT feelings did the boy take with him as he ran off, Shin'ichi wondered. If such treatment occurred every day, then the boy's heart must have been cruelly assaulted time and again, leaving a gaping wound that bled with anger and sadness. When Shin'ichi thought of the boy's future, his own heart ached.

Around this period in America, the civil rights movement was gaining momentum, marking a major turning point in the long struggle to secure equal rights for African Americans. In 1954, the U.S. Supreme Court ruled that racial segregation in public schools violated the Constitution, a decision that led to a rapid heightening of public sentiment against discrimination and toward the abolition of segregation.

In December 1955, the following year, an African American woman named Rosa Parks was arrested in Montgomery, Alabama, an incident that led to the Montgomery bus boycott.

Around that time, African Americans, especially in the southern states, were openly subject to unjust discrimination. Not only was there inequality in terms of jobs and wages, but African Americans were segregated from white Americans in schools, transportation, cafeterias and other public facilities. Segregation was institutionalized by city ordinances at every turn, even extending to the segregation of bus seats.

On that December day, Mrs. Parks, exhausted from a hard day's work, got on the bus and sat down in an empty seat. The seats at the rear of the bus were designated for African Americans and the seats in the front for whites. However, if all the seats for white passengers were filled, African American passengers were commonly asked to stand and give up their seats. That day, all the seats were taken when some white passengers boarded the bus. The bus driver ordered Mrs. Parks and three other African American passengers to stand up. The other three complied, but Mrs. Parks refused, responding with a firm "No." The driver began heaping loud abuse on her. "Get over there!" he roared, but she just kept repeating, "No." For this, Mrs. Parks was arrested.

When word of Rosa Parks' arrest got out, the anger of the city's African American population exploded. There were calls to impose a boycott on the bus company for its policy of unjust discrimination. The leader of this movement was Martin Luther King Jr., who was to wage a tenacious struggle against discrimination through an unwavering commitment to nonviolence.

One year later, with the bus company driven to the brink of bankruptcy and the supreme court ruling that discriminatory treatment on buses was in violation of the Constitution, the intractable Montgomery city authorities were finally forced to abolish ordinances that permitted racial discrimination.

*V*ICTORY in the bus boycott added impetus to the civil rights movement, which spread to every corner of the United States.

Shortly thereafter, the u.s. government passed the Civil Rights Act of 1957, which promised to facilitate equal voting rights for African Americans. Many whites, however, remained opposed to this move. The powerful rights of the constituent states meant that not all federal government decisions were necessarily implemented.

For example, despite a federal decision ruling school segregation to be unconstitutional, more than a few state legislative bodies in the South invoked the doctrine and power of states' rights to oppose this ruling. The American system of federalism is a double-edged sword. It is a great bulwark for humanity, protecting people against the abuse of centralized power. It also provides protection from locally generated injustices.

Even when schools were desegregated, there were cases in which African American students were barred from using facilities such as campus dining halls and dormitories. Whites also conducted vocal demonstrations against allowing African Americans to enter white schools and universities, and there were numerous lynchings of African American students.

Having witnessed the treatment meted out to the boy in the park, Shin'ichi Yamamoto turned over the problem of racial discrimination in his mind: To abolish unjust discrimination in America, securing the civil rights of African American citizens would be essential. But would that be enough to bring people happiness?

The answer was clearly no, because the fundamental cause lay in the prejudice and bias rooted deeply in people's hearts. Unless people were liberated from these chains of prejudice, discrimination would only manifest itself in even more devious and despicable forms.

Beyond distinctions of race and ethnicity, Shin'ichi thought, all human beings are equal. This was the spirit of America expressed in its Declaration of Independence. Nevertheless, the sense of superiority and fear many white Americans felt toward African Americans would not permit genuine equality.

The question boiled down to how to change people's hearts and minds. The Buddhism of Nichiren Daishonin teaches the inherent dignity and equality of all human beings, deeming all people to be children of the Buddha and what the Lotus Sutra terms "treasure towers." Shin'ichi realized it would be vital to establish in each person's heart the profound view of the human being espoused by the Daishonin. There was no other solution to the problem of racial discrimination than realizing a human revolution in each individual. In other words, an inner reformation in the depths of people's lives to transform the egoism that justifies the subjugation of others and replace it with a humanism that strives for coexistence among all peoples.

Shin'ichi keenly sensed how vitally important it would be to achieve kosen-rufu in America.

President Toda had often spoken of the concept of "a global family," which he espoused as a basis for achieving the coexistence of humanity. Now, Shin'ichi vowed to make that ideal a reality.

In his heart, he addressed the young boy in the park: "I promise you that I will build a society truly worthy of your love and pride."

SHIN'ICHI Yamamoto's guidance tour of the United States continued without respite. That afternoon's discussion meeting was held at the same place as that of the previous day—a member's house located on Newport Street near Clark.

The participants split up into English- and Japanese-speaking groups and conducted separate discussions. Shin'ichi joined the English speakers, with Nagayasu Masaki acting as interpreter. Many of the participants in this group were men whose wives were from Japan; more than half had started practicing faith on their wives' recommendations.

Shin'ichi decided to turn the discussion into a question-and-answer session. "How do we go about advancing kosen-rufu?" He fielded such questions one after another—questions filled with the spirit of construction.

As he answered the members' questions, he made a point of looking at the harmonious way in which a white American and an African American sat together in the front row. When the eyes of these two met, they smiled and nodded at each other. The African American youth's hand then went up.

"As a Buddhist, I would like to contribute to American society. How should I go about doing so?" he asked.

Shin'ichi could not conceal his pleasure at this question.

"That's a wonderful way to think. I sense a loftiness and beauty in your spirit," he said. "The most important thing is to become one who is respected and trusted by all those around you, in your local community and your place of work. This is the struggle you have to wage. Next, it is vital to spread the humanistic philosophy of Buddhism, which expounds the freedom and equality of all people, here in American society. This will lead to the revitalization of the founding spirit of your nation, the greatest contribution you can make to society."

The youth nodded solemnly. Shin'ichi thought he would like to speak with and encourage him more later on.

After the question-and-answer session, Shin'ichi proposed they take a short break. This was out of consideration for the American participants who had been sitting on the floor along with the Japanese members, a posture that they were not used to.

Joyous conversations sprang up naturally among the members. There were people of many different races and ethnic groups at the meeting. They were delightedly shaking hands and sharing the determinations they had made with one another. From their behavior, at least, one could not sense the slightest bit of prejudice or discrimination.

They appeared totally unconscious of one another's skin color or other differences.

If the incident in the park that had sent the African American boy running away in anger and humiliation had spoken of racial discrimination, then this discussion meeting could be called a model of human harmony. To Shin'ichi, the scene at this meeting was like a priceless and inspiring painting; he felt as if he were glimpsing a ray of hope for the future.

*S*HIN'ICHI joined in the joyful discussion. He asked the members frankly, "I know that racial issues are highly controversial here in America, but what do all of you think about the problem?"

Nagayasu Masaki translated this for the members.

One white youth replied: "Racial discrimination exists everywhere throughout American society. I cannot in all honesty say that I myself am completely free of prejudice. However, since taking faith in the Daishonin's Buddhism and coming into contact and doing activities with all kinds of people, I've come to feel that we are all people who are striving together with one mind to achieve kosen-rufu."

"I see. That's very important," said Shin'ichi. "The concept of 'humankind' itself encompasses great diversity. There are many different races, ethnic groups, languages, cultures and nationalities. Also, just as no two people look exactly alike, each person differs in terms of birth, occupation, position, way of thinking and personal preferences. Human society—or what Buddhism terms our 'realm of existence'—is built upon this diversity.

"In reality, however, human beings have tended to emphasize each other's differences, classifying people into categories and practicing discrimination. History has seen members of the same human family divided again and again and led into one endless conflict after another because of their stubborn attachment to differences. The Daishonin's Buddhism is a teaching capable of unifying all humanity, bringing together hearts that have long been separated by deep schisms."

No one's eyes sparkled more brightly at these words than those of the African American youth who had earlier asked Shin'ichi a question.

The youth now inquired again: "President Yamamoto, you said that Buddhism will bring people's hearts together. What exactly does Buddhism teach with respect to how people are connected with one another?"

"That's a very good question," said Shin'ichi. "One of the fundamental tenets of Buddhism is that of dependent origination. All phenomena arise from mutually interdependent relationships of various causes and conditions. In other words, Buddhism teaches that nothing can exist entirely on its own, in complete isolation; all things are mutually dependent upon and influence one another."

With earnest expressions, the members listened intently to Shin'ichi's explanation.

SHIN'ICHI Yamamoto went on to further clarify the Buddhist doctrine of dependent origination. "In the same way, Buddhism teaches that no human being can exist in a state of total isolation; instead we congregate and live by supporting and helping one another. This philosophy opposes the idea of rejecting or shutting out certain persons or groups of people. If anything, the principle of dependent origination leads us to give the utmost consideration to how to enable others to reveal their potential, how to establish better human relations and how to create the greatest possible value."

Nodding his agreement, the youth who had asked the question then opened up and expressed what was in his heart.

"Until I started practicing Buddhism," he said, "I was constantly obsessed with my roots. I couldn't shake off the thought that we had been brought to America as slaves by the white man. I'm sure that white people harbor similar thoughts about us. They are loathe to treat people who were once slaves as their equals or grant us exactly the same rights as they have. For that reason, I despised white Americans. It was impossible for me to like them when I recalled how we, our parents, our grandparents and our ancestors before them had been exploited, abused and discriminated against by the white man.

"From childhood, each time I was bullied or suffered discrimination, it was driven home to me that I was black. I even came to deplore the blood running through my own veins. Then I joined the Soka Gakkai. There, everyone treated me as an equal and warmly encouraged me. It made the whole issue of racial difference seem so trivial. I came into contact with the altruistic spirit of the members. And, as you just mentioned, I realized that I had been caught up in stressing the differences in the color of our skin."

"I see," said Shin'ichi, smiling. "It's quite understandable that you should have placed great importance on your own roots. But Buddhism teaches that we are all Bodhisattvas of the Earth, the most praiseworthy of all bodhisattvas. As children of the Buddha from time without beginning, these bodhisattvas emerged at their own wish from the vast earth of life to fulfill a mission to realize kosen-rufu and to save all people of the Latter Day of the Law. These, if you will, are our ultimate roots."

The youth gazed at Shin'ichi with grave intensity.

*I*N short," Shin'ichi continued, "we—indeed, all people —are brothers and sisters from the infinite past who share a mission to bring peace and happiness to the world we live in. What we decide to base ourselves on has a drastic influence on the meaning of our own individual lives.

For instance, a large tree with leafy, green branches will not grow in the desert or on top of solid rock; it will only thrive in rich, fertile soil.

"Similarly, if we are to become great human beings capable of realizing a rich blossoming of humanity and a fruition of glory in our lives, then it is vital that we stand firm and prosper in whatever soil we may find ourselves. Establishing this kind of solid basis is to have an awareness of our mission as Bodhisattvas of the Earth.

"The earth belongs equally to everyone. It revitalizes all human beings, transcending racial, ethnic and national distinctions, and supports the flourishing of culture. A vibrant wellspring of pure altruism, of compassion, surges forth from its soil. If everyone were to awaken to their missions as Bodhisattvas of the Earth and take action based on it, there would not be the slightest doubt that we could build true world peace and human harmony."

The youth's eyes sparkled brightly. Gazing at him intently, Shin'ichi spoke with powerful emphasis: "I'm sure you must have suffered many bitter sorrows and hardships in your life. But now you have awakened to your identity as a Bodhisattva of the Earth. You have started a new life. Don't dwell on the past; live strongly, turning your eyes to the future! And to eradicate the root causes of the suffering you have experienced because of unjust discrimination, let's stand together, as champions of the cause of human liberation."

Shin'ichi extended his hand to the youth, who clasped it in a firm, strong handshake. The youth's spirited expression broadened into a bright smile.

This joyous discussion became a forum for the members to exchange vows of friendship and make a new departure toward the future.

After the Japanese-speaking group finished their discussion, they rejoined the English-speaking group. Shin'ichi

then announced the formation of two new districts: one in Chicago and one in Kentucky.

Miyako Coleman, who had been active as a central figure in the city, was appointed Chicago District chief. Shin'ichi took the gold Soka Gakkai pin he wore on his lapel and presented it to Miyako's husband, Mark. This gesture expressed Shin'ichi's wish that the Colemans pool their energy and strive for the happiness of the people of Chicago with an awareness and determination equal to his own.

*A*FTER the discussion meeting, Shin'ichi and the other leaders, accompanied by the Colemans, went for a walk around Chicago's downtown area.

Trains rumbled by on the elevated circular railway tracks known as The Loop, which snake their way between the city's towering skyscrapers. In the trains' reverberations, Shin'ichi could hear the dynamic pulsing of the bustling city of Chicago. Shin'ichi's heart, too, was beating vibrantly. He was overjoyed to have witnessed at the discussion meeting clear proof that heart-to-heart bonds could be formed among people, which could heal the deep rifts of racial discrimination that ran through American society.

Shin'ichi stopped at a camera shop and bought an instant-picture camera. He wanted to take snapshots of the people he met on his travels and then present them with the photographs on the spot. With his new camera, Shin'ichi wasted no time in taking a picture on Michigan Avenue. He called out to a young boy who was passing by and asked one of the other leaders to take a photo of them together. Shin'ichi wanted to speak to all the children in America who would one day shoulder their country's future; he wanted to share with them his great expectations for the future and to offer them his best wishes.

The group then decided to go to the top of the Prudential Building, renowned at that time as one of the tallest buildings in the United States. Lake Michigan, spreading out before them, shone like a golden mirror in the light of the setting sun.

The blue waters of the lake glowed with golden brilliance, Shin'ichi observed, because they were bathed in the sun's rays; human beings, too, when infused with the light of Buddhism, become "golden Buddhas." Gazing out over the city of Chicago in the twilight glow, Shin'ichi vowed to bring the sun of the Mystic Law—which illuminates the darkness of hearts obscured by clouds of prejudice and hate —to shine over America. He was painfully aware that this could only be achieved by gaining many new members and thoroughly fostering each person.

By the time the group had dined and returned to the hotel, it was around 8:00 P.M. Shin'ichi was still running a fever and felt increasingly fatigued as night approached. Walking to their rooms, the leaders noticed a group of four women and two children sitting on the floor in the hallway. They were Japanese members who had traveled to Chicago from Kentucky. Dearly wishing to see Shin'ichi one more time before making their way back home, the women had waited patiently for his return.

"Why are they sitting in the hallway?" muttered Yukio Ishikawa to himself in an undertone, clicking his tongue in annoyance. "They could have sat in the sofas in the lobby and waited. If people saw them here, they'd think it was very strange."

Shin'ichi paid no heed to his remarks.

*H*ELLO there! Is something the matter?" Shin'ichi asked the women who sat in the hallway. "Sensei! Thank goodness we caught you. We very much wanted to receive guidance from you before we went back."

"I see," said Shin'ichi. "Thank you for waiting all this time. Well, then, please come to my room. You must be exhausted."

He led them to his hotel room, but when they reached the door, the Japanese women hesitated, apparently not wishing to intrude. Shin'ichi courteously invited them in, saying, "Please, there's no need to stand on ceremony."

The women were not well dressed, but to Shin'ichi each appeared as a golden Buddha who would lead her friends in America to happiness. Buddhas do not exist in some far-off realm; they dwell here in this very real, strife-ridden *saha* world. A Buddha dwells within each living, breathing human being who experiences problems, sufferings and joy. Shin'ichi had resolved that his personal responsibility as president was to protect and serve such Buddhas—not fictitious ones, but real Buddhas—the people who dedicate their lives to fulfilling their missions for kosen-rufu. This was his conviction and his philosophy.

The discussion had barely begun when the children started whimpering. Guessing that they must be hungry,

Katsu Kiyohara quickly went to buy a large assortment of snacks and sweets for them. Having scrimped and saved to pay for their trip to Chicago, the women from Kentucky obviously had no money left over to buy their children sweets. Shin'ichi was deeply gladdened by Kiyohara's thoughtfulness.

It was evident from their stories that the women were grappling with momentous problems in their daily lives. Yet the announcement of a district being formed in Kentucky had filled their hearts with joy and a vibrant spirit of construction that far transcended their personal suffering.

Just as a river courses over rocks and stones, life is filled with problems and sufferings. If the river flows strongly, the rocks and stones will not only be submerged but eventually be eroded, washed away. The profound inner joy and dynamic vitality of a life dedicated to achieving the mission of peace known as kosen-rufu resembles the powerful flow of a river. With the joy of faith, one can calmly sweep away and triumph over all sufferings, no matter how numerous they may be.

Shin'ichi continued to give wholehearted encouragement to the women until it was time for them to leave to catch their bus. He strove with all his might to create a turning point for each person so that she could embark on a course toward happiness in life, much in the way that a plane soars upward in response to the brief, well-timed movement of the flight controls.

THE group set aside their third day in Chicago for an extensive tour of the city. Shin'ichi Yamamoto felt that the great metropolis of Chicago could show them what Japan might look like in the future.

In the car, Shin'ichi chanted daimoku continuously. Since taking his first step in Hawaii on this overseas trip, he had tried to chant daimoku at all times. He was determined to permeate the new land of America with his daimoku, offering prayers for its prosperity.

Shin'ichi and the other leaders visited various sites in Chicago's industrial area, including an automated factory where electrical appliances were manufactured. As they strolled down the street, their eyes were drawn to some election posters covering the window of what appeared to be a campaign office for the Democratic Party.

A presidential election was to be held on November 8. American voters would go to the polls to elect not only their new president, but many state governors and members of both the Senate and the House of Representatives. The Japanese group's visit thus coincided with the most intense period of campaigning before the election.

In particular, the presidential campaign saw a neck-and-neck race between Republican candidate Richard M. Nixon, who was then vice president, and Democratic candidate John F. Kennedy. With Nixon at age 47, and his opponent Kennedy at 43, it was a contest between two youthful nominees.

The U-2 affair earlier that year had led to the scuttling of a planned East-West summit meeting, and the Cold War seemed to be right back where it had started. This prompted people to place their hopes and expectations on a new president who could restore America's prestige and usher in a bright future. Perhaps not surprisingly, then, interest in the election was extremely high.

Nixon had taken the lead, appealing to his political experience and referring to himself as President Eisenhower's successor. Kennedy, meanwhile, stressed a new program, which he hailed as the "New Frontier," aimed at revitalizing American society. Their televised debates, in particular, saw the unfolding of an intense battle as one candidate asserted his experience, while the other retorted that experience was fine, but the most important thing was a philosophy and vision for the future.

In the youthful image of Kennedy that was presented on their TV screens, many people found a fresh sense of hope and of new possibilities for the future.

Every new era is ushered in by fresh talent and ability.

As he listened to Nagayasu Masaki describe the progress of the presidential election campaign, Shin'ichi thought: "The American people are yearning for a new leader and new ideals. And just as surely they must be longing for the profound and yet-still-unknown philosophy of the Daishonin's Buddhism."

He gazed silently at Kennedy's poster.

*T*HAT afternoon, Shin'ichi and the other leaders took a drive to the rural areas outside of the city. A quiet rustic landscape stretched out all around them. "It would be great if we could talk with some of the farmers and ask them about how they live," Shin'ichi remarked.

As they drove past a farmhouse, they saw a young woman standing outside. She appeared to be a farmer's wife. Nagayasu Masaki stopped the car and Shin'ichi stepped out and greeted the woman with a bright smile and a warm hello. Masaki followed him, explaining in English, "Good afternoon, we're interested in learning a little bit about the lives of farmers here in the Chicago area." He then added: "This is Mr. Shin'ichi Yamamoto from Japan. He is the president of the Soka Gakkai, a Buddhist organization dedicated to realizing world peace and human happiness."

The woman was happy to respond to Masaki's questions, describing the Chicago farmers' daily lives, the crops they grew, and even sharing the history of her own family, which she said had immigrated from Germany.

Hearing the conversation, an elderly woman then came out of the house to join them. She seemed to be somewhere in her late 60s. "Oh, this is Grandma," said the younger woman. "Today is her birthday."

Hearing this, Shin'ichi took the elderly woman's hand and said in Japanese: "Is that so? Congratulations! My very best wishes! Please live a long, long life. Nothing could be a greater source of joy for your family than your staying in good health; it will make everyone happy. I also hope that your whole family will please cherish you above all. This spirit not only strengthens the bonds of affection among you; it is a source of enduring prosperity for your family. Happiness is not in some faraway place; it is found within the family."

Masaki translated for Shin'ichi. The elderly woman smiled in delight at the good wishes conveyed by this stranger from Japan. Gazing at the woman's bright face, Shin'ichi proposed, "Let's all celebrate by singing 'Happy Birthday'!"

Enveloping the woman in his warm gaze, Shin'ichi began to sing.

T HE others joined with Shin'ichi in a chorus, their voices soaring into the air above the green fields. It was a heartwarming interlude of friendship and good will. Tears came to the woman's eyes as she stood in their midst.

When they had finished singing, Shin'ichi took a photo of everyone with his instant-picture camera, and gave it to the woman.

Looking deeply moved, she said: "Thank you. You don't even know me, yet here you are celebrating my birthday. This has been the happiest day of my life."

"I hope you will go on to create still many more happy memories in the future," Shin'ichi said. "Just because our bodies may age and our faces may become wrinkled, this doesn't mean that our hearts have to wither as well. Depending on our attitude, our hearts can remain eternally young. I hope that you will enjoy a life of perpetual youth and stay ever young at heart. Please promise me that you will live at least to 100."

When Nagayasu Masaki translated Shin'ichi's words, the woman blushed and looked somewhat doubtful. "I don't think I can live that long," she said. "But I promise to live with a youthful heart, as you said. Thank you so very much."

Her voice choked with emotion and no other words would come. She then held out her arms and embraced Shin'ichi. Though this was their first encounter, in that brief time their hearts resonated harmoniously together in a beautiful symphony of friendship.

The depth of human interaction or relations between people is not necessarily determined by the length of their acquaintance. The air of humanism emanating from a person's character inspires an echoing response in others' hearts, nurturing bonds and friendship. It paves the way for the forging of spiritual bonds that transcend ties based on kinship, locality and personal advantage.

As they drove off, the elderly woman stood waving until their car had disappeared from sight.

Shin'ichi always strove to treasure each encounter. Whether or not the other party was a Soka Gakkai member, Shin'ichi poured his heart into each meeting, planting seedlings of hope, encouraging luxuriant leaves of friendship to grow, and creating new value. This is the true way of life for a Buddhist who is aware of the principle of dependent origination that unifies all human beings.

THE next day, October 11, the group left Chicago for Toronto, Canada. At that time, there were no members in Canada.

The purpose of their visit was to purchase construction materials for the Grand Reception Hall that was scheduled to be built at the Head Temple Taiseki-ji, and to observe local conditions in Canada.

From the plane window, they gazed down upon a vast expanse of brilliantly blazing autumn foliage. The land, dyed in vivid hues of red and gold, resembled a sea of flames. It was truly a golden autumn.

The group arrived at Toronto Airport just before noon. As expected, the Canadian air was rather chilly. As soon as they reached the airport lobby, Nagayasu Masaki went to rent a car. While the others were waiting, some distance away a young Japanese woman with large eyes, wearing a green coat and a scarf around her head, gazed intently in their direction.

The woman came up to them and asked in a quiet voice, "Excuse me, are you members of the Soka Gakkai?"

They were not expecting anyone to meet them here in Toronto. Though somewhat puzzled by her presence, their hearts leapt hopefully at the thought that she might be a member.

"Yes, we are," Kiyoshi Jujo answered. "Are you a member, too?"

"No, I'm not."

They gazed at the woman somewhat bewildered and waited for her to continue.

"My mother is a Soka Gakkai member in Japan, and I'm here because she asked me to come and meet you.

"Is that so?" said Shin'ichi, smiling. "Thank you for taking the trouble to come all this way to greet us. I am Shin'ichi Yamamoto, president of the Soka Gakkai. May I ask your name?"

"Yes, it's Teruko Izumiya."

"And what chapter does your mother belong to?"

"I think she said it was Kamata Chapter."

"It says a lot about your mother's character that she should worry about our arrival and ask her daughter to come and welcome us. She's a wonderful person. How do you come to be in Canada, by the way?"

"My husband works for a trading company and he was transferred here. We arrived six months ago."

Izumiya answered Shin'ichi's questions cheerfully, a bright smile lighting her face.

*T*ERUKO Izumiya lived in a Toronto suburb that was about twenty minutes by car from the airport. Her mother, concerned about her daughter who had married and gone to live in Canada, had sent her letters urging her to take faith in the Daishonin's Buddhism. However, all the talk of punishment and benefit that filled these letters had sounded questionable and terribly outdated to Izumiya and had made her feel resistant to the idea. She didn't even feel inclined to look through the copies of the *Seikyo Shimbun*, the Soka Gakkai's newspaper, which her mother sent her regularly.

Then, just that morning, she had received an airmail letter from her mother informing her that President Yamamoto and a group of leaders from the Soka Gakkai would be visiting Toronto on the 11th. Her mother had written: "President Yamamoto will be an internationally renowned leader some day. Please go and meet him at the airport."

For a moment, Izumiya had wavered over whether to go. She was six months' pregnant and hadn't been feeling well all morning. It would be more than she could bear if, after going all the way out to the airport, she was then proselytized to. Yet, not to go would be disrespectful of her mother's wishes, a thought that made her feel remorseful and disloyal. Thus she had decided to go to the airport.

Shin'ichi asked Izumiya about her life in Canada and outlined for her why faith was important, explaining that Buddhism constituted the law of life itself. There was nothing highhanded in his manner nor was he pushy or overly insistent about her taking faith. Moreover, what he said made clear and perfect sense.

She began to feel that perhaps she had been wrong about the Soka Gakkai after all.

"In any event, should you be faced with a problem, please chant daimoku," Shin'ichi advised.

Izumiya accepted his words without resentment.

Presently, Nagayasu Masaki returned with a rented station wagon. The group then took a commemorative photo together with Izumiya.

Shin'ichi asked Izumiya how she had come to the airport. She replied that she had come by taxi.

"We'll drive you home then," Shin'ichi offered.

"No, that won't be necessary. I'll take a taxi home."

Shin'ichi was loathe to allow Izumiya, the only person who had come to welcome them at the airport, to travel home alone by taxi. However, when they had loaded all their luggage into the station wagon and the leaders themselves got in, the car was packed.

"Please wait for a moment. I'll make some room," Shin'ichi said.

They took out the luggage and tried to rearrange it several times, but no matter how they tried they could not make enough space to accommodate Izumiya.

TERUKO Izumiya's heart was warmed by the sincerity and thoughtfulness that Shin'ichi Yamamoto showed her in wanting to give her a lift home.

"I'll be all right. Please don't worry. Please go ahead without me," she said.

Shin'ichi apologized deeply, stating repeatedly how sorry he was that they could not drive her home. As they were leaving, he gave her the name of the hotel where they were staying. "If you have any questions, please don't hesitate to contact me. I'll make sure to let your mother know that you are well and doing fine when I return to Japan."

Izumiya waved goodbye to the group until their car had disappeared from view. Sitting in the taxi on her way home, she felt lighthearted and refreshed. In contrast to the heavy feeling that had weighed upon her as she left the house, she now felt as if warm rays of morning sunlight were streaming into her heart, clearing away the mist that had earlier enshrouded it. This was not merely due to a sense of relief at having dutifully fulfilled her mother's request to go to meet President Yamamoto and his party. Her joy actually came from having encountered, suddenly and quite unexpectedly, something very precious and important that she had not known before.

Izumiya realized that this first encounter with the reality of the faith her mother practiced so wholeheartedly left her feeling very pleased and happy. Coming into contact with the sincerity, thoughtfulness and conviction that emanated from President Yamamoto's being, as well as his rational and logical explanation of Buddhist theory, she could sense that the faith her mother practiced was quite special. Izumiya was aware that something had changed fundamentally in her own heart.

A few weeks later, a parcel containing several books on the Soka Gakkai arrived in the mail. They were from Shin'ichi Yamamoto.

One year and seven months after her first meeting with the Soka Gakkai president at Toronto Airport, Teruko Izumiya took faith in the Daishonin's Buddhism of her own accord. At that time, the seed sown by Shin'ichi sprouted and, in time, would herald the arrival of spring for kosen-rufu in Canada.

Shin'ichi and the other leaders arrived and checked in at the King Edward Hotel on King Street. Everyone then decided to go sightseeing around the central city area, except Shin'ichi, who stayed in the hotel because he was still feeling under the weather. The fever that had plagued him since Seattle tended to peak in the afternoons.

Shin'ichi knew that all he needed was some rest. However, he had resolved to exert a year's effort in each day on this overseas trip, so he had to content himself with snatching a few moments' rest whenever time permitted and in such a way that did not adversely affect his schedule; he had to continue at this strenuous pace, aware all the time that he was pushing himself to unreasonable limits.

KIYOSHI Jujo and the others who had gone to have a look around the Toronto central city area came back to the hotel early that evening. They were accompanied by a middle-aged Japanese man—a Soka Gakkai member who, as president of a trading company, spent six months of each year in Montreal on business. When he learned that President Shin'ichi Yamamoto would be visiting Toronto, the man had decided to go and meet him, making a ten-hour bus journey from Montreal.

Shin'ichi spoke with the businessman for some time; he was delighted that a fellow member had shown up here in

Canada, where he had expected to find none, and that this person had traveled from Montreal just to see him.

Shin'ichi asked the man about conditions in that Canadian city. He explained that Christianity was deeply rooted in every aspect of society and how difficult it was to spread a correct understanding of Buddhism among people under such circumstances. Though he gave an objective appraisal of the situation in Montreal, his words failed to impart any sense of what he himself would do to challenge these obstacles as an active player in the kosen-rufu movement.

"I guess we'll have to postpone kosen-rufu in Montreal then," Shin'ichi said.

The man looked perplexed.

Wherever it may be, the advancement of kosen-rufu depends on the presence of one person with the lion's courage to stand alone. Without someone who is determined to boldly confront all obstacles and take on full responsibility for kosen-rufu, there can be no progress or development.

Shin'ichi thought: "Difficulty and hardship are part and parcel of blazing new trails. If we think something is difficult then it will be difficult; and if we think something is impossible, then it will be impossible. The path to kosen-rufu, however, can be forged only with a burning fighting spirit and a passionate struggle to pierce through all obstacles that stand in our way."

But Shin'ichi held back from expressing these thoughts. He had placed his hopes on this man who could be described as a solitary seed of kosen-rufu in Canada. Yet Shin'ichi felt hesitant to instruct him on the strict path of faith that required lionlike courage. This member had obviously had no opportunity to learn the Soka Gakkai's "stand alone" spirit. For that reason, Shin'ichi felt he deserved to be praised simply for having traveled all the way to Toronto to see him. Shin'ichi thanked the member for his efforts and offered words of encouragement. After they had said good-bye, Shin'ichi prayed that the man would be a victor in faith, practicing steadfastly throughout his life.

Through this encounter, Shin'ichi realized that he would have to wait for the appropriate time for the curtain to rise on the kosen-rufu movement in Canada—for a time when a steady stream of like-minded friends, whose mission in this life was to realize the widespread propagation of the Daishonin's Buddhism, would emerge and develop one after another.

*I*T was thus in Toronto that Shin'ichi Yamamoto ushered in the morning of October 12, 1960, the 681st anniversary of Nichiren Daishonin's inscription of the Dai-Gohonzon for all humanity. He felt deeply moved to be celebrating this day on Canadian soil on his first visit to the North American continent—a trip inspired by his determination to spread the Law throughout the world in accord with the original Buddha's decree.

Despite his ill health, Shin'ichi's heart overflowed with fresh resolve for kosen-rufu.

That day, riding in a car driven by Nagayasu Masaki, the group visited various sites in Toronto to inspect possible construction materials for the Grand Reception Hall. Afterward, they went to Niagara Falls, located midway along the Niagara River, which flows between Lake Erie and Lake Ontario [along the border between the United States and Canada].

Stepping from the car, Shin'ichi and the others were struck by the thunderous, almost earth-shattering roar of the giant falls that spread before them, its waters crashing down to churn up great clouds of spray.

Niagara Falls was split in two by Goat Island, a small island lying in the middle of the Niagara River. The crests of the falls on both sides were several hundred yards long, and the sight of water plummeting over sheer drops of around 165 feet was truly spectacular.

Shin'ichi was entranced by the breathtaking beauty of this natural phenomenon. He sat down on the stone fence that ran along the edge of the cliff overlooking the river. Set off by a magnificent clear blue sky and the distant forest cloaked in colorful autumn hues, the falls shone with pristine brilliance as the water thundered down with powerful intensity. Mist from the crashing water danced into the air, creating a vivid rainbow.

To Shin'ichi, the monumental and unceasing flow of water seemed somehow symbolic of the advance of kosen-rufu, while the shimmering rainbow it gave rise to represented boundless hope. As he gazed at the majestic sight, he said with deep feeling to Eisuke Akizuki who stood next to him:

The rainbow above this waterfall would disappear in an instant if the flow of water were to stop. Similarly, the rainbow of hope in our lives shines only when we advance energetically toward kosen-rufu. People who never lose hope have the strength to remain undefeated by any difficulty. Once a person loses hope, however, life becomes dark. Despair is the same as spiritual death. Youth must live with constant and unflagging hope. I want to create a rainbow of hope in the hearts of the world's youth.

Akizuki, the Soka Gakkai youth division chief, could feel in Shin'ichi's words his boundless compassion and fervent expectation for young people. He thought how fortunate he and the other members of the youth division were to practice together with such a leader.

BY the time the group returned to the hotel, darkness had fallen. Shin'ichi went to the front desk to pick up his room key and then sat on a sofa in the lobby where he casually reached for a local newspaper lying nearby. What he saw made him gasp. "That's Chairman Asanuma of the Socialist Party!" The paper carried a photograph of Inejiro Asanuma[2] being attacked by a knife-wielding youth wearing a loose jacket over a school uniform. The picture actually captured Asanuma, his glasses askew, as he was about to crumple to the floor.

Nagayasu Masaki hurriedly translated the accompanying article for Shin'ichi: "It says that at shortly past 3:00 P.M. (Japan time) on October 12, Mr. Asanuma, chairman of the Japan Socialist Party, was fatally stabbed with a short sword by a 17-year-old right-wing youth identified as Otoya Yamaguchi. At the time of the attack, Mr. Asanuma was delivering a speech at an interparty meeting attended by rival party heads from the ruling Liberal Democratic, the Socialist and the Democratic Socialist parties, which was held at the Hibiya Civic Hall in Tokyo."

The other leaders from Japan gazed in shock at the picture in the paper. "How terrible," said Shin'ichi.

He chanted three daimoku in his heart and prayed for the repose of the deceased politician. Although Shin'ichi had never met Asanuma personally, and their philosophies and beliefs naturally differed, the late Socialist Party chairman's affinity for the common people and his energetic actions struck a chord of sympathy within him.

Despite serving in such top party posts as secretary-general and later chairman, Inejiro Asanuma had maintained his residence in a humble apartment in Shirakawacho in Fukagawa, Tokyo, living a very modest lifestyle. He traveled energetically around Japan, marched at the head of demonstrations and made it his motto to always fight alongside the people—activities that had earned him the nickname, "the human dynamo."

Shin'ichi was deeply saddened that a person like Asanuma should have been felled by a terrorist's knife.

He deplored this cruel and inhuman crime. He also felt intense pity for the young assailant who had sunk into the dark and bloody depths of terrorism.

In that same year, there had been a number of similar incidents of senseless violence related to the ratification of the new u.s.-Japan Security Treaty. On June 17, a 20-year-old youth, armed with a knife, had entered the National Diet compound and stabbed Jotaro Kawakami,[3] a member of the House of Representatives and an advisor to the Socialist Party, inflicting minor injury. Then, in the following month, on July 14, Prime Minister Nobusuke Kishi also sustained minor wounds when he was attacked at his official residence by a 65-year-old man, the former head of a prewar right-wing group, who was brandishing a short sword. The assailant in this case committed his crime with the intent of forcing the authorities to reflect on their conduct, convinced that the uproar over the new security treaty pointed to problems with the way the government was running the country.

*A*T first, no one believed that the assassination of Socialist Party Chairman Asanuma was the work of a lone 17-year-old youth. Police investigators took the view that other shadowy figures had masterminded the attack. Suspicion fell on members of a right-wing organization with which the young man had once been affiliated. Much to everyone's surprise, however, it later came to light that the youth, although influenced by the organization ideologically, had planned and carried out the assassination on his own.

It was reported that he had been a well-mannered young man who was gentle and pure of heart. His father was an officer in the Japan's Self Defense Forces. His early adolescence coincided with a time when the very existence of the Self Defense Forces was harshly criticized by the left wing. Given these conditions, it is not at all surprising that an anti-communist attitude should gradually have grown in his heart.

One day, the youth happened to hear a speech given by a right-wing leader. The speaker declared that the Soviet Union and China were aiming to spread communism in Japan. Their henchmen in this endeavor, he claimed, were the members of the Japan Communist Party, the Japan Socialist Party, the labor unions, the Zengakuren and other groups. Pointing to the corruption and degeneracy of conservative politicians, he asserted that Japan was now standing on the brink of revolution. Demanding that resolute action be taken to bring about a political restoration, the leader called on the youth of Japan to rise up. This passionate appeal, which rang with clarity and simplicity, rocked the young man to the very core of his being. He voluntarily joined a right-wing organization and became an active member.

In the meantime, the anti-security treaty movement was beginning to grow in scope. The young man participated in rightist activities to oppose anti-security treaty rallies and protest meetings, and he was always one of the first to storm the demonstrators. He was arrested time and again.

As the anti-security treaty movement broadened and intensified, drawing many ordinary citizens to its fold, it provoked a growing sense of crisis in this youth who feared the outbreak of a communist revolution. He came to feel that because the right wing had far fewer numbers than the left, it would be impossible for it to gain control of the government by legitimate means. It was then that an idea began to germinate in his mind: the only way to protect Japan from becoming a communist state would be to assassinate the leftist leaders.

The youth was already dissatisfied with right-wing leaders who spoke of toppling their counterparts on the left yet never actually made any move to do so. As a result, despair and disillusionment washed over him, fueling his sense of crisis and panic. He thought to himself, "I'll have to kill them myself."

*T*HE young man drew up a list of several politicians he considered possible targets for assassination. Of these, he finally chose Inejiro Asanuma, chairman of the Japan Socialist Party (JSP). He saw this political party as an even worse threat than the Communist Party and was convinced that it was deceiving the people and attempting to sell Japan out to communism. In particular, he felt that a remark made by Asanuma, then JSP secretary-general, during a visit to China in March of the previous year, that "American imperialism is the common enemy of Japan and China," clearly exposed the Socialist Party's communist leanings.

Yet for the youth to embark upon and carry through with his terrorist plan, he needed some kind of spiritual support. He surely must have vacillated over whether to proceed with his plan when he thought of the suffering it would inevitably cause his family.

It was later found that a short time before committing his crime, the youth had borrowed a copy of the book *Tenno Zettai Ron to Sono Eikyo* (The Theory of the Emperor's Supremacy and Its Influence), authored and edited by Masaharu Taniguchi, the leader of a religious group known as Seicho no Ie[4] (House of Growth). The book stated that loyalty was the means by which to become one with the emperor, asserting that "Selflessness is the essence of loyalty." Sadly, these words seem to have spurred the impressionable youth in making his decision to proceed down the path of terrorism. He finally carried out his assassination plan on October 12, at a meeting where leaders of the three main political parties were to deliver campaign speeches in preparation for Japan's 29th general election scheduled for November 20.

Misguided ideology is truly frightening.

On November 2, twenty-one days after assassinating Asanuma, the youth ended his own short life by hanging himself in his solitary prison cell in the Tokyo Juvenile Classification Center. On the wall he had written in toothpaste: "Serving my country with seven lives. Long live the Emperor!"

Back in the hotel lobby in Toronto, Shin'ichi was overcome by a sense of frustration at this news of Chairman Asanuma's assassination.

It appeared that the youth had tried to force reality to fit within the framework of his own abstract ideals. Reality, however, is fluid and alive and filled with contradictions. It never conforms to the standards of abstract idealism. When a person's ideals do not accord with reality, the ultimate outcome is panic or hopelessness. It is not difficult to imagine that the youth had been overwhelmed by despair and a growing sense of urgency as he rushed blindly toward violence, fully prepared to sacrifice his own life.

Many of the students who had poured their passion and energy into the struggle over the security treaty had become so weary and defeated that they were already turning their backs on the idea of achieving a reformation. Though the beliefs and arguments of those on both sides of the security treaty issue were diametrically opposed, Shin'ichi felt that they all shared something in common.

He pondered the tragedy of those pure-hearted young people who had dreamt of change only to lose hope and be cruelly disillusioned, their spirits growing blighted and withered. Shin'ichi was keenly aware that it is only possible to create a new era when youth, with their dynamic power, sink roots into the soil of society and are allowed to flourish.

*I*T was morning and a station wagon sped along the highway. At the steering wheel sat Nagayasu Masaki. It was the car carrying Shin'ichi and the other leaders to the airport so that they could continue on to their next destination, New York. Masaki's face was covered with a fine film of perspiration. Their flight to New York was scheduled to leave at 10:00 A.M. Though the group had planned to leave the hotel at 8:00, by the time everyone had assembled, they were running some twenty to thirty minutes late.

Masaki was doing his best to make up for lost time. With a road map in one hand, he drove at high speed toward the airport. But it seemed to be taking forever to get there. His watch showed that it was already ten minutes past nine.

"Aren't we there yet?" Yukio Ishikawa asked from the back seat.

"Masaki, this isn't the same road we took from the airport two days ago," observed Eisuke Akizuki.

Masaki became increasingly anxious. But as far as he could tell from the map, they were heading in the right direction. He continued on the highway a little further and then exited. Stopping at a nearby farmhouse, he went up to the door and asked if he could use the phone.

He rang Molton Airport (now Toronto International Airport) for directions. He was totally unprepared for the response: The airport was in exactly the opposite direction from the one they had been heading.

"But the road map says there is an airport out this way."

"Yes, that's Milton Airport, the military air force base."

Masaki was aghast. He had been utterly convinced that Molton Airport lay in this direction, never suspecting for a

moment that there was another airport with a name whose spelling differed by only one letter.

If Shin'ichi and the other leaders missed their flight, it would wreak havoc with their entire schedule. Moreover, many members would be waiting to meet them at the airport in New York. Just as the time in Hawaii when he realized that no one had gone to meet Shin'ichi and his party, Masaki felt his blood run cold.

A deathly pale Masaki returned to the car and said to Shin'ichi: "I'm sorry, I'm on the wrong road. I'll turn back right away."

After bowing deeply in apology, he jumped into the car, revved the engine and took off again at breakneck speed.

*A*S he drove, Nagayasu Masaki could hear Yukio Ishikawa and Chuhei Yamadaira talking in the back seat: "Will we make it on time? It will cause real problems if we're late."

"Mmm, we might not make it."

The words stabbed at Masaki's heart. He drove even faster.

"Masaki, there's no need to be in such a hurry," said Shin'ichi, knowing how he must have felt. "You mustn't have an accident. If we're late, we're late."

Masaki was doubtlessly filled with remorse over having made such an awful mistake. Shin'ichi wanted to relieve his mental anguish, even if only a little.

At long last, Molton Airport came into view. Masaki grasped the steering wheel with earnest resolve, chanting daimoku in his heart.

It was already a few minutes after 10:00 A.M. when they arrived at the airport and rushed to the check-in counter, hoping against hope that the plane had not left. Masaki was gasping for breath as he told the flight number to the clerk on duty.

"That flight has just left," the clerk informed him apologetically.

The clerk was quite young—somewhere in his 20s. Masaki asked the time of the next flight and whether there were any seats available.

"The next flight is at 12:15, but unfortunately there are no seats left. In fact, all flights to New York are fully booked right through to final flight this evening at 10:15."

Masaki regretfully told Shin'ichi the news. The party was at a loss as to what to do next. Masaki went back to the counter and explained their situation to the clerk.

"That's a real problem. I'll see what I can do to make sure you make it to New York as soon as possible."

After making two or three phone calls, the young clerk left the counter. The group watched his retreating figure with anxious and worried expressions.

"All kinds of things happen when you travel," Shin'ichi said, hoping to lighten the atmosphere.

However, he too wanted by all means to avoid causing any more inconvenience to the members who would be waiting for them at the airport in New York.

The clerk returned about ten minutes later.

Masaki looked at him anxiously. Smiling, the clerk said: "Please wait just a little longer. I can probably work something out for you."

A few moments later, the phone on the counter rang. The clerk picked it up as if he had been waiting for the call. He then engaged at length in what seemed to be a negotiation with the person on the other end.

*S*MILING, the young clerk at the airport hung up the phone and informed Masaki: "It will be on a different carrier, but we've managed to secure seats for all seven of you. That's great, isn't it? The flight will depart at 12:30 P.M. Please put your luggage over there."

Masaki felt like jumping for joy. When he informed Shin'ichi and the other leaders of this news, there were relieved smiles all round. Masaki then placed a call to the airport in New York to ask that the change in their flight be announced over the P.A. system.

More than anything, Shin'ichi was profoundly grateful for the young clerk's kindness. It was their fault that they had been late and missed their flight. The clerk was not in any way obligated to show them special consideration. Nonetheless, he had taken a warm personal interest in their dilemma and done everything possible to find them seats on another flight. Moreover, there had been nothing in his manner to make them feel as if he were doing them a great favor. Accompanied by Masaki, Shin'ichi went over to the young clerk to express his heartfelt appreciation.

"Thank you very much," he said in English and then continued in Japanese, "I deeply appreciate your sincerity." The youth smilingly shook the hand that Shin'ichi held out to him. It was a handshake that communicated the warm spirit of friendship.

"Bon voyage!" the clerk wished the group cheerfully in parting. Shin'ichi felt he would never forget this young man for as long as he lived.

It is easy to speak of loving one's fellow human beings. But it is difficult to lend assistance to a stranger who is in trouble. All too often people shun involvement by pretending not to see what's going on. It may seem like a small thing, but coming to the aid of a total stranger in difficulty is an act that requires human compassion and courage. The realization of ideals such as world peace and love for all humanity starts from the way in which each individual deals with situations and problems in his or her immediate environment.

In any event, Shin'ichi thought it unfathomably mystic that such a person should have appeared to help them out of their dilemma. He keenly sensed that the members in Japan were sending daimoku for the success of his overseas visit. As Shin'ichi reflected on the moving good will the youth had shown them, the plane rose into the air. The brilliant autumn colors of the maple leaves below seemed inexpressibly beautiful to him. To his eyes, the vast earth, cloaked in red and gold autumnal hues, appeared as a dazzling, richly colored tapestry of human harmony woven from the threads of sincerity. A renewed pledge for world peace resounded like a sonorous bell in his heart.

"Golden Autumn" Notes:

1. "Desiring little and contenting ourselves with what we have.": This is a quality the Daishonin assigns to honest priests. In the Gosho, he writes: "True priests are those who are honest and who desire little and yet know satisfaction" (WND-I, 747), and "A good teacher is a priest who is free from any fault in secular affairs, who never fawns upon others even in the slightest, who desires and is satisfied with little, and who is compassionate" (WND-I, 880).

2. Inejiro Asanuma (1898–1960): Japanese social activist and politician. After World War II, he participated in the forming of the Japan Socialist Party (JSP), serving in a number of key party posts. He was appointed JSP chairman during the turbulent period of the 1960 Security Treaty ratification and was assassinated while giving a speech on October 12, 1960.

3. Jotaro Kawakami (1889–1965): Japanese politician. Also involved in the formation of the Japan Socialist Party. He served as chairman of the party's right wing (1951–55). After the assassination of Asanuma, he became party chairman (1960–65).

4. Seicho no Ie: A religious organization founded in 1930 by Masaharu Taniguchi (1893–1985), whose teachings incorporated a blend of doctrines of Shinto, Buddhism and Christianity as well as modern philosophy and psychoanalysis, with particularly strong Shinto overtones. His writings formed the basis of the religious organization's propagation activities, with claims being made that reading his book *Seimmei no Jisso* (The Truth of Life) could cure illness. During World War II, Seicho no Ie supported the emperor-centered ideology of the military regime.

Light of Compassion

*T*HE compassionate light of Buddhism was now about to illuminate the skyscrapers of the United States' largest city, New York.

Shin'ichi Yamamoto's flight from Toronto arrived shortly after 2:00 P.M. at New York's Idlewild (now John F. Kennedy) International Airport. He and the other leaders were about two-and-a-half hours behind schedule. Despite this delay, more than ten Soka Gakkai members were on hand to greet them with an energetic rendition of the song "Ifu Dodo." Amid the members' welcoming applause, a young girl of about 4 or 5 presented Shin'ichi with a bouquet of flowers.

True to the global economic center that it was, the city of New York overflowed with energy and activity. Shin'ichi gazed in awe at the forest of skyscrapers with the Empire State Building standing tallest among them. The party was staying at a Manhattan hotel at Broadway and 34th Street.

The hum of endlessly flowing traffic could be heard even in Shin'ichi's room on the 19th floor. When he closed his eyes, it sounded like the roar of the ocean or the cheering of a great crowd. He pictured in his mind the samurai of the first Japanese delegation to the United States, which had paraded down Broadway 100 years earlier.[1]

After exchanging ratification papers for the u.s.–Japan Treaty of Amity and Commerce in Washington, D.C., the delegation had visited New York, where they received a grand welcome from its citizens. The delegation went down Broadway in carriages, surrounded by an honor guard 7,000 strong. Tens of thousands packed the sidewalks, their cheering echoing in the skies. A witness to this parade, the poet Walt Whitman, praised it in verse as the meeting of a youthful and free America and the ancient, all-embracing motherland of Asia:

> *Over the Western sea hither from Niphon[2] come,*
> *Courteous, the swart-cheek'd two-sworded envoys,*
> *Leaning back in their open barouches, bare-headed, impassive,[3]...*

Whitman had cherished a vision that this encounter with the East would supply America with something it lacked, thereby making it whole and complete. Now, 100 years later, Shin'ichi took his first step on Broadway as an emissary of the Eastern philosophy of Buddhism. In stark contrast to the enthusiastic throngs that had greeted that first mission of envoys a century earlier, Shin'ichi and his party were met by only a handful of members. Shin'ichi, however, was determined to make his visit the dawn of true interaction between America and the all-encompassing philosophy of the East, the fusion of which Walt Whitman had so yearned for.

THE next morning, October 14, the group visited the U.N. Headquarters. The fifteenth U.N. General Assembly, which had begun on September 20, was in regular session. It was attended by ten heads of state, thirteen prime ministers and fifty-seven foreign ministers, including the leaders of the Eastern and Western blocs—Prime Minister Nikita S. Khrushchev of the Soviet Union and President Dwight D. Eisenhower of the United States. With the conspicuous attendance of the world's leaders, this session of the General Assembly took on the air of a summit, matching the United Nations' purpose to serve as a "parliament of humankind."

During the session, seventeen nations, including Cameroon, Togo and Madagascar, were admitted as members. With the exception of Cyprus, all of these countries were newly independent African states. This brought the U.N. membership to ninety-nine nations, of which forty-five belonged to the Asia-Africa bloc. This represented a major redrawing of the political map of the world, since it gave the members of the Asia-Africa bloc a greater influence in the deliberations of the General Assembly.

This session, though it saw the increase of U.N. membership and the attendance of many of the world's leaders, was a stormy one, marked by a renewed deepening of the schism between Eastern and Western blocs. The tense mood in the General Assembly was particularly pronounced following the speech that Khrushchev had delivered on September 23, the second day of the general debate.

After welcoming the newly admitted African states to the United Nations, Khrushchev launched on a pointed attack of the United States. Citing the spy flights by American U-2 reconnaissance aircraft over Soviet territory earlier that year, he slammed the United States for obstructing an easing in international tensions. In addition, he called for the immediate and complete dismantling of colonialism. The

Soviet premier also turned his attack on U.N. Secretary-General Dag Hammarskjold,[4] saying that all secretaries-general of the world body to date had been selected from among Western-leaning candidates. He proposed a plan for restructuring the United Nations, in which the position of secretary-general would be abolished and replaced with an executive council of three—one from the Western powers, one from the Socialist bloc and one from the nonaligned countries.

These hard-line proposals came amid an atmosphere of deepening mistrust between East and West. For the Western countries, none of the elements of these proposals was in any way acceptable. Rather, they appeared to be a deliberate provocation. In particular, the idea of eliminating the position of secretary-general was viewed in the West as a direct challenge to the United Nations. Unlike the previous year's General Assembly, when a mood of detente had prevailed, this year's session was marked by an atmosphere of turbulence and discord.

When Dag Hammarskjold indicated that he had no intention of acceding to the demand that he resign as secretary-general, Khrushchev expressed his dissatisfaction by loudly pounding on the table in front of him.

*F*ROM the start of the session, opinion was divided as to whether disarmament issues should be taken up in committee or in plenary session. When the Soviet Union insisted that it be treated as a plenary topic, the Western countries objected, saying that the Soviet request was for propaganda purposes only.

Standing at the speaker's podium and waving both arms, Soviet Prime Minister Nikita Khrushchev embarked on a verbal counterattack, saying that it was a question of whether disarmament was to be pursued in earnest. If the West wanted an arms race, he said, then that was fine with the Soviet

Union; Soviet rockets were capable of reaching any place on Earth or even outer space. He hinted of dire consequences should the present situation continue.

The American and French representatives fiercely rebutted the Soviet leader's statement. When, on the subject of colonialism, the American representative stated that there were many countries in eastern Europe without freedom, the representatives of the Eastern bloc began pounding on their tables en masse. The representative from Romania ran up to the chairman's seat, adding to the uproar. Outraged, the chairman pounded his gavel and declared a recess. In his fury, he struck the gavel with such force that it broke.

People the world over long for peace. This simple desire, however, was never given true voice by the representatives of the member states attending the General Assembly. The shouted cries of the mouthpieces of rival ideologies, estranged from human reality, resounded meaninglessly in the assembly hall. For the United Nations to truly function as a parliament of humankind, it is vital that the representatives of each nation, through a spirit of friendship and dialogue, remember that they are all members of the same human family.

Shin'ichi and his party visited the U.N. Headquarters the day after Khrushchev, who had been at the United Nations for twenty-five days, left for the Soviet Union. The group observed both committee and plenary proceedings. They were particularly impressed by the vibrant expressions worn by the representatives of the newly independent African states. These countries, which had been subject to colonial rule, were faced with many difficult problems in such fields as politics, economics, education and human rights. Many of their leaders, however, were youthful, proud and brimming with fresh energy. They were free of the arrogance and craftiness so often seen in the aged leaders of great powers.

Shin'ichi was filled with hope for the future of Africa. He saw there the beginnings of a new current of history. Turning to Eisuke Akizuki, he said: "The twenty-first century will be the century of Africa. The world should support the growth of this young sapling." His eyes were fixed on the distant future.

*A*FTER visiting the U.N. Headquarters, the party traveled to New Jersey, where a discussion meeting was to be held. The meeting place was the home of Yukiko Nishino, the elder sister of Nagayasu Masaki. Yukiko had moved to New Jersey from Washington, D.C.

Just outside the house, Shin'ichi Yamamoto met a woman and a young man, both of them Japanese. He greeted them politely and handed them his name card. The young man, who introduced himself as Mitsuo Sugihara, was an employee of a Japanese trading company who had been stationed in the United States. He had brought the woman, the wife of an adjunct university professor, to the meeting at Nishino's request. The woman was a Soka Gakkai member, but Sugihara was not. It was thus clear that the local members had asked even their non-member friends to lend their cooperation to ensuring the success of the discussion meeting. The meeting was scheduled to start at 6:30 P.M., and the time until then was put to use making plans for the establishment of a district.

The discussion meeting began, attended by more than ten people, including guests. Most of the participants were Japanese women, almost all of whose husbands had been stationed in Japan with the U.S. military. Fatigue from the strain of daily living was clearly visible on the members' faces. Shin'ichi spoke to each of the participants, asking about their home lives. The first woman he addressed responded in a small and forlorn voice.

"My husband is in the military and is stationed overseas. My child and I are waiting for his return."

"Is that so? You must miss him very much. When your husband returns, please show him how much you care for him. Until then, although it will be very difficult for you all alone, please do your best to raise your child to be a fine young person. Nothing will make your husband happier than knowing that your child is growing up healthy and strong. This is the greatest possible encouragement for him. If your husband knows that you are cheerful and in high spirits, he will feel reassured and can display his full capabilities at work.

"On the other hand, if your husband thinks that you are lonely and depressed, he will be concerned and unable to devote himself wholeheartedly to his work. Therefore, please be cheerful and vibrant; please become strong enough so that you can write and tell him that you are fine and that he, for his part, should also do his best. Unless you yourself are strong, you cannot be kind and considerate of others."

A slight trace of color had returned to the woman's earnest face.

SHIN'ICHI Yamamoto then addressed the next woman, who was around 30. Her hair was disheveled, and she wore an air of careless resignation, as if her heart had grown desolate from living without hope.

"What kind of work does your husband do?" asked Shin'ichi.

"He hardly does any at all," the woman responded. "When he was stationed in Japan with the military, he told me tales about how I'd have a maid and a wonderful life when I returned to America with him. But my life here has been awful. He drinks all the time, never works and becomes violent—it's horrible! Basically, I was fooled. I guess you could say it's my fault for believing him in the first place, but I've had just about all I can take."

As she spoke, several of the other women nodded in sympathy.

At every discussion meeting Shin'ichi and the others attended in the States, there were members who had expressed discontent with their circumstances, but it was clear that these women of New York were suffering more than most.

Her face flushed with agitation, Katsu Kiyohara, the Soka Gakkai women's division chief, addressed the woman pointedly: "But you're doing gongyo, aren't you? You're praying to the Gohonzon, aren't you?"

"No."

"What do you mean 'No'? When you joined, you were told the importance of doing gongyo and chanting daimoku every day, weren't you?"

"I was never told any such thing. When I was leaving for America, my mother said: 'You're going to a country that was Japan's enemy in the war. Who knows what could happen to you. You'd better receive the Gohonzon and pray to it if you have a problem.'"

It seemed that there had been virtually no guidance in faith in New York up to that point. Until the arrival of Yukiko Nishino, there had been no one to act as a central figure around whom the members could gather, no one to encourage them and give them direction.

Kiyohara began speaking with great force, "Well, leaving aside how you came to this point, the only way for you to accumulate good fortune is to do your best for American kosen-rufu."

"Kosen-what?"

Kiyohara was at a loss for words. "This is serious," she thought. "I'll have to teach them the very basics of faith equaling daily life."

Out loud she said: "You...you don't know what that is? It means teaching people throughout this land about the

Daishonin's Buddhism and enabling them to become happy. This is the mission you all have!"

Even as she said this, Kiyohara found herself wondering how to guide these members.

ATSU Kiyohara took a deep breath and began to speak with renewed determination. "It looks like you've never had the opportunity to learn the basics of this faith. That can't be helped. Now, please listen carefully. The Buddhist practice consists of practice for oneself and practice for others. Practice for ourselves means doing gongyo and chanting daimoku, while practice for others means teaching people about this Buddhism. The Daishonin has promised us that when we practice faith correctly in this way, we can achieve a state of supreme happiness. If you do so, not only can your husbands find jobs, but you yourselves can realize a truly regal state of life where you can travel to Japan any time you wish."

"That's unbelievable!"

"Impossible!"

The room was filled with the sound of members voicing their disbelief.

A young woman who had been silent until then suddenly cried out: "You say we can visit Japan whenever we want some day, but I can't wait that long. Please take me back with you! I can't stand it anymore!" She burst into tears.

The leaders accompanying Shin'ichi stared at the woman with stunned expressions. Shin'ichi's eyes, however, were bright and penetrating. He was now pushing the limits of physical exhaustion, and the leaders accompanying him were well aware of this. Removing his jacket, Shin'ichi began speaking in a quiet, yet powerful tone.

"You have all truly suffered. You have endured in silence. There must have been times when you felt like giving up. There must have been times when you felt that death would bring a welcome release. I can deeply appreciate how much pain and sadness you must feel. However, this Buddhism has the power to transform your suffering into happiness, to change the tears you have shed into glittering jewels of good fortune. Those who have wept the most bitterly have the right to become the happiest people of all. My purpose in coming to the United States is to help you turn that into a reality."

Shin'ichi burned with a determination to shine the compassionate light of Buddhism into the darkness of suffering in people's lives. Passion and energy issued forth from his entire being and his powerful words deeply shook the lives of all in attendance.

The atmosphere of the meeting was now completely different. Driven by an earnest determination to encourage the members, Shin'ichi continued: "I'm sure you're all wondering whether you can really become happy through this practice. Am I right?"

The women all nodded in agreement.

*H*E continued with powerful conviction: "There's nothing to worry about. So long as you persevere in your practice, each of you, without exception, can become happy. In Japan, there are actually more than a million of our fellow members who have become happy. Isn't that the greatest possible proof?

"The Buddhist scriptures contain the following parable. There was once a man who visited the home of a close friend. He was entertained until he became quite drunk and fell asleep. While he was sleeping, his friend took a jewel of the highest imaginable value and sewed it into the lining of the guest's robe, hoping to protect him from a life of want or worry."

The participants in the meeting listened attentively, thoroughly absorbed by what Shin'ichi was saying.

"The guest then set off for other parts. He fell on hard times and became so desperately poor that he was often forced to go hungry. Throughout this time, he remained completely unaware of the priceless jewel sewn inside his robe. It was in this state of extreme poverty that the man again encountered his friend. The friend informed him of the precious jewel affixed to his garment. Naturally, once the man learned of the jewel's existence, he could become happy.

"This is 'The Parable of the Priceless Jewel' from the Lotus Sutra. The precious jewel is an allegory for the life of the Buddha, the state of ultimate happiness, which exists in the hearts of each of you. This life-condition can be brought forth and made manifest by praying to the Gohonzon and fighting for kosen-rufu. If, despite having taken faith in this Buddhism, you fail to understand this and remain submerged in sadness, you are just like the man in the parable."

The eyes of the participants were shining. Smiling, Shin'ichi continued:

"A few moments ago, Miss Kiyohara said that you could attain a regal state of life. Nichiren Daishonin has declared unequivocally that we are all children of the Buddha. From the perspective of Buddhism, it is clear that each of you is a human treasure, possessing supreme good fortune and the highest mission. Your status surpasses even that of kings or queens. In light of this, there is no way you will remain mired in unhappiness."

Shin'ichi then introduced each of the leaders accompanying him, asking them to share their experiences and to explain why benefit can be realized through the practice of faith.

In sharp contrast to the situation of a few moments earlier, the expressions of the participants were now filled with the energy of an awakened seeking spirit.

When the leaders from Japan had finished speaking, Shin'ichi asked, "Now do you understand why this practice is important?"

With bright faces, the participants nodded in affirmation.

WITH an embracing smile, Shin'ichi continued speaking: "All of you are still young, your husbands are in good health and your children are small. It is not unusual, however, for women to outlive their husbands and to be left to fend for themselves. That is a critical time in a woman's life. This Buddhism enables you to create a palace within your hearts, to establish a condition of absolute happiness that cannot be destroyed under any circumstances. That is why it is vital to practice faith throughout your entire life. I look forward to meeting you again, this time in Japan."

Shin'ichi then announced the formation of the New York District, after which he handed the participants the *fukusa* he had brought as gifts.

At this point, one woman who had come to the meeting as a guest expressed her decision to start practicing. While listening to Shin'ichi speak, she had begun to embrace the hope that she, too, could become happy. And she had decided that she very much wanted to take faith in the Daishonin's Buddhism.

The room reverberated with congratulatory applause.

Another guest, Mitsuo Sugihara, the young trading company employee Shin'ichi had met earlier, had also been paying close attention to the proceedings. He had already heard about this Buddhism from Nagayasu Masaki and Susumu Aota on many occasions. At the time, he was facing a personal crisis at work, having been forced to take responsibility for a management blunder. Nevertheless, he had steadfastly refused to join the Soka Gakkai because he felt that to do so would be an admission of defeat.

At first, he had watched the proceedings as an observer, curious to see how Shin'ichi would respond to the women's

outbursts of discontent. But he gradually felt himself being moved by the force of Shin'ichi's guidance, by the sincerity and passion with which he strove to encourage the members. Sugihara thought: "This person is working desperately for the happiness of complete strangers! I never thought there could be a world of such warmth!"

Having experienced the coldness and indifference of people in society, Sugihara was astounded by what he was witnessing. One month later, Sugihara began practicing. He became the first young men's division member in New York.

At the discussion meeting, Shin'ichi had not made any explicit attempt to urge Sugihara to take faith. He had simply given his all to communicating the way to realize a life of victory and human glory. This was done out of his deep desire for the happiness of his fellow members who had gathered at the meeting.

As in Aesop's fable "The Sun and the Wind," it is not the bitter chill of the north wind that causes people to remove the cloaks from their hearts. Rather, this is only achieved by the warm, compassionate light of the sun, caring and all-embracing. For it is such warmth that gives rise to the melodies of true human empathy.

S INCE arriving in New York, Shin'ichi's condition had taken a turn for the worse. Chills constantly racked his feverish body, and his legs were shaky when he walked. The punishing schedule of the group's overseas trip was taking an incredible toll on Shin'ichi's already frail health. Not wanting his companions to worry about him, Shin'ichi took pains to conceal his discomfort and distress.

No meetings were scheduled the next day, October 15, so the group could prepare for their trip to Brazil. Shin'ichi stayed at the hotel to rest while the others went shopping and sightseeing around the city. That evening, however, he was scheduled to attend a dinner with representatives from various Japanese trading companies in New York who had assisted in the purchase of construction materials for the Grand Reception Hall, which the Soka Gakkai planned to donate to the head temple.

On October 16, Shin'ichi and his party traveled by train to the nation's capital, Washington, D.C., a trip that took a little more than four hours. Shin'ichi found it restful to gaze quietly out at the deepening fall landscape reminiscent of the woodlands of Tokyo's Musashino area.

It was around 1:00 P.M. when the train pulled in at D.C.'s Union Station. About twenty people, lined up neatly in four rows, welcomed the party with a Gakkai song. Some Japanese women in the front row held a large banner emblazoned with the words *Soka Gakkai* in Japanese. As soon as the members caught sight of Shin'ichi, their eyes grew moist and their singing faltered.

Standing to one side of the chorus was a middle-aged American man, who wore an armband on which someone had inadvertently written the Japanese word *unsohan* (freight group), instead of *yusohan* (transport group).

Also, attached to the antenna of one of the cars waiting for them outside was a triangular pennant, which proclaimed in English, "Soka Gakki"—the word *Gakkai* having been misspelled. Shin'ichi was nevertheless moved by the members' sincerity, which he treasured above all else.

"Thank you for your welcome. I am deeply touched. Shall we go?"

Because they were in the middle of the station, Shin'ichi kept his words brief, but he did not neglect to express his heartfelt appreciation for the members' earnest efforts.

THE car driven by the American man in charge of transportation bore Shin'ichi toward the house of Fumie Shearing, where a discussion meeting was to be held. When Shin'ichi had taken his seat in the car, the man had greeted him with a friendly smile and a cheerful "*Konnichi-wa* (Good afternoon)!"

Washington, D.C., was a tranquil city set amid abundant greenery, with none of the towering rows of skyscrapers or the noise and bustle of a great metropolis like New York.

The Shearings' house was located in a quiet residential area and fronted by a well-tended lawn. Fumie Shearing, who was acting as the central figure for the members in Washington, D.C., came out to greet Shin'ichi and his party. Her arm was bandaged, and she wore sunglasses and a scarf around her head.

"What happened?" Shin'ichi asked in concern.

"Excuse me for looking like this," she began, and then went on to explain somewhat hesitantly what had happened: Her gas oven had exploded when she tried to light it earlier that day—the result, apparently, of an undetected gas leak. She had sustained burns to her face and arm.

"Are you all right?" asked Shin'ichi anxiously.

"Yes, the doctor said the burns are minor."

"Well, I'm glad to hear that," said Shin'ichi, relieved.

He continued: "Buddhism teaches the principle of lessening karmic retribution. Through the benefit of faith, we can transform heavy, negative karma accumulated from our past lives and receive its effects in a much lighter form in this lifetime. Your accident today may be an example of this principle. For all you know, you may have been saved from a much bigger tragedy. It is important that you dedicate yourself to your practice with this conviction and with a corresponding sense of gratitude. This will open a path toward good fortune and courage.

"At the same time, however, please make a determination not to have any more accidents and pay keen attention to preventing them. If we think we will be protected just because we chant and allow ourselves to grow careless, we cannot be said to be practicing faith correctly. Rather, because we are practicing faith, we must stay alert at all times, doing everything we can to avoid accidents.

"This is true faith. When we practice this way, the power of our daimoku will come alive as wisdom and good fortune."

Shin'ichi wanted to refute the kind of faith that placed hope for salvation in an external power—a trap that the members could easily fall into.

*T*HE discussion meeting began at 2:00 P.M. The first question came from a Japanese woman whose husband was a non-member.

"My husband is very supportive of my practice, but he rejects the idea of becoming a member himself because he is Catholic. I can't help feeling that as long as he refuses to take faith, it will be impossible for me to become happy. What can I do to make him start practicing?"

This was a common dilemma shared not only by the Washington, D.C., members but also by those in other parts of the United States.

This woman's husband was the man who, as a member of the "freight group," had driven Shin'ichi to the meeting.

Hearing this, Shin'ichi replied with a smile: "You have a husband who is making sincere efforts for kosen-rufu; he displayed the Soka Gakkai flag and happily provided us with transportation. That's wonderful! There's no need to worry about whether he is a member. Such formalities are not important.

"Some of you may have husbands or other family members who are opposed to your practice. However, it is foolish to become emotional and embroiled in arguments with them over faith. Should your husband become deadlocked or make a serious mistake at work, I would ask you particularly to refrain from telling him, 'It's because you don't practice faith.'

"It may be lonely being the only person practicing, but if you exert yourself diligently, your benefit and good fortune will extend to and be shared by your entire family. Your presence will be just like a huge umbrella sheltering them from the rain. It is a mistake, therefore, to think that you and your family cannot become happy because no one but you practices.

"Offering prayers for your family members to take faith in the Daishonin's Buddhism so they may become happy is certainly important, but the most fundamental thing is for each of you to demonstrate the greatness of faith with your own life. If you continue to strive in faith as wives and mothers, growing as human beings and becoming sunny presences overflowing with good cheer, wisdom, warmth and consideration, then your families will naturally come to approve of this Buddhism. Thus, to be loved and respected by your families is the first step to winning them over to this practice."

Shin'ichi tried to drive home the fact that Buddhism is the height of good sense and reason.

*O*NE question followed another. Sometimes Shin'ichi let the other leaders accompanying him respond. A young Japanese woman spoke: "My daughter is 5 years old, but she hasn't learned to speak yet. I am praying for her with all my might, but my prayers remain unanswered. Do you really think she will speak some day?"

Answering in Shin'ichi's place, Yukio Ishikawa said: "The Gohonzon is absolute; it is certain that all prayers will be answered. The problem is that you doubt the Gohonzon. In that case, no matter how much daimoku you may chant, your daughter's situation will not improve. How would you like it if someone were disrespectful toward you? You wouldn't feel motivated to exert yourself for his or her happiness either, would you?"

At this arrogant response, the woman uttered a stunned "Oh" and lowered her head.

Embracing her with a warm smile, Shin'ichi added reassuringly: "But there's no need to worry. If you earnestly persevere in faith, your daughter will definitely learn to speak. This, however, will depend on the strength of your faith.

"Let us take, for example, one of those giant bronze temple bells that are so common in Japan. The sound it emits will depend on what you strike it with. If you use a great log and strike the bell with powerful force, it will reverberate loudly. But if you strike it with a matchstick or a wooden chopstick, it will emit only a feeble and ineffective sound.

"Similarly, we have the Gohonzon, which is endowed with the immeasurable power of the Buddha and the Law. If, however, our faith and practice are weak, it will be like striking a giant bell with a matchstick; it will be impossible to bring forth any great benefit.

"If you exert yourself wholeheartedly in your Buddhist practice, you can definitely transform your negative karma and see an improvement in your daughter's condition. So please don't give up; strive with all your might to the very end!"

By skillful use of analogy, Shin'ichi had given clear and precise guidance.

The next question was from a woman who wore a rather troubled expression.

"Actually, one of my friends who lives in the same neighborhood occasionally asks me to mind her children so that she can go to church. It would ruin our friendship if I told her, 'I'm not going to look after your children while you go off to church!' What should I do?"

Shin'ichi answered with a smile: "This is America. Therefore, please have a big, magnanimous heart as vast as this great land itself. What your friend chooses to do while you mind her children is up to her. You are looking after her children out of friendship. In the process you are also enabling your friend to form a connection to Buddhism. So there's absolutely no need for you to be anxious or nervous about what you're doing."

*A*LTHOUGH the woman who had asked the question nodded in response to Shin'ichi's guidance, she still looked somewhat doubtful. Evidently she was having trouble reconciling the Daishonin's propagation spirit of "refuting the erroneous and revealing the true" (shakubuku) with a spirit of generosity toward others; she felt it was a contradiction in terms.

Sensing her misgivings, Shin'ichi continued: "As disciples of Nichiren Daishonin, it is natural that we take a strict stance in clarifying what is true and what is erroneous in terms of the Law. At the same time, however, our interactions with others must be based on a spirit of tolerance and generosity. This is the true way of life for a Buddhist."

The participants listened intently; the leaders from Japan also waited expectantly for his next words, notebooks in hand.

"To take a strict stance in distinguishing between good and evil and to show generosity toward others—these two things are in no way incompatible and are essentially part of the same whole.

"Let's suppose, for example, that someone eats poisonous mushrooms and is rushed to a doctor. Irrespective of who the patient may be, the doctor naturally exhausts all possible means to save the person and also offers sincere words of encouragement. This, we might say, is an example of 'generosity toward others.'

"It is also likely, however, that the doctor will warn the patient not to eat harmful mushrooms in the future. I am sure there is no doctor who would stand by indifferently while the patient declares, 'But poisonous mushrooms are delicious; I want to eat them again.' This corresponds to 'taking a strict stance toward the Law.'

"In both these instances, the doctor is motivated by his compassion and commitment to removing the patient's suffering. This is also the behavior of a Buddhist."

Shin'ichi then went on to recount how Nichiren Daishonin embarked on his bold campaign of refuting erroneous teachings and clarifying the true out of his profound compassion to enable all humankind to realize happiness.

The Daishonin, he said, realized that if people were to persist in believing the provisional pre–Lotus Sutra teachings constitute the highest teaching, they could not embrace faith in the Lotus Sutra of the Buddhism of Sowing, which contains the ultimate truth, and thereby they would destine themselves to unhappiness. Determined to stop this, the Daishonin, holding aloft the four dictums, waged a formidable battle against the corrupt, degenerate priests of his time who, with the support of ruling authorities, spread false doctrines throughout the land. He knew that if he ignored or failed to fight such evil, he would only be encouraging it, allowing it to run rampant.

His struggle, however, took the form of dialogue known as shakubuku. From beginning to end, his struggle was based on the power of speech and the written word. And despite being subjected to life-threatening persecutions, he upheld the spirit of nonviolence.

SHIN'ICHI addressed the woman: "For that reason, there is no contradiction between the spirit of shakubuku—that of 'refuting the erroneous and revealing the true'—and true friendship. The spirit of compassion is fundamental to both. Consequently, it is the Buddhist ideal that the more we exert ourselves in faith, the greater the generosity with which we can embrace our friends and deepen our friendships. Because shakubuku is an endeavor to touch others' lives through dialogue, trust and friendship are essential.

"Please become a person who transcends differences of religion and prays for the happiness of her fellow human beings, who forges deep ties of friendship with many people. Your doing so will also testify to the depth and breadth of Buddhism."

This was the first time that the Buddhist way of life had been outlined to the members; they were struck by its freshness and engraved it in their hearts.

After fielding several more questions, Shin'ichi then announced the establishment of Washington, D.C., District. Fumie Shearing, who had allowed her home to be used for the discussion meeting, was appointed district chief. Groups were also established in Washington, D.C., the Carolinas, Pennsylvania and Florida.

When Shin'ichi prepared to leave the room at the end of the meeting, an American man, his face showing deep emotion, addressed him in English. Nagayasu Masaki, who was standing at Shin'ichi's side, acted as their interpreter.

"I was deeply moved by what you said," the man said. "I think the teachings of Buddhism are wonderful. I'd like to join your religion, but I cannot—I am a Catholic. It's really too bad. I'm very sorry."

"Whether you formally belong to the organization is not an issue," Shin'ichi reassured him. "If you believe in the Buddhist teachings and chant even one daimoku, if you warmly embrace and support your wife and the members while sharing our spirit and aspirations—that is enough. Through this, you will come to have an even greater appreciation of Buddhism."

Smiling, the man held out his hand to Shin'ichi.

Kosen-rufu translates directly into the happiness of humanity and the realization of world peace. It is simply revealing and cultivating the positive state of Buddhahood inherent in all people's lives and enveloping the world in the brilliance of friendship forged on the basis of humanism. In a sense, kosen-rufu is a movement that transcends the narrow confines of sectarianism in order to realize a renaissance of life in the universal realm of the human being.

*F*UMIE Shearing ushered Shin'ichi to a room on the second floor, where an elderly woman with a dignified bearing soon brought him some refreshments. It was Fumie's mother, Tomino. Since taking faith some two years before, mother and daughter had been steadily exerting themselves in practice. Tomino, despite being almost 80, was filled with a sincere desire to do anything at all to assist the Soka Gakkai, and she supported Fumie behind the scenes in her energetic activities for kosen-rufu.

Tomino greeted Shin'ichi with a smile and said: "Thank you very much for the meeting. I know how tired you must be. Please have some refreshments."

Shin'ichi thanked her.

Tomino then began to speak in a quiet, relaxed manner: "Listening to you speak impressed upon me what a truly noble organization is the Soka Gakkai. I'm sure it will develop by leaps and bounds here in America, too. As it grows, however, the organization is sure to encounter strong opposition and criticism in society. Long experience tells me that periods of adversity are inevitable in life. The crucial question, I think, is who will protect our precious Soka Gakkai at that time."

Shin'ichi was surprised and at the same time pleased that this elderly member of only two years' practice should give such detailed thought to the Soka Gakkai's future.

Tomino continued in a pleasant yet firm tone: "But, no matter what happens, as long as I'm alive, Washington, D.C., will be fine. Please rest assured, I will do my best!"

Shin'ichi keenly felt that the children of the Buddha were beginning to emerge steadily one after another from the soil of America.

"I am grateful," he said. "Thank you. Please stay in good health and live a long, long life; please continue to protect the Soka Gakkai."

The elderly woman then noticed the beads of perspiration on Shin'ichi's face.

"Sensei, you're sweating! Are you sick?"

Shin'ichi was running a fever, but he answered: "No, there's no need for alarm. I'm just perspiring a little from the exertion of having spoken so energetically earlier."

"I see. Still, you look fatigued. Please rest here for a while. I worry about your health more than anything." She then discretely withdrew from the room.

For a brief time, Shin'ichi lay back against the sofa to rest his weary body, his heart soothed by the warmth and thoughtfulness Tomino had shown him.

*T*HAT evening, Shin'ichi and his party stayed at a hotel in Washington, D.C. After breakfast the following morning, Eisuke Akizuki dropped by Shin'ichi's room.

"Sensei, I'll be returning to New York ahead of you and the others," Akizuki informed him.

"Ah, yes, that's right," Shin'ichi said. "You were going to visit a newspaper today, weren't you?"

As managing editor of the *Seikyo Shimbun*, the Soka Gakkai's newspaper, Akizuki had an appointment to visit the offices of *The New York Times*.

"Please observe carefully and try to learn what makes *The New York Times* an internationally respected newspaper. It will be important to actively incorporate anything you find useful into our paper's operations. Eventually, we'll have to publish the *Seikyo Shimbun* daily and, above all, develop it into a publication that will be universally accepted as one of the world's leading newspapers."

Indelibly engraved in Shin'ichi's heart were the many times that Josei Toda had voiced his desire to "enable people throughout Japan and throughout the world to read the *Seikyo Shimbun*." Shin'ichi had vowed to realize his mentor's wish without fail. Thus he was constantly trying to think of ways to develop the *Seikyo Shimbun* into an internationally renowned newspaper.

Akizuki replied, "I'll do my best!" But frankly he had been surprised and somewhat overwhelmed when he heard the words "one of the world's leading newspapers."

Until August that year, the *Seikyo Shimbun* had been published as an eight-page weekly; it was only since September that it had begun to be published twice a week—a four-page issue on Wednesdays and an eight-page issue on Saturdays.

Expressing the great dreams he held for the paper, Shin'ichi said: "The *Seikyo Shimbun* is the organ of the Soka Gakkai. At the same time, I see it as a journal for the people."

"A journal for the people?"

"That's right. A news journal for humanity. Ordinary papers are filled with dark and dismal news. To some extent this can't be helped because it's a reflection of society. Nevertheless, none of these newspapers applies any thought or editorial effort to enabling people to find hope and experience joy while living in such a society. None of them teaches its readers how to truly challenge and overcome life's sufferings. But it is just this kind of newspaper that society needs most. Isn't the *Seikyo Shimbun* the only newspaper fulfilling this function? For that reason, it is truly a newspaper for humanity."

Shin'ichi's words brought a flush of excitement to Akizuki's face.

*L*OOKING earnestly at him, Shin'ichi leaned toward Akizuki and emphasized: "The *Seikyo Shimbun* has a truly immense mission. For the Soka Gakkai, it must be a textbook of faith as well as a medium for forging heart-to-heart bonds among the members. Its mission in society, meanwhile, is to fight injustice and wrongdoing and, with the compassionate light of Buddhism, to illuminate the true way for people to live while guiding the way to genuine peace and happiness for humanity. Our paper inherits the spirit of Mr. Makiguchi and Mr. Toda who risked their lives to take a stand against the militaristic government during World War II. In that respect, there is no newspaper more uniquely suited to communicating the true path to peace than the *Seikyo Shimbun*."

Shin'ichi looked out the window; it seemed as if he were gazing up at Josei Toda. "Did you know," he continued, "that even while he was being persecuted as a Buddhist during the war, President Toda continued to fight in the shadows against the government as a magazine publisher?"

"No, I didn't," replied Akizuki.

"I heard from President Toda that in January 1940, he launched a monthly children's magazine called *Elementary Students' Japan*. This might be called a forerunner of *Boys' Adventure*, which was subsequently renamed *Boys' Japan*, the publication that I later came to edit."

Josei Toda began publishing *Elementary Students' Japan* in 1940. That year marked the 2,600th anniversary of the beginning of the Japanese Imperial line, an event that was celebrated by a series of major festivities that were held with great pomp and splendor throughout the country. The Imperial Rule Assistance Association also was formed that year. Japan was now already more than two-and-a-half years into a full-scale war with China, and the National Mobilization Law, which had been enacted in 1938, was in full force. In short, it was a time when the Japanese government was intent on solidifying the overall framework for securing the cooperation of the country's entire civilian population in the war effort.

Even schoolbooks from the first grade on contained exhortations such as "Advance! Advance, soldiers, advance!"

It was an era in which militarism was relentlessly drilled into the pure and tender hearts of children.

Magazines of all varieties also vied with one another to extol and glorify the war. Freedom of speech and thought were subject to strict government regulation, and nothing could be published unless it endorsed the war. Constraints on newspapers and magazines were further amplified by an extreme shortage of paper needed for their manufacture. These developments foretold the arrival of a dark, forbidding age devoid of freedom.

Toda was deeply concerned that the prevailing militaristic propaganda would distort the hearts and minds of children destined to shoulder the future and cause them to become narrow and intolerant in their outlook and thinking.

*O*UR children," Josei Toda thought, "will grow up without knowing of the splendid cultures, industries and national characters of other countries. If they continue to be tainted with xenophobia and come to regard fighting and dying for their country as the highest virtue, then their whole lives will be ruined. The country's future will also be extremely bleak."

As a Buddhist and a human being, Toda's conscience compelled him to take action to rectify this situation. He settled upon the idea of publishing a magazine that would open children's eyes to the world and nurture in them an ability to discern the truth. Government regulation of the print media, however, had become increasingly strict. The severe paper shortage also led the authorities to deny, in principle, permission for the launching of new magazines.

Toda, however, tirelessly lobbied the relevant government departments and finally succeeded in getting his new magazine, *Elementary Students' Japan*, onto the newsstands. The magazine, of course, had to comply with the government's policies.

The table of contents of the first issue displayed in bold type two or three suitably rousing titles that were in keeping with the prevailing wartime mood. But closer examination of the actual articles revealed that they were only very short essays. The magazine's main feature article, part of an ongoing monthly series, meanwhile, was extremely pacifistic in content. Furthermore, the two or three war-related columns that had started in the first issue disappeared from the magazine's pages within a short time. This made *Elementary Students' Japan* exceptional among other magazines of the time in that it did anything but glorify the war.

Particularly noteworthy was the magazine's global outlook, featuring reports about the fine cultures and industries of other countries and stories from Europe. The magazine also carried a few short stories on war themes, but the characters painted war as being far from the glorious adventure it was made out to be in other fiction. It was a startling departure given the times.

Even in an age when publications were threatened with closure if they failed to sing the praises of war, Toda did not compromise his editorial policy. He wanted to teach the children, who were so precious to him, the correct way for human beings to live.

When the Japanese government changed the name of elementary schools to "citizens schools," Mr. Toda was forced to rename the magazine. During the war, the military government referred to children as "junior citizens," but Toda boldly rejected this designation. Substituting *junior* with the word *small*, he renamed his magazine *Small Citizens' Japan*. Though this may seem trifling, it was a definite sign of Josei Toda's firm refusal to capitulate to the authorities' demands. His choice of the term *small citizens* was also perhaps an expression of his determination to staunchly protect and raise these young successors with every last ounce of his energy.

WITH the March 1941 issue, Josei Toda began publishing the magazine under the new name, *Small Citizens' Japan*. That issue contained a special feature, "Shedding Light on the Secret and the Mysterious." In his editorial for that month, which he titled "The Mother of Science," Toda wrote:

> The peoples of ancient times, devoid of learning and civilization, worshiped what they found wondrous or inexplicable, for these things inspired in them a sense of fear and awe. Lacking a scientific mind, the ancients were deeply superstitious, ignorantly believing in that which they didn't understand.
>
> In the realm of science, however, we pursue the various questions that arise in our minds—the whys and the hows—and strive to bring them to their correct conclusion. It is a realm that enlightens and illuminates the world and leads it toward progress and development.
>
> Seeing an apple fall from a tree in the garden, Isaac Newton discovered the theory of universal gravitation. By gazing at water boiling in an iron kettle, James Watt was inspired to invent the steam engine. Didn't Thomas Edison and Marie Curie, too, pursue their doubts and questions honestly and single-mindedly? Wonder and doubt are the mother of science.

In an era overshadowed by spiritualism centering on State Shinto, Toda spoke to the children of Japan of the folly of "ignorantly believing in that which they didn't understand." He urged them to have inquiring, scientific minds with which to "pursue their doubts and questions honestly and single-mindedly." In these words we cannot help but sense the cry of Toda's conscience as he fought undaunted amid the impenetrable darkness of the times.

The October issue of *Small Citizens' Japan* included a feature titled "Protect Our Skies" (for students of the higher grades of the citizens schools). This bold title belied the article's actual content, which outlined how children should go about protecting themselves during air raids and gave detailed instructions for making gas masks and building air-raid shelters. The feature also contained an article on the air-raid drills carried out by children in Great Britain and the Soviet Union. A portion reads:

"What pain and misery air raids have inflicted, especially on the small citizens of Britain! The constant news reports we hear hint that their tragic plight is far worse than we can imagine. In the beginning, many British parents sent their children to America or to take refuge in the countryside from the danger of the air raids over urban areas. However, many children still remain in the dangerous cities. When they see a bomb being dropped, even some distance away, they quickly fall flat onto the road to protect themselves. So used to this state of affairs have they grown that they are quite calm and matter of fact about it."

*T*HE issue of *Small Citizens' Japan* in which this feature appeared came out on October 1, 1941—only two months before Japan declared war on America and Britain. Anglo-Japanese relations were already extremely strained, with Japan viewing Britain increasingly as a hostile nation. It was an extremely dangerous time to be printing an article on the hardships and brave struggles of British children to protect themselves from air raids.

Josei Toda recognized that all the world's children, not only those in Japan, had to be protected. Nor was there any need for children to hate one another. Rather, he clearly asserted that children should come to understand one another's suffering and join hands in friendship.

Although the article was titled "Protect Our Skies," Toda actually was striving to protect the precious lives of the children who would be responsible for the next generation. In this article, we can also clearly sense Toda's fervent appeal to these young people, how he desperately urged them to live with all their might.

Small Citizens' Japan ceased publication in April 1942. With censorship growing increasingly strict, Toda chose this course rather than continuing to produce a magazine that, by complying with government directives, would be forced to extol the war and incite people to rush off to die for their country.

In a dramatic turnabout after the war, the Japanese media, without exception, became pacifistic. It was easy to make loud declarations for peace in a world where freedom was now guaranteed in speech, news reporting and publishing. But to ascertain whether this pacifism was genuine, one had to question what the news media and their journalists had done during the war.

This applies not just to the realm of journalism but to religion, also. No matter how much a religious organization may speak of peace and democracy and assume the guise of justice today, it is vital to remember that the organization's true nature is revealed by how it behaved during the war.

Shin'ichi Yamamoto told Eisuke Akizuki everything he knew about this children's magazine published by Toda.

"During the war, President Toda fought to the very limit as a journalist, walking a razor's edge. This is the spirit the *Seikyo Shimbun* must perpetuate. Speech and writing not based on philosophy and conviction are as insubstantial as smoke. The *Seikyo Shimbun*, however, is based on the great philosophy of life known as Buddhism."

Akizuki, with an earnest expression, listened intently to Shin'ichi's words.

T HE sunlight filtering through the trees shimmered on the hotel window. "President Yamamoto," Eisuke Akizuki asked, "what is the most important point to bear in mind in writing articles that will enable the *Seikyo Shimbun* to become a top international newspaper?" Behind his glasses, Akizuki's eyes shone with a burning intensity.

Shin'ichi replied: "First, because the *Seikyo Shimbun* is the journal of our organization, it is natural that we strive to write articles that will enable members to have confidence and conviction in faith and to summon forth courage. Beyond that, our fundamental aim should be to pursue world peace and the happiness of humankind, based on the compassionate spirit of the great Buddhism of Nichiren Daishonin. It is important to stress in our articles that, instead of promoting national interests or ideologies, we must search for and try to build a common path of humanity, as a global race or global family. I have long thought that the *Seikyo Shimbun* must become a newspaper that will be known as a voice of global conscience and global common sense. For this accords with the original spirit of the Daishonin's Buddhism."

Akizuki felt the limitations of his own way of thinking dissolve. He had pondered how best to produce the paper in terms of content and subject matter, but he had never considered it from such a broad perspective.

"Furthermore," Shin'ichi continued, "it is important to express the universal philosophy of Buddhism — which upholds the equality of all people — in a way that is fresh and easy to grasp, and that accords with society and our modern age. We have to discuss Buddhism in terms that are accessible and comprehensible to all people. A newspaper only understood by Soka Gakkai members will not spread in society.

Similarly, a paper so complex that even members can't understand it exists only for the gratification of the editorial staff.

"In addition, we must accurately discern what society is searching for and what it holds to be important. All of the answers society is now seeking can be found within Buddhism and within the real essence of the Soka Gakkai. The question is whether we can always express these in a way that accords with the issues that concern society and our times.

"We have to aim for daily improvement and innovation. The times are always changing. Society, too, is in motion, as are people's minds. It is vital that we continue to offer guidelines that inspire and draw understanding, while being sensitive to these changes and responding appropriately.

"Therefore, whether it be with respect to headlines, articles or design and layout, it is important not to fall into a rut and just content ourselves with doing things the same old way. A newspaper is a living thing. No one is interested in buying fish that is no longer fresh. In the same way, readers will discard a paper that is hackneyed or has grown stagnant."

Shin'ichi's guidance was clear and to the point.

*E*ISUKE Akizuki's face brightened. "Ultimately," Shin'ichi continued, "whether we can keep innovating our newspaper depends solely upon whether our writers can keep 'innovating' their personal determination. We could have thousands or tens of thousands of journalists, but if they forget the spirit of challenging themselves and instead become stagnant, failing to make creative efforts and performing their work passively, then it will be impossible for the *Seikyo Shimbun* to compete with the world's leading newspapers.

"What we need are writers with unsurpassed, lionlike courage, who are prepared to bear full responsibility for the Soka Gakkai and take up their pens with a resolve to change the world. If we have just one or two, or better still, five or ten such journalists, then that's all we need. Success in communicating our message through speech or writing does not depend on the number of people involved.

"Becoming an internationally respected newspaper means producing journalists who are also internationally respected. Let's raise writers of true caliber. After all, the struggle for kosen-rufu is waged through the written and spoken word."

Full responsibility for the *Seikyo Shimbun* effectively rested on the shoulders of managing editor Eisuke Akizuki. In addition to carrying out pivotal activities as the Soka Gakkai youth division chief, Akizuki also earnestly poured his energies into the production of each issue of the Soka Gakkai's newspaper. And as one of the leaders accompanying Shin'ichi Yamamoto on this overseas trip, he did his utmost to guide and encourage the members. At the same time, he took photos and wrote articles, often staying up until dawn to complete them, then posting his work to the *Seikyo Shimbun* headquarters in Japan.

In the months since the inauguration of President Yamamoto and the opening of a new era for the Soka Gakkai, Akizuki had given deep thought to the future of the *Seikyo Shimbun*. But it had been like feeling his way through a heavy mist; he had found it impossible to form a clear vision. Sensing Akizuki's dilemma, Shin'ichi had taken time to speak with him at length about the *Seikyo Shimbun* on this day.

"In ten or fifteen years," Shin'ichi continued, still voicing his hopes for the future, "the *Seikyo Shimbun* will steadily dispatch reporters and correspondents overseas. The day will also surely come when it will be quite commonplace for our writers to interview heads of state and leading scholars in many fields, confidently discussing with them the pacifistic philosophy and ideals of Buddhism. Let's also solicit articles from outstanding world leaders in all spheres of human endeavor and strive together with them to find the path to lasting peace. Imagine how exciting that will be!"

"Yes," responded Akizuki with a smile.

Listening to Shin'ichi outline his hopes and dreams for the *Seikyo Shimbun*, Akizuki felt as if a ray of light had illuminated the future. The clouds had been swept from his heart, and he felt lighter in both body and mind. Akizuki set off for New York deeply encouraged.

*A*FTER he saw Eisuke Akizuki off, Shin'ichi Yamamoto joined the other leaders for a tour of the city of Washington, D.C. The clear blue sky made a stunning backdrop for the gleaming white buildings that stood along streets lined with shade trees beginning to show the first signs of autumn.

Washington, D.C., was a capital renowned for some of the finest parks in the world. Thus, it was a city where architecture and nature blended in splendid harmony.

The party visited the Capitol, the White House, the Washington Monument, the Lincoln Memorial and other sites of interest. With the imminent construction of the Grand Reception Hall at the head temple, they all took a keen interest in these buildings. They were especially captivated by the Lincoln Memorial, its marble columns and steps resembling a classic Greek temple.

"It has a wonderful grandeur, doesn't it?" said Kiyoshi Jujo admiringly.

"Yes, it certainly conveys strength. It would be great to incorporate this kind of style into the Grand Reception Hall," said Shin'ichi, gazing up at the memorial.

"I think that should be possible. I'll have a talk with the architects," said Jujo happily, making a note in his book.

Shin'ichi's proposal was later realized in the form of the great stone steps at the entrance of the Grand Reception Hall.

The group then walked along the Tidal Basin—the name given to the area around the banks of a lake fed by the Potomac River. The autumn breeze felt pleasant on their faces.

Cherry trees fringed the edge of the Tidal Basin, and the white dome of the Jefferson Memorial, gleaming in the sunlight, was visible on the opposite bank. Stained a deep reddish brown, the leaves of the cherries were beginning to fall. How beautiful it must be in the spring when the trees proudly displayed their blossoms in full bloom!

"I'd love to come here when the cherries are in bloom," Shin'ichi remarked.

"These cherry trees," Katsu Kiyohara explained, "were planted at the request of Helen Taft, the wife of the twenty-seventh U.S. president. Perhaps you already know the story. When her husband was inaugurated as president, she supervised the development of Potomac Park and came up with the idea of planting Japanese cherry trees."

"I see you've been doing your homework!" said Shin'ichi.

"Yes," Kiyohara admitted.

"This story is well known," Shin'ichi observed. "Mrs. Taft sent a request to Japan for the cherry trees, and, if I remember correctly, the then mayor of Tokyo, Yukio Ozaki, readily responded to her request."

"Yes, in January 1912, he sent some 3,000 cherry-tree saplings as a token of U.S.-Japan friendship," Kiyohara offered, smiling.

KATSU Kiyohara continued to speak knowledgeably on the origin of the cherry trees of Washington, D.C. "The cherry tree saplings sent by Yukio Ozaki arrived safely in the American capital. First Lady Helen Taft and the wife of the Japanese ambassador to the United States planted the first two saplings. As the years passed and the

took root and began to bloom, they became a popular attraction, with many people coming to view the cherry blossoms each year. The trees came to be loved not only by the citizens of Washington, D.C., but by many throughout the United States. Later, between 300 and 400 of these trees were slated to be cut down to make way for the construction of the Jefferson Memorial. The people of Washington, D.C., however, organized a protest and finally succeeded in forcing the city authorities to change their plans. As a result, only a small portion of the original number of trees had to be cut down."

"That's a wonderful story," Shin'ichi said after Kiyohara had finished. "The garden of the house where I lived as a child in Kojiya, in Tokyo's Kamata Ward, also had a big cherry tree. Our family later moved away, but toward the end of the war, I had occasion to visit the neighborhood again. It had been quite some time since I last was there. When I stopped by the house in which we had once lived, I found that it had been converted into a munitions factory. The house had been demolished and the cherry tree that

"The hearts of people had been so bitterly wounded by war that they probably had no time to think of cherry blossoms. I remember standing there, overwhelmed by a sense of loss and sadness.

"Shortly after that, the great air raids began over Tokyo, and many people were burned out of their homes. The entire landscape was turned into a hellish blackened wasteland. But in one corner of the city there remained several cherry trees that bore fragrant blossoms. The sky was a dazzling blue and the branches of these magnificent cherry trees, heavy with blossoms in full bloom, swayed with regal serenity in the spring breeze.

"In the dark, chaotic days of the war, they seemed to me to radiate with the light of hope. These cherry blossoms, blooming so gloriously only to fall so quickly, also seemed to symbolize life's transience. This was something I often reflected on because my eldest brother had been killed in the war, as had so many other young people.

"As the cherry blossom petals fluttered gently down around me, I was filled with powerful emotions. A poem came spontaneously to my mind. As soon as I arrived home, I quickly wrote it down."

Shin'ichi spoke with a nostalgia and feeling characteristic of the youthful poet that he was.

*F*ALLING Cherry Blossoms" was the title that Shin'ichi had given to the poem he had been inspired to write on seeing the cherry trees blooming amid the burned-out ruins of war:

> *Surviving*
> *The disaster of war*
> *To bloom*

Cherry blossoms
Against the blue sky
Petals fluttering

. . . .

Fallen cherry blossoms
Blossoms that remain
Too shall fall
So people say

Cherry blossoms of youth
How many untold millions
Why do you fall,
Why do you fall?

In the distant southern seas
The fallen cherry blossoms
Never blooming to the full
The branches ache

Friends remaining
One day
Witnessed by no one
Will you fall?

Are all things transient
Or eternal?
Without knowing even that
Will you fall?

O fallen cherry blossoms
Blossoms that remain!

Blossoms that remain!
Forever
Bloom fragrantly
In stormy profusion
In spring.

Life and death, transience and eternity—these were inescapable issues for the 17-year-old Shin'ichi. It was from this time that he began his quest for philosophy—a journey that would eventually bring his path to cross that of Josei Toda and to encounter the great Law of life that is the Buddhism of Nichiren Daishonin.

Looking up at the cherry trees growing along the edge of the Tidal Basin, Shin'ichi said reflectively: "At the very moment I stood gazing at those cherry trees abloom amid the charred wartime landscape and composed that poem, people here in Washington, D.C., too, were probably savoring the flowering beauty of these cherry trees from Japan. Though our respective countries may have been at war, people in both nations share the capacity to be moved by the sight of beautiful flowers."

"Yes, that's so true," said Katsu Kiyohara, nodding in agreement. "Visitors to Japan who have seen our cherry blossoms extol their unforgettable beauty."

"Seeing that many of our fellow members from overseas will come to visit the head temple in the future," Shin'ichi said, "I'd like to adorn the grounds there by planting many flowering cherry trees. The sight of cherry blossoms in full bloom will be eternally engraved in their hearts as a wonderful memory of their visit to Japan as well as a symbol of the rich blossoming of the benefit of faith."

Shin'ichi pictured in his mind's eye the spectacular vista of the Head Temple Taiseki-ji lined with row upon row of cherry trees blooming together in magnificent profusion.

In just over ten years from that time, Shin'ichi realized

cherry blossoms and presented the members, who traveled from all corners of the world to make their pilgrimage there, with a breathtaking landscape of dazzling beauty.

The day would come, however, when these cherry trees would be felled ruthlessly by a callous high priest who had become the manifestation of the Devil of the Sixth Heaven.

SHIN'ICHI Yamamoto and the other leaders left Washington, D.C., just after noon, arriving in New York toward nightfall. The next day they would finally be departing for São Paulo, Brazil. They decided to devote that evening to packing and making preparations for their departure.

After dinner, the other leaders went out to do some shopping. Shin'ichi, however, stayed back at the hotel. His condition was still far from satisfactory. If anything, it looked as if it would only grow worse.

First, the flight from New York to São Paulo was a little more than ten hours. Moreover, their attempts to contact members in the Brazilian city had so far been frustratingly unproductive, leaving them in the dark as to what to expect when they arrived. The journey was certain to be a trying and exhausting one for Shin'ichi, both physically and mentally.

Shin'ichi took out the picture of his mentor, Josei Toda, that he kept in the inside pocket of his suit jacket. As he lay on the bed resting his weary body, Shin'ichi gazed steadily at it. The events of November 19, 1957—some five months before Toda's death—came vividly to his mind. It was the day before Toda had collapsed, overtaken by illness. On that day, Shin'ichi had tried to stop his mentor from leaving for Hiroshima, fully aware that he risked incurring stern rebuke for doing so. Toda was gaunt as he never had been before. His physical strength was at its lowest ebb, and his body showed signs of painful debilitation. It was clear that if he continued to overexert himself, he would be placing his life in jeopardy.

As Toda lay resting on the sofa in one of the meeting rooms at the Soka Gakkai Headquarters, Shin'ichi knelt on the floor before him and bowed deeply to his mentor. "Sensei, please cancel your trip to Hiroshima. I beg you," he implored desperately. "Please rest for a while."

Toda responded resolutely: "How do you expect me not to go? I have to. As an emissary of the Buddha, I can't turn my back on something once I've decided to do it. I will go even if it kills me! Can't you see that this is the real meaning of faith, Shin'ichi? What's gotten into you?"

Even now, the impassioned tones of his mentor still rang clearly in his ears.

That cry, Shin'ichi thought to himself, summed up the way a leader of kosen-rufu should live—a way of life that Toda had shown him through his own example.

Brazil was on the opposite side of the world from Japan, one of the countries lying the furthest distance away. When he thought of the many members waiting there to see him, Shin'ichi knew he absolutely had to go. He resolved to encourage them and to strive with all his might as long as there was still breath left in him. The fighting spirit he had inherited as a disciple of Josei Toda blazed brightly in his heart.

*E*VER since he had fallen ill, Shin'ichi had made conscious efforts to rest whenever time permitted to regain his health. He did this so that he could go ahead with his plans to visit Brazil.

Rising from his bed after some time, Shin'ichi sat in a chair and began to earnestly chant daimoku to his *omamori* Gohonzon. His prayers were directed single-mindedly toward the goal of tapping powerful life force from the depths of his own being to conquer the devil of illness. He chanted for a long time. When he finished, there was a knock at the door. It was Kiyoshi Jujo, the Soka Gakkai vice general director.

For several days Jujo had been debating with himself over whether it might not be wise to stop Shin'ichi from traveling to Brazil. He sensed that the young Soka Gakkai president's condition was deteriorating daily. In particular, there appeared to be a marked drop in his physical strength and stamina compared to when the group had first arrived in New York. Nor could he help noticing the dark circles under Shin'ichi's eyes.

Jujo had given long, solitary thought to what he should do. He was fully aware that President Yamamoto's visit to Brazil had been planned and organized with careful thought and consideration, based on an overall perspective of the future development of the kosen-rufu movement. He knew, too, that to bring this visit to a halt could easily jeopardize those plans for kosen-rufu altogether.

However, Jujo was convinced that if Shin'ichi went ahead with his itinerary, he would certainly collapse. His responsibility as one of the leaders accompanying the Soka Gakkai president would not permit him to stand by silently and watch that happen. After giving the matter a great deal of thought, Jujo had discussed it with the other leaders. He now stood outside Shin'ichi's room, hoping to persuade him to give up the idea of going to Brazil.

Shin'ichi opened the door and invited Jujo inside.

"Hello, Mr. Jujo!" Shin'ichi said. "Did you get everything you wanted?"

"Yes, thank you," Jujo replied.

"Where did you go?"

"To a department store. I was surprised at the large number of Japanese-made goods they had on display there."

Jujo now straightened his posture and began, with a rather hesitant expression, "Sensei, I don't know how to say this to you."

"Did something happen?" asked Shin'ichi in concern.

Jujo continued with an agonized look: "I've come to talk with you about your departure for Brazil tomorrow. To get straight to the point, I would like you to remain here in the United States, Sensei. I think it better that only I and the other leaders should go."

Shin'ichi looked at Jujo with surprise.

KIYOSHI Jujo summoned his nerve and explained fully: "It's obvious to everyone that you're terribly ill. If you push yourself unreasonably, the consequences could be disastrous. If you were to fall seriously ill, the Soka Gakkai would lose its main pillar. I don't dare contemplate what would happen then.

"I wanted to talk with you about this earlier, but every time I tried to, I just couldn't bring myself to mention it. And I know I'm being terribly presumptuous by doing so now, but I dearly wish to see you get some rest. The other leaders also share my sentiments on this point." The vice general director gazed imploringly at Shin'ichi.

"Jujo, I'm very grateful," said Shin'ichi, steadily returning Jujo's gaze. With a burning determination in his eyes, he continued adamantly: "I'm going. There are members waiting for me. I absolutely refuse to cancel my plans when everyone is waiting. One of the main purposes of this overseas trip was to visit Brazil. That's why we've come all this way. I can't abandon everything now, when we're almost there. Did President Toda ever once retreat in the middle of a campaign or struggle? I am his disciple. I will go. I will definitely go. If I collapse, then so be it!" He spoke with great force, his words ringing with an impassioned fighting spirit.

For a moment there was silence. Shin'ichi and Jujo looked at each other, their eyes gleaming.

Jujo swallowed. He tried to find words to persuade Shin'ichi, but none were forthcoming. Having heard the young president's heartfelt resolve, he knew there was nothing more he could say. And when he realized this, he felt a burning surge of emotion rise within him.

"President Yamamoto," said Jujo, deeply moved and with tears in his eyes. "I understand. Please forgive me. I am determined to accompany you always, no matter what or where."

A smile now returned to Shin'ichi's face. "Let's go—let's go to the end of the ocean! On President Toda's behalf."

A serene picture of the new and unknown land of Brazil had already emerged within Shin'ichi's mind.

"Light of Compassion" Notes:

1. In June 1860.

2. Niphon: Nippon, meaning Japan.

3. Walt Whitman, "A Broadway Pageant," *Leaves of Grass*, (London: J.M. Dent & Sons LTD., 1968), p. 205.

4. Dag Hammarskjold (1905–1961): Swedish politician and diplomat. Became the second secretary-general of the United Nations in 1953. Worked tirelessly in the cause of international peace, bringing about a cease-fire in the Suez Canal crisis. He was killed in a plane crash in 1961 en route to Africa to find a solution to the conflict in the Congo. He was posthumously awarded the Nobel Peace Prize.

Pioneers

*T*HE jet airliner broke through the thick cloud cover and rose powerfully into the clear sky above. Its silver wings glinted brilliantly in the sunlight, while below a sea of clouds stretched out in all directions. The ascent was somehow reminiscent of the struggles of the members, who, as bold champions of justice, fought their way through obstacles and hardships to soar serenely, like a noble eagle, into the victorious and joy-filled skies of kosen-rufu.

Pan American Flight 203, with Shin'ichi Yamamoto and the other leaders on board, left New York shortly after 10:00 A.M. on October 18, destined for São Paulo, Brazil.

Sometime later, the clouds parted to reveal the beautiful azure waters of the Caribbean sparkling below. But this was to prove short-lived. Soon clouds obscured the ocean once more, and the plane began to be buffeted wildly by what appeared to be the effects of a hurricane. The turbulence was particularly rough on Shin'ichi, whose physical exhaustion was already at a critical level.

The group had received almost no information on what they could expect to find in São Paulo. After their visit had been officially decided upon, the staff of the Overseas Affairs Section of the Soka Gakkai Headquarters had sent several letters to the members who were serving as the organization's main contacts in Brazil but had received no response.

That was not surprising given that of the many letters the Headquarters sent, only one had actually reached the members; and even that had been as late as September 20. Although the local members forwarded a reply right away, Shin'ichi and the others had already left for overseas by the time it arrived in Japan.

Nevertheless, from the one letter that had reached them, the local members in Brazil learned the group's arrival date and flight number. They thus spread the happy news of the Soka Gakkai president's imminent visit among their fellow members.

Before their departure from New York, as well, Shin'ichi and the others had sent a telegram to São Paulo but again received no response. It had taken the local members quite a bit of time to arrange for an international wire to be sent in reply. It, too, eventually arrived after the group had already departed for Brazil.

The only information Shin'ichi and the others did have concerning conditions in Brazil was that the membership numbered some 100 households, spread throughout the country, and that the members there had held several discussion meetings.

Since Brazil's national language was Portuguese, the in-flight announcements were in Portuguese and English. Neither

Shin'ichi nor any of the others could speak Portuguese, and Nagayasu Masaki, who could speak English, had remained in New York to await their return. This leg of their trip was filled with constant uncertainty, like trying to feel one's way blindly in the dark. They felt anxious and alone.

*S*HIN'ICHI looked haggard and pale. Kiyoshi Jujo, who sat next to him on the plane, peered anxiously at his face and asked, "How are you feeling?"

"I'm fine. Please don't worry," said Shin'ichi, offering him a reassuring smile. "In olden days, Christian missionaries would often sail across the ocean, being rocked and tossed about for weeks on end, journeying to unknown shores without knowing the language of the natives. Then, all alone, they would strive to propagate their faith. Even though I may be feeling a little under the weather, compared to what they had to go through, I am quite fortunate to travel like this by plane."

"Yes, well…," said Jujo, at a loss for something else to say.

"By the way," Shin'ichi continued, "I've been thinking about this for some time, and I'd like to establish a chapter in Brazil."

"Establish a chapter?" exclaimed a stunned Jujo, as if wishing to confirm that he had heard Shin'ichi correctly.

"Yes, the first chapter outside of Japan. I realize that the membership in Brazil is still small. However, the history, culture and temperament of South Americans are very different from North Americans. We must think of South America as distinct and separate. Brazil will become the cornerstone for our activities in this region. I also believe that this will heighten the local members' self-awareness and above all strengthen their unity."

It was not the idea of establishing a chapter in Brazil that had surprised Jujo. Rather, he had been taken aback by

Shin'ichi's powerful sense of mission, his tenacity of purpose. For in spite of his dire health and being confined in a plane that continued to pitch and heave violently in the turbulence, Shin'ichi calmly outlined his sincere hopes and vision for the kosen-rufu movement in Brazil.

The plane landed in the early evening at an airport surrounded by palm trees. According to the itinerary they had received from the travel agency, Shin'ichi and his party were not scheduled to arrive in São Paulo until 10:45 P.M. It was obvious, then, that they had not landed there. An announcement came over the P.A. system, but the group from Japan had no idea what was being said and were left completely in the dark as to where they were or why they had landed.

In the row behind Shin'ichi, Chuhei Yamadaira, glancing about restlessly, said to Eisuke Akizuki, who was sitting next to him, "Where do you think we are?"

Eisuke Akizuki, using the few words of English that he knew, asked some of the passengers sitting near them where they were and the reason for their landing. He repeated the same question five or six times before someone finally seemed to understand what he was trying to ask. They replied in English, but Akizuki could not understand the full gist of their explanation. Nevertheless, he managed to catch the name "Port of Spain" and the word *gas*.

*E*ISUKE Akizuki took out the English dictionary he had packed in his hand luggage and looked up the word *gas*. He found that in American usage it also meant "gasoline." Next, he pulled out a world map and tried to locate Port of Spain. This he discovered was the main city of the island of Trinidad lying off the northeastern coast of Venezuela in South America.

Akizuki promptly conveyed this information to Shin'ichi, who was sitting in the row in front of him. "Sensei, we appear to be in Port of Spain, Trinidad. And I think we've made a stop for refueling."

"So, we're in Trinidad! This island is famous in Europe as one of those considered to have been 'discovered' by Christopher Columbus," remarked Shin'ichi.

Shortly after the plane resumed its flight to Brazil, it was enfolded in the dark embrace of nightfall. As they flew over the Guiana Highlands, the turbulence worsened, buffeting the plane violently. Some of the passengers had turned pale with nausea.

It was after 11:00 P.M. São Paulo time when the plane finally landed.

"Finally, we've made it to São Paulo!" Chuhei Yamadaira said, then yawned heavily.

An announcement came over the P.A. system. After listening to the English, Akizuki said to Kiyoshi Jujo, "It seems to me they're saying this is Brasília and that we've landed here because of some kind of problem with the plane."

"Yes, I also got the impression they said something like that," Jujo agreed.

The passengers then started to leave the plane.

Shin'ichi and the other leaders also got off, but they had no idea where to go.

An airport employee stood in front of the terminal building. He appeared to be of Asian descent. Jujo tentatively addressed him in Japanese: "We're going as far as São Paulo. What plane do we take?"

The clerk replied with a smile, "In that case, it's the plane next to this one." He spoke Japanese; everyone gave a sigh of relief.

The next leg of their journey was by propeller plane. By the time they finally reached São Paulo, it was 1:00 in the morning — more than two hours behind their original schedule.

Their entire journey from New York to São Paulo, which was two hours ahead of New York time, had taken around thirteen hours.

*A*S Shin'ichi Yamamoto and the other leaders came into the airport lobby, they were greeted by the unexpected strains of the Gakkai song "Ifu Dodo." Coming after the group's anxious and somewhat forlorn journey, it filled their hearts with a sense of homecoming and courage.

Between twenty and thirty people were lined up in the lobby. The members sang with all their hearts while gazing at a large lyric sheet attached to wooden dowels. As if they had only just learned the song and were not yet familiar with the words, their singing was out of rhythm and far from powerful.

The well-wishers who had gathered to greet Shin'ichi and the others in North America had been mainly women, but here more than half were men. Many of them, having emigrated to Brazil from Japan, were farmers. These friends, their sunburnt faces shining brightly and tears flowing from their eyes, were singing this newly learned Soka Gakkai song with all their might. When Shin'ichi thought of the long hours the members had already waited for their arrival, he was filled with an overwhelming sense of affection and tenderness toward them.

"Thank you," said Shin'ichi when they had finished their chorus. "I apologize for being so late. You must have been waiting for hours." He then sat down on a nearby bench.

The airport lobby was dimly lit, most of the lights having been turned off due to the late hour.

The majority of the men who had gathered wore suits and ties, but they seemed rather unaccustomed to such attire. The ties on some of them stuck out from under collars that were somewhat askew, while others wore their suit jackets with all of the buttons fastened.

After the leaders accompanying Shin'ichi had introduced themselves, Shin'ichi rose to his feet to speak to the members. Out of consideration for the lateness of the hour, Shin'ichi kept his words brief, simply expressing his appreciation.

"Thank you very much for coming to the airport to meet us. I am deeply grateful for your sincerity. Seeing that it's already very late, let's meet again tomorrow."

Among the local members were a number of youth whom Shin'ichi had encouraged back in Japan. He now asked one of them, "How many hours did it take those living furthest away to get here?"

"About three or four hours by bus," came the response.

"What will they do tonight?" he asked.

"It's been arranged that they stay with members who live in and around the city. We've also taken the liberty of booking a hotel for you and your party," the youth informed him.

The party had already reserved their own hotel accommodations, but when Shin'ichi heard of the local members' sincere gesture, he said: "That's very kind of you. Thank you very much. We'll stay at that hotel tonight, then."

Shin'ichi did not wish in any way to reject the members' kindhearted intention. He decided to cancel their own reservations for that night and spend at least one night at the hotel arranged for them by the members.

SHIN'ICHI Yamamoto and the other leaders caught taxis to their hotel. Traveling quickly through the streets of São Paulo in the early hours of the morning, they finally arrived there around 3:00. The hotel was very modest and the rooms were small.

When Shin'ichi got to his room, he gazed at his reflection in the mirror. His eyes looked hollow, shadowed by dark circles.

"My goodness!" he thought, afraid that the Brazilian members would worry if they saw him in this condition.

Although they would be staying in Brazil for three nights, they actually only had two full days to conduct their activities. In his mind, Shin'ichi went over all that he must achieve during that time.

The night wore on quietly; outside, everything was shrouded in deep darkness. In Shin'ichi's heart, however, there burned the bright crimson flame of his fierce resolve to usher in the dawn of Brazilian kosen-rufu.

At 10:00 the following morning, Shin'ichi and his party split into two groups and set off on a tour of the city. Katsu Kiyohara, Chuhei Yamadaira and Yukio Ishikawa visited the Tozan Farm in Campinas, some 100 kilometers northwest of São Paulo. Shin'ichi Yamamoto, Kiyoshi Jujo and Eisuke Akizuki went to visit the Cotia Industrial Cooperative and other sites.

The Cotia Industrial Cooperative was an association formed by Japanese immigrants in Cotia, in the state of São Paulo. At the time, it was actively promoting emigration to Brazil among Japanese youth and making great contributions to the development of Brazilian agriculture.

In the evening, Shin'ichi and the other leaders held a gongyo meeting at a member's home in São Paulo. By the time gongyo was completed, the room was filled beyond capacity with members.

Shin'ichi asked each person about his or her work and daily life. Many had moved to Brazil as farmers after World War II. Their lives, however, were far from easy. One, who had worked as a farmer under a four-year contract, related how he had been assigned to live in an old barn with neither electricity nor running water, and how snakes would crawl in during the night while he was asleep. If you had a bad harvest, he added, then debts were all that were left you.

Another member, who had been a farmer in Japan, had sold all his property to buy land in São Paulo, wishing to migrate there and start a farm. On his arrival, however, he discovered there was no record of the land he thought he had purchased; he had been the victim of a fraud. He was thus forced to become a tenant farmer, growing peaches and some potatoes, but had not been very successful with either. Now, he said, he had started to grow vegetables.

From each of the members' stories, Shin'ichi could keenly sense the hardships they had undergone since arriving in Brazil.

*T*HE first Japanese "contract emigrants" had moved to Brazil in 1908. On April 28 of that year, the ship *Kasatomaru* left the port of Kobe with 781 passengers on board and arrived in the Brazilian port of Santos on June 18, after fifty-two days at sea.

Brazil had abolished slavery in 1888. However, as if to compensate, immigrants were often treated little better than slaves. The Italian government had conducted an investigation into the matter and subsequently banned its citizens from emigrating to Brazil. Italy was not alone. Many countries in Europe, seriously concerned about the virulence of yellow fever and malaria in Brazil, were curtailing emigration of their citizens to the South American country. With fewer immigrants, the owners of coffee plantations in São Paulo were left severely short-handed; they sought cheap labor to do the work that slaves had formerly done.

It was against this backdrop that an ambassadorial minister from Japan visited Brazil. He received a lavish welcome and later reported to the Japanese government that the country was "a fertile paradise bequeathed by the heavens." Shortly thereafter, Japanese emigration to Brazil began.

A recruitment notice described the conditions awaiting would-be emigrants as follows: The land around São Paulo is extremely fertile. Crops such as coffee, sugar, cotton and rice can be grown "without using any fertilizer." The climate closely resembles that of southern Europe and, irrespective of race, all people are "guaranteed full and equal rights."

The language of the notice seemed specifically designed to give people the impression that Brazil was a present-day utopia. Moreover, the usual Chinese characters that had been used to transliterate the word *Brazil* into Japanese in the past were replaced with a new set of characters, the individual meaning of which conjured up vivid images of an exotic paradise.

At the time, Japan was in the throes of a serious recession following the Russo-Japanese War, and not a few of its citizens sought to find a better life by migrating to another country. In addition, anti-Japanese exclusionist sentiment had begun to surface in the United States, the country that had until then been the main destination for Japanese emigrants. This prompted the Japanese government to discontinue emigration to the United States. As a result, people's attention focused on Brazil as a promising new land.

No doubt these emigrants dreamed of Brazil, embellished with such effusive words of praise, as an earthly paradise. They traveled there with hope in their hearts and filled with visions of making their fortunes and bringing glory and prestige to their hometowns in Japan.

Brazil remained the principal destination for Japanese emigrants until 1932, when Japan began its campaign to recruit settlers for Manchuria and Mongolia.

*S*OMEONE once observed that it may be the eternal paradox of human beings to show great cleverness when they deceive and great foolishness when they are deceived.

Cherishing dreams for the future, Japanese emigrants flocked to Brazilian coffee plantations, but all that awaited them was a wretched existence, a far cry from the paradise they envisioned. They were called *colono* (settlers) by the locals, and work on the land was unimaginably hard. They had to build their own homes, even their own beds.

There was no running water, electricity or toilets. They were also plagued by sand flies, which burrowed under people's nails and caused painful, oozing infections that itched unbearably.

On many farms, the immigrants were treated like slaves, spurred on by the cracking of whips. In some places, they were not even called by their own names but referred to by number. Many immigrants fled under the cover of night, but to do so was to condemn themselves to the life of a wandering peasant. At some point, the following song had become popular among the Japanese immigrants:

> *Who was it that said*
> *Brazil's a great place?*
> *Duped by the emigration company,*
> *We traveled halfway 'round the world*
> *Only to find*
> *The paradise we'd heard of*
> *Was in fact hell.*
> *My, oh, my!*

Some referred to themselves not as "immigrants" but "vagrants."

Gradually, however, a few Japanese immigrants did manage to work their way up, toiling in earnest silence under extremely harsh circumstances, advancing from employed laborer to contract laborer and eventually becoming independent farmers who owned their own land. Later, too, some of them would establish businesses that came to be known as *colônia*.

However, the winds of destiny were incredibly cold and harsh. In 1930, a military coup d'état gave birth to the Vargas regime,[1] which promoted a series of nationalistic policies that started a growing tide of anti-Japanese sentiment. This led to the enactment of legislation restricting Japanese immigration, the banning of foreign-language publications and prohibiting schools from teaching their curricula in languages other than Portuguese, Brazil's national language.

The year after the outbreak of the Pacific war in 1941, Brazil severed diplomatic ties with Japan. In June 1945, it declared war on Japan. This only exacerbated the hardships suffered by those of Japanese descent living in Brazil. Gatherings of more than three persons of Japanese ancestry were banned, individual assets were frozen, and many were driven from the land they had worked so hard to cultivate.

Later, Japan's surrender would also unleash unexpected confusion among Brazil's Japanese community.

TUNING in to a crackling and indistinct broadcast from Japan on their shortwave radios, Japanese Brazilians heard the news of Japan's defeat. Having been taught that not a single soldier of the Imperial Army must ever surrender, however, many of them just could not believe — or, more precisely, did not want to believe — that the Japanese emperor, the generalissimo of the Army and Navy, had capitulated to the enemy. Rumors began to circulate that Japan had won the war.

Left largely uninformed about news and events in society following the Brazilian government's ban on the publication of Japanese-language newspapers, many Japanese Brazilians avidly seized on this rumor. Others who did believe the news of Japan's defeat launched a movement to make their fellow Japanese Brazilians recognize the truth. The Japanese-Brazilian community split into two opposing camps: those who believed Japan to be victorious and those who acknowledged Japan's defeat. Thus one Japanese Brazilian was pitted against another.

The "victory" camp was led by an ultra-nationalistic group called the Shindo Alliance. Individuals associated with this alliance formed a "special commando unit" that instigated a succession of terrorist attacks against the leaders of the "defeat" camp. This prompted the victimized group to lodge an appeal with the Brazilian president to halt the terrorism perpetrated by the "victory" group, which it denounced as "spreading poison in Brazilian society." Although these efforts paid off with a full-scale crackdown on the activities of the Shindo Alliance, it had the unfortunate effect of adding further fuel to the country's exclusionist sentiment toward all Japanese Brazilians.

The false rumors circulated by the "victory" group immediately after the war — even going so far as to proclaim that the United States had unconditionally surrendered to Japan — plunged the Japanese-Brazilian community into deep confusion. This escalated into talk of a Japanese military occupation of Brazil and the total repatriation of all Japanese citizens in Brazil.

These unfounded rumors also spawned numerous incidents of malicious fraud. The most noted was the so-called "yen-selling" incident. Hearing the news that all Japanese citizens were preparing to leave the country en masse, many Japanese in Brazil sold off their homes and land and practically vied with one another to change their money into yen. By seeming coincidence, there happened to be a large volume of Japanese yen available to be sold. After the war, however, Japan had issued new currency. The notes that were circulating in Brazil were thus obsolete and nothing more than useless scraps of paper. Day after day, endless lines of people, their pockets filled with worthless bills, could be seen standing at the docks waiting in vain for the ships they thought would take them back to Japan. When it finally came to light that they had been swindled, some people took their own lives. This was a truly despicable case of fraud in which unscrupulous Japanese Brazilians took advantage of the confusion of the times to prey on their compatriots.

THE antagonism among Japanese Brazilians, who had divided themselves into "victory" and "defeat" camps, continued for several years after the war. It was only when this conflict had abated that Brazil formally reopened its doors to Japanese immigration in February 1953 — some seven-and-a-half years after Japan's surrender.

Compared to the situation before the war, a much more favorable environment awaited postwar Japanese immigrants to Brazil. Would-be immigrants were subjected to a strict screening procedure. There were far fewer Japanese wishing to move to Brazil temporarily to earn money and then return to Japan. Now, many Japanese sought to settle there permanently. And this was not just to engage in agriculture.

As more and more Japanese enterprises began venturing into Brazil, an increasing number of technicians joined the ranks of immigrants. Japanese Brazilians came to be active in all spheres of Brazilian society, gradually winning for themselves a deepening trust and respect among the population as a whole.

Nevertheless, living in a foreign country entailed many hardships. Depending on where the newcomers settled, discord sometimes arose between them and Japanese Brazilians who had immigrated before the war.

As he spoke with the local members who had come to the gongyo meeting, Shin'ichi Yamamoto gained a clear picture of each person's occupation, condition of faith and even his or her personality and character. Almost all of the members had started practicing the Daishonin's Buddhism in Japan within the last four or five years. Quite a few had striven within the organization in such front-line leadership positions as unit chief. While taking the lead in activities for kosen-rufu in their respective regions, they had spoken to friends and acquaintances about the Daishonin's Buddhism. As a result of their efforts, one or two people in each area had begun to join them in chanting daimoku. Discussion meetings were also now being held regularly in São Paulo. Tiny buds of kosen-rufu were beginning to sprout. It was at this time that the members received news that the newly inaugurated third president of the Soka Gakkai, Shin'ichi Yamamoto, would be visiting Brazil with several other top leaders.

Local members who had been playing leading roles in activities literally danced for joy when they heard this. They threw themselves wholeheartedly into preparations for the group's arrival. Since they would be welcoming the Soka Gakkai president, they made elaborate plans to bring all the members in São Paulo together for the occasion. Knowing that there must still be some members who had not been contacted, the key local members came up with the ingenious idea of placing an announcement of the Soka Gakkai president's visit in the Japanese-language newspapers. This proved even more effective than hoped, and it led to contact with a host of hitherto unknown members. Filled with joy and excitement, the members waited impatiently for Shin'ichi and his party to arrive.

*A*FTER hearing the members' reports, Shin'ichi Yamamoto said, smiling brightly: "The dawn of kosen-rufu in Brazil is now approaching. I have come to Brazil with the intention of establishing the first chapter outside of Japan."

There were gasps and cries of surprise from among the participants.

Shin'ichi continued: "This means that Brazil will assume the mission of a pioneer of worldwide kosen-rufu. Each of you is a pioneer. Opening new frontiers naturally entails great trial and hardship. But if you succeed in surmounting these obstacles, a paradise of happiness will unfold for you here in Brazil. Together, let's blaze the trail of kosen-rufu for the sake of this country and the prosperity of all of your families."

After their evening meal, Shin'ichi and the other leaders met to discuss the formation of the new chapter. They deliberated carefully over where to establish districts and whom to appoint to leadership positions, taking into account the number of members who lived scattered throughout each region.

It was past midnight when Shin'ichi returned to his room. Although he was so physically exhausted that he felt dizzy, he reached into his bag for some writing paper. He then sat down at the table and began to write a letter of encouragement to a fellow member in Japan. Indeed, he wrote several such letters.

Despite his extreme physical weakness, Shin'ichi's heart beat vibrantly, filled with delight at being here in Brazil, breaking new ground for the development of kosen-rufu in place of his beloved mentor, Josei Toda. This joy and fighting spirit became a passionate cry for kosen-rufu that filled his entire being and caused his pen to fly across page after page.

To one chapter leader, he wrote: "Right now, my sole thought is to carry on President Toda's intent and dedicate myself to completing the foundation for kosen-rufu, even if it costs me my life. People are vital to this endeavor — people of outstanding ability. I fervently hope you will always join me in this task and courageously walk the path of your mission to the very end. And on my behalf, I hope you will love every member of your chapter with all your heart and guide them all toward happiness."

The members in Japan had no idea of the circumstances under which he wrote these letters. Later, however, when they learned of the ill health that had plagued him during his overseas journey, tears welled in their eyes as they fiercely renewed their vow to struggle alongside him for kosen-rufu.

It is only sincere actions that have the power to move people's hearts.

A DISCUSSION meeting was held on October 20, the following day. The site was the second floor of Chá Flora, a restaurant located in a primarily Asian section of São Paulo. Japanese Brazilians often used the place to hold gatherings and events.

Although the discussion meeting was not scheduled to begin until 1:00 P.M., members started filtering in before noon. Every face was bright and cheerful. Some members had come from regions as far as 900 miles away. Traveling on a succession of trains and buses, it had taken them three full days and nights to reach São Paulo.

By 12:30, all of the several dozen or so seats in the room were filled and people began to stand in the back.

When Shin'ichi Yamamoto and the other leaders arrived, there was a spontaneous burst of applause. Many who attended had tenaciously kept the flame of their faith alive while struggling all alone in regions far from the city, without other members to depend on.

"President Yamamoto has come all this way to see us. Our president has come to Brazil!" When they thought of this, they could not hold back their tears.

One woman murmured: "I can't see President Toda anywhere. I wonder if he'll be coming later?"

The woman sitting next to her whispered back: "Haven't you heard? President Toda passed away. Mr. Yamamoto has become the third president."

Communication in Brazil in those days was poor. Mail from Japan sometimes took three months to reach an address in São Paulo. It was not rare for mail addressed to more remote areas never to reach its destination. Given this situation, it was not strange that some members, having no contact with others in the organization, had remained unaware of Toda's death.

Standing before the gathering, Shin'ichi bowed and sat down at the long narrow table in the front of the room. "Thank you all for coming today. Let's begin, shall we?"

At this meeting, Shin'ichi devoted even more time to answering members' questions than he had at any other place thus far on his journey. He was well aware of how hard life was for the immigrant farmers. He wanted to offer appropriate guidance and encouragement to those desperately struggling to find a way out of their difficulties without leaders in faith to guide them or anyone with whom they could discuss their problems.

"Please feel free to ask me anything you like. That's why I have come," said Shin'ichi.

Four or five hands immediately shot up; everyone had been longing for such an opportunity.

*M*ANY of the questions were about serious issues related to the members' very survival. One man in his early 40s began speaking nervously. "Occupation: Farmer!" he introduced himself, his tone resembling that of a soldier reporting his rank.

"Please relax," said Shin'ichi. "This isn't the army. We're all friends, all a family. Just relax as you would in your own home."

The members laughed. A bright smile also lit the man's sunburnt face.

He then explained that he had recently started to farm vegetables, but his crop had failed. As a result, he was now heavily in debt. He wanted to know what he could do to overcome this situation.

"What was the reason for your crop failure?" Shin'ichi Yamamoto asked.

"I think it might have been partly due to the weather," the man replied.

"Are there other farmers growing the same vegetables as you who produced a successful crop?"

"Yes, but most people's crops failed."

"Was there some problem with the fertilizer you used?"

"I'm not sure…."

"Was there a problem with the way you tended your crop?"

Silence.

"What about the relationship between the soil and the vegetables you are trying to grow in it?"

"I don't know."

The man could not reply satisfactorily to any of Shin'ichi questions. As a farmer, he had clearly been working hard and trying to do the best he could. But so was everyone else. He was unaware of his own complacence in thinking that what he had been doing was enough.

Shin'ichi began speaking in a penetrating tone: "First, it is vital that you thoroughly investigate the cause that led to your crop failure so that you don't make the same mistake again. You might want to talk with farmers who have been successful and take note of what they have to say.

"It is also important that you take sufficient measures to prevent failure. People who are deadly serious about what they are doing are always studying and exerting their ingenuity to solve problems. You will not be successful if you neglect such things. You will be greatly mistaken if you think that just because you practice faith, your fields will yield abundant crops without any effort on your part.

"Buddhism is a teaching of unsurpassed reason. Therefore, the strength of your faith must manifest itself in the form of studying, exercising your ingenuity and making twice as much effort as anyone else. Earnest daimoku is the wellspring for the energy to challenge these things. Your daimoku must also be a pledge."

"A pledge?" asked the man. None of the members had ever heard of such a concept before.

"Yes, a pledge." Shin'ichi replied. "This means to make a vow of your own accord and pray to fulfill it."

SHIN'ICHI Yamamoto emphasized strongly: "Of course, there are many ways of praying. Some people may pray that everything just falls into their laps without having to make any effort. But a religion that encourages such prayer will lead people to ruin.

"Prayer in Nichiren Daishonin's Buddhism means to chant daimoku based on a pledge or vow. At its very core, this vow is to attain kosen-rufu. It means chanting resolutely with the determination: 'I will realize kosen-rufu in Brazil. Therefore, I will show magnificent actual proof in my work. Please enable me to somehow bring forth my greatest potential.' This is what our prayer should be like.

"It is also important that we establish clear and concrete goals for what we hope to achieve each day and then pray and challenge ourselves to achieve each of them. This earnest determination gives rise to wisdom and resourcefulness, thereby leading to success. In short, to win in life we need determination and prayer, effort and ingenuity. It is misguided to dream of getting rich quick, expecting to encounter a rare stroke of luck or some shrewd money-making scheme. This is not faith. It is mere fantasy.

"Our work is the mainstay that supports our lives. Unless we show real evidence of victory in our work, we cannot demonstrate the principle that faith manifests itself in daily life. Please rid yourself of any laxness and reapply yourself wholeheartedly to your work with a fresh determination."

"I'll do my best!" said the man, his eyes filled with resolve.

Shin'ichi was well aware of the hardships these immigrant farmers were facing. To be successful under such circumstances, they would above all have to battle their own complacency. The enemy they had to face was within.

The greater the adversity, the more important it is to resolve that now is the time to achieve a victory in life and to keep challenging oneself. It is here that the beneficial power of the Gohonzon becomes manifest. Adversity is therefore an opportunity to prove the power of Buddhism.

Toward the end of the question-and-answer session, Shin'ichi noticed a woman in the back row who had been hesitantly raising her hand and putting it down again throughout the session. Somewhere in her mid-30s, her face was gaunt and tired-looking.

"You have a question, don't you? Please go ahead," he encouraged her.

She stood up listlessly and said: "Um, you see, my husband died from illness. I just don't know how I'm going to survive from now on."

*T*HE woman had emigrated with her husband and children under a contract labor agreement and had been working the land. Deprived of her husband's crucial participation, however, it was impossible to continue farming alone. She still had several small children to look after.

Just as she was entertaining thoughts of suicide, she heard about the Daishonin's Buddhism from a Soka Gakkai member living nearby. She had started her practice just one week before the meeting. In that short space of time, she found employment at a factory in São Paulo, which also provided her lodging.

"But," she continued, "when I think of living here in a foreign country I know nothing about, struggling to provide for my children, I can't help feeling anxious. I think I must have awfully deep karma. And I have no idea what may happen in the future. Just thinking about it is unbearable."

Shin'ichi smiled at her and said: "Please don't worry. As long as you're practicing this faith, you can definitely become happy. That's what Buddhism is for. Also, your current suffering and misfortune exist so that you may fulfill your own unique and noble mission. Everything will turn to defeat if all you do is worry about your karma and let it make you miserable."

The woman gazed at Shin'ichi with a look of puzzlement. The member who had introduced her to the practice had told her that the reason she had to suffer the loss of her husband was because of negative karma she had accumulated from offenses committed in past lifetimes.

It is true that Buddhism teaches that one who commits evil deeds against others will receive the negative effects of those actions and live an unhappy life. This is just one aspect, however. Were it the entire teaching on karma, then people would be doomed to live under a cloud of guilt and vague anxiety, not knowing what offenses they might have committed in past lives. It would also mean that people's destiny was fixed — a concept that could easily rob them of their energy and passion. It might also cause people to lapse into a passive way of life, simply concerning themselves with not doing anything bad.

The Buddhism of Nichiren Daishonin goes far beyond the framework of superficial causality. It elucidates the most fundamental cause and shows us the means for returning to the pure life within that has existed since time without beginning. This fundamental cause is to awaken to our mission as Bodhisattvas of the Earth and dedicate our lives to the widespread propagation of the Law.

Shin'ichi said: "Buddhism teaches that its practitioners 'voluntarily choose to be born in evil circumstances so they may help others.' This means that although we have accumulated the benefit through Buddhist practice to be born in favorable circumstances, we have purposely chosen to be born in the midst of suffering people and there propagate the Mystic Law."

*H*E continued in easily comprehensible terms: "For example, if someone who had always lived like a queen and enjoyed every luxury were to say 'I became happy as a result of taking faith,' no one would bat an eye. But if a person who is sick, whose family is poor, and who is shunned by people because of these things becomes happy through practicing faith and goes on to become a leader in society, this will be splendid proof of the greatness of Buddhism. Don't you agree that this would make others want to practice Buddhism, too?

"By triumphing over great poverty, a person who has been poor can give hope to others who are struggling with financial hardship. By regaining vitality and good health, someone who has been battling illness can light a flame of courage in the hearts of those in similar straits. By creating a happy and harmonious family, a person who has suffered great anguish over discord in the home can become a model for others plagued by family problems.

"Similarly, if you, a woman who has been left widowed in a foreign land where she does not speak the language, become happy and raise your children to be fine adults, you'll be a shining example for all women who have lost their husbands. Even those who don't practice faith will admire you and come to seek your advice. So you see, the deeper and greater the suffering, the more magnificently one can show proof of the powerful benefit of Buddhism. You could say that karma is another name for mission.

"I myself am the son of a poor seaweed processor. I worked by Mr. Toda's side throughout the bitter trials of his company's bankruptcy, even though I was suffering from frail health and a tubercular condition at the time. Because I have experienced hardship and suffering just like everyone else, I can take the lead for the kosen-rufu movement in this way as a representative of the common people."

As she listened to Shin'ichi's explanation, the woman nodded repeatedly.

The faces of the participants had also grown increasingly animated. All of them had been through great hardships, groaning under the weight of each day's arduous challenges.

Shin'ichi took a sip of water and said with even greater force: "Each of you may think you have just happened to come to Brazil as a result of your respective circumstances. But this is not the case. You have been born as Bodhisattvas of the Earth in order to achieve kosen-rufu in Brazil, to lead the people of this country to happiness and to create an eternal paradise in this land. Indeed, you have been chosen by Nichiren Daishonin to be here.

"When you realize your great mission as Bodhisattvas of the Earth and dedicate your lives to kosen-rufu, the sun that

has existed within you since time without beginning will begin to shine forth. All offenses you have committed in past lifetimes will vanish like mist, and you will embark upon wonderful lives permeated by deep joy and happiness."

SMILING warmly at the woman, Shin'ichi Yamamoto continued: "Viewed from the profound perspective of Buddhism, your suffering is like that portrayed by a brilliant, highly paid stage actress cast in the role of a tragic heroine. When the play is finished, the actress goes home to a life of ease and comfort. Your life is the same. Moreover, the story you play out on the stage of life's theater will have a happy ending. There is no need to worry. You will definitely become happy. I say this with absolute certainty. Just as a great actress relishes performing her tragic role, please rise from the depths of your sorrow to boldly act out a magnificent drama of human revolution.

"All people are pioneers traveling the unknown frontiers of life. Therefore, it is up to you alone to cultivate and develop your own life. You must wield the hoe of faith, sow the seeds of happiness and persevere tenaciously. The sweat of your efforts for kosen-rufu will become precious gems of good fortune, brilliantly dignifying your life forever. Please become the happiest person in Brazil!"

When Shin'ichi had finished speaking, the woman responded cheerfully, "Yes, I will!"

The audience broke into applause, expressing not only their agreement with what Shin'ichi had said but also their genuine delight at the woman's newfound resolve.

Shin'ichi fielded two or three more questions before it was time to announce the establishment of the new chapter. The first chapter outside of Japan was about to be born.

"I hereby announce the establishment of a chapter here in Brazil!" Shin'ichi's proclamation was met with a wild storm of applause.

This discussion meeting was therefore effectively the first Brazilian general meeting as well as an inaugural chapter meeting.

Three districts were also established on this occasion: the São Paulo, Campinas and Alujá districts.

Appointed to the positions of chapter chief and women's division chapter chief were a married couple who ran a business manufacturing and selling transistor radios. The position of young men's division chief, meanwhile, went to Eiji Gohno, a youth who had been a member of the Soka Gakkai brass band while still in Japan.

Shin'ichi closed his words by saying: "Brazil is now a forerunner in the kosen-rufu movement among countries outside Japan. There is infinite potential here. As pioneers of peace and happiness, please blaze the path of kosen-rufu in Brazil in my stead. Please do your best."

There was more applause.

Each of these humble pioneers, dressed in shabby suits that had seen better days, made a passionate new pledge;

warm tears welled in their eyes, glittering brightly against their deeply sunburnt faces.

The sun of kosen-rufu had now truly risen over the untamed frontiers of Brazil.

*A*FTER the discussion meeting had ended, an elderly man approached Shin'ichi, accompanied by one of the members. The man was sturdily built, with a calm and dignified demeanor. Throughout the meeting, he had sat listening with a slightly defiant posture, his expression serious as if carefully trying to discern something.

Shin'ichi had been wondering who he was.

The man was president of the Japanese Society in an area not far from São Paulo. His face flushed with enthusiasm as he said to Shin'ichi: "I really heard something wonderful today. Many religions from Japan have made their way to Brazil. During the war, I was a member of one of these religious organizations. But it just turned out to be a sham, concerned only with glorifying the war and making money by cleverly gaining favor with people.

"If you gave a lot of money, the leaders of the organization would visit you frequently and talk to you about various things, but if the amount you gave was small, they looked openly disgruntled and would then completely ignore you. Nor did they make the slightest effort to lend a helping hand to the poor. Religion ought to have compassion and serve all people, but this group just behaved as I have described. The corruption of Japanese religion at work here in Brazil is deplorable.

"I hope you will forgive me, but I must admit that I listened to today's meeting thinking that you people must be exactly the same as all the others."

Shin'ichi said to the man with a smile, "I'd be most happy to hear any opinions or criticisms you might have."

"No, no. I was most favorably impressed. After I listened to everything that was said, I thought to myself, 'This is the genuine article; there's no doubt about it.'

"I'd heard about the Soka Gakkai from others, but everyone apart from the members was very negative about it. Some leaders from other religious organizations even came to warn me that the Soka Gakkai propagates a religion that condones violence and that we mustn't let it spread. But witnessing today's meeting, I believe I have obtained ample evidence that your group upholds a religion genuinely concerned with helping ordinary people."

"That's very kind of you to say so."

"Therefore, as of today, I would like to join you and exert myself diligently in the practice of this faith," he declared, gazing steadily at Shin'ichi, his intelligent eyes shining brightly.

"Taking faith is no small matter," Shin'ichi responded. "It requires considerable resolve."

*T*HE man looked at Shin'ichi questioningly. "What is it that you mean by 'considerable resolve'?"

"A true religion," Shin'ichi said, "is invariably subject to attacks, to persecutions. Unless you are resolved to endure these things, you will be unable to carry through with your faith. Are you prepared to accept this?"

The man held an important position in one of the local Japanese societies. Most members would have delightedly accepted his decision to join. Shin'ichi, however, considering the man's situation, held back from doing so.

There is no special or easy path in faith. Those who begin faith halfheartedly are often swayed by trivial things. If this should cause them to forsake their practice, then it is meaningless for them to have taken faith in the first place. In that case, it would only make them unhappy.

The man replied resolutely: "Of course. If people's hearts have grown hard and cynical, they will naturally try to oust and heap abuse and criticism on that which is correct. Particularly if the Soka Gakkai keeps growing the way it is, fear and jealously will prompt increasing attacks against it. I'm ashamed to say that back-stabbing is rampant in the Japanese community in Brazil. Perhaps because they are conscious of being foreigners and having a weak position in society, they are quick to side with those who wield authority and, borrowing their strength, try to bring others down. It's truly lamentable.

"Therefore, I am fully prepared for the Soka Gakkai to be subject to persecution, especially since there are so many spurious religions all around. For that same reason, however, I would like to practice correct faith." The man was completely earnest.

"I understand. If you have the solid determination to do so, then please join us and do your best to exert yourself in faith. I congratulate you from the bottom of my heart on the start of your new life."

The man then firmly shook the hand Shin'ichi held out to him. Shin'ichi had deep respect for the man's keen perception.

The first and most important mission of religion is to save those who are suffering. A true religion is one that extends a helping hand to the poor and the sick. The Soka Gakkai was devoting its entire energies to saving those who were suffering. Nevertheless, in Japanese society, the organization was constantly derided as "an organization of the poor and sick."

It was a testimony to the man's outstanding vision that, despite all this, he concluded in light of the true mission of religion that the Soka Gakkai was indeed promoting a genuine religion.

THAT evening, Shin'ichi Yamamoto invited some of the newly appointed leaders out for dinner at a Japanese restaurant to celebrate this fresh beginning for Brazil. He wanted to wholeheartedly encourage and show his appreciation to the friends who would shoulder the future of this new realm for kosen-rufu.

The conversation during the dinner with Shin'ichi was lively and amiable.

Shin'ichi spoke with Eiji Gohno, the new leader of the young men's division, a sensitive-looking youth.

"What kind of work are you doing now?" he asked.

"I play the trumpet."

"I see. It must be hard making ends meet. Do you speak Portuguese?"

"I attended Portuguese language classes in Japan for two or three months, so I understand a little."

"That's not enough if you hope to become an asset for kosen-rufu. Please study hard and master Portuguese. This will be the first step in fulfilling your mission."

Shin'ichi had met and encouraged the young man a number of times in Japan. At that time, Gohno was not only an active member of the Soka Gakkai's brass band but working hard as a group chief in the young men's division.

The young man had one dream — to become a jazz musician. In those days, however, few in Japan appreciated jazz as a valid form of music; the word *jazz* usually evoked looks of disapproval. Even Gohno himself wondered how he could contribute to kosen-rufu in his chosen field.

Finally, after a lot of soul-searching about his future, he sought guidance from Shin'ichi Yamamoto, then the youth division chief of staff.

At that time, Shin'ichi told him: "If jazz really strikes a chord in your heart, and if you are absolutely determined to proceed in this field, then go ahead and challenge it. Even if by some chance you should not be successful, as long as you always cherish a desire for kosen-rufu in your heart, then all your experiences in life will serve you well. In Buddhism, nothing is ever wasted."

Gohno made up his mind. If he were to study jazz in earnest, he would have to go to the United States, the birthplace and center for that musical form. But he didn't have the money to do so. After doing some checking, however, he found that people wishing to emigrate to Brazil were eligible to apply for a loan to cover their travel expenses.

Gohno thought he would first go to Brazil and then make his way to the United States from there. In mid-July of that year, two months after Shin'ichi had become Soka Gakkai president, Gohno set sail from Yokohama, arriving in the port of Santos, near São Paulo, at the beginning of September.

*O*NE day shortly after his arrival in São Paulo, as he was wandering through the Asian section of town, Eiji Gohno came across a youth wearing a Soka Gakkai pin on his lapel. From this member, he learned of President Yamamoto's imminent visit.

Gohno joined in the preparations to welcome the Soka Gakkai leader; it was he who had taught the members Gakkai songs and conducted the chorus that greeted Shin'ichi at the airport.

Looking at him now, Shin'ichi thought that Gohno's true mission had all along been to work for kosen-rufu right here in Brazil. The question was when he would come to realize that. Shin'ichi had earlier mentioned the importance of learning Portuguese to Gohno out of his sincere hope that the youth would awaken to his mission as soon as possible.

As the meal was drawing to a close, Shin'ichi spoke, his words conveying profound expectations: "The kosen-rufu movement here in Brazil will develop dramatically in the future. It is important that, as leaders, you be determined to serve as the 'soil' for kosen-rufu in Brazil, in which members who appear later can grow and blossom, rather than strive to become 'flowers' and 'fruit' yourselves. It is also important to clearly convey to others how wonderful it is to be a part of the Soka Gakkai and dedicate your lives to the cause of kosen-rufu.

"A drop of dew on a leaf soon vanishes, but the waters of the ocean encompass the globe. The Soka Gakkai, the organization of kosen-rufu, allows us to open the vast, oceanlike potential within our lives and elevate our state of life. I hope each of you will make a personal determination that, no matter what happens, you will never leave the Soka Gakkai. When leaders whose job it is to guide others in faith stop practicing and let down or betray their fellow members, they commit a grave offense.

"It is quite likely that the Soka Gakkai will encounter various forms of attack in the future. There will definitely be those who seek to undermine and disrupt the solid unity of our organization. However, true practitioners of Buddhism are those who have been forged and tested through many trials; such people will savor glory in life.

"Benzo Yoda, an early pioneer of Japan's northernmost island of Hokkaido, wrote the following poem:

> *Young hero*
> *Heart resolved*
> *Facing the northern seas —*
> *Wind, howl as you like!*
> *Waves, rage as you will!*

"I hope all of you will embrace this same spirit and always dedicate yourselves to blazing the trail for kosen-rufu, and in doing so write a brilliant poem of your pioneering struggles."

Shin'ichi had left his meal practically untouched, his intense fatigue robbing him of any appetite. His heart, however, was happy and refreshed. His entire being was filled with a deep sense of satisfaction at having striven with every ounce of his energy to secure the foundations for the great future development of the kosen-rufu movement in Brazil.

ON October 21, the following day, Shin'ichi Yamamoto and his party left Brazil to return to the United States. At 11:30 that morning, around two dozen members saw Shin'ichi and the others off as they boarded a bus in front of the Pan American office in São Paulo for the trip to the airport in Campinas.

Arriving at the airport, the group learned that their flight had been delayed considerably; it was 3:00 P.M. by the time they were finally airborne.

As the onset of night darkened the sky around them, they landed for refueling at El Dorado Airport in Bogotá, Colombia. There, they had to disembark and wait in the lounge.

The airport was deserted. Shin'ichi stepped outside the airport building for a moment. He looked up at a night sky filled with countless shimmering stars that stretched as far as the eye could see. The airport was named after El Dorado, the mythical city of gold fabled to exist in the New World. Gazing at a beautiful sky dusted with silver light, he felt as if he were indeed standing in the land of El Dorado.

Shin'ichi recalled that the French philosopher Voltaire (1694-1778), in his novel *Candide*, had written of a wondrous land known as El Dorado hidden deep in South America. It was portrayed as a land of fabulous riches where children wore robes of gold and played with gems as other children played with stones. In addition to enjoying immense material wealth, everyone — from the king down to ordinary citizens — was a stranger to conflict and discord.

In El Dorado, there were no lawsuits, courts or prisons. In Voltaire's portrayal, it was a kingdom overflowing with trust and goodwill, a place where people's hearts were even richer than the material wealth they possessed. Without spiritual wealth it would not be a true El Dorado.

Shin'ichi's goal of accomplishing kosen-rufu was nothing other than the construction of just such a golden realm.

Right now, he thought, there are no members here in Colombia. But some day, the time would definitely come when courageous Bodhisattvas of the Earth would — no, must — appear in this land and joyously conduct their activities.

Shin'ichi chanted daimoku as he gazed up at the sky.

From that time on, while praying for the peace and prosperity of Colombia, Shin'ichi, as an ordinary citizen, began working to foster friendly ties with the South American country. In 1990, thirty years after he first set foot on Colombian soil, an exhibition of Colombian gold artwork was shown at the Tokyo Fuji Art Museum, which he founded. As a result, 517 priceless Colombian treasures — including some of the world's largest uncut emeralds never before shown outside Colombia — were displayed to the Japanese public, symbolizing the trust and friendship between the two countries.

In 1993, Shin'ichi made his first official visit to Colombia and established the first SGI chapter in that country.

THE plane carrying Shin'ichi and his party arrived at New York's Idlewild International Airport shortly after 2:00 A.M. on October 22, several hours behind schedule.

Susumu Aota and Nagayasu Masaki were waiting to welcome them at the airport, along with Yukiko Nishino and other members from the New York area.

When Shin'ichi saw their faces, he smiled and said: "Sorry to have kept you waiting so long. We're all back safe and well. Thank you."

Although he looked drawn, the members were relieved to see Shin'ichi in such high spirits. The sight of his gallant presence filled them with courage.

"Sensei, you must be exhausted. Please accept these rice balls," said Yukiko Nishino, offering Shin'ichi a small bundle she had prepared for him and his party.

"Thank you, that's very thoughtful. I'm deeply touched by your kindness."

When Shin'ichi and the others ate them later back at their hotel, these rice balls, with their centers of pickled plum, seemed exceptionally delicious.

About ten hours later, Shin'ichi and his party were on their way from New York to Los Angeles. Their plane arrived in the West Coast city at 2:30 P.M. The group had spent most of the time during their short stopover in New York discussing the formation of a chapter in Los Angeles and carefully deliberating over the selection of leaders.

On arriving at the airport in Los Angeles, they were greeted by a chorus of about two dozen members singing a Gakkai song. As he approached where they were standing, Shin'ichi joined them in their passionate singing. The members' voices faltered repeatedly as they tried to stem the tears that welled forth out of their joy to be welcoming their president.

In the meantime, several more members raced up to them, heavily out of breath. It was the very first time that many of them had been to the airport, and finding their way around the large terminal had made them late. Because travel from Japan to the United States in those days was primarily by sea — a journey of about two weeks — the airport was a totally unfamiliar place for most of them. Quite a few weren't even aware that there were different lobbies for arrivals and departures.

When the singing ended, Shin'ichi said: "Thank you very much. I appreciate all your hard work!"

From the back of the group, someone suddenly called out, "Sensei!" Making her way through the small crowd of people, a woman approached Shin'ichi. A man was accompanying her.

"Sensei, I've brought my husband!" she declared cheerfully.

WHEN Shin'ichi saw the woman, he smiled and said, "Thank you for coming to see me!" The woman's name was Takae Hanamura. She had moved to the United States several years before, where she had somehow managed to maintain her practice. In the spring of the previous year, during a short visit to Japan, she had stopped by the Soka Gakkai Headquarters with her mother. Shin'ichi had encouraged her on that occasion and promised, "I'm thinking of visiting America in October of next year; let's meet again over there."

The woman had been surprised to hear that Shin'ichi was planning to visit the United States. She had never imagined that the top leader of the Soka Gakkai would travel all that way.

She had also told Shin'ichi on that occasion that her husband was not a member.

"Well then, could you introduce me to him when I come?" he had asked.

"Yes, I'd be delighted to!" said the woman.

Eighteen months had passed since then.

Now, Takae Hanamura introduced her husband, who had been standing behind her, to Shin'ichi. "This is my husband, Michiaki."

"I'm pleased to meet you. Thank you very much for coming all this way. I'm Shin'ichi Yamamoto, president of the Soka Gakkai." Shin'ichi greeted him courteously and shook his hand.

The man gazed at Shin'ichi in stunned surprise.

"I hope to see you again later at the discussion meeting," said Shin'ichi, smiling.

Michiaki Hanamura nodded silently. His mind was in turmoil. He had always thought there was something questionable about the Soka Gakkai. Then his wife had insisted that they go to the airport to meet the president of that very organization. He had gone only with the greatest reluctance. Having met Shin'ichi in person, however, Michiaki found him to be a well-mannered and stalwart young man, a far cry from the image he had formed of him as an authoritarian "religious leader." He actually found something appealing about Shin'ichi. Hence his bewilderment and confusion at the seeming disparity.

Many people in society form their image of the Soka Gakkai based on prejudiced reports and spurious rumors circulated by segments of the mass media. Once preconceptions are in place, it is difficult for people to make a fair and impartial appraisal. The ultimate means of breaking through such bias is dialogue — dialogue with someone possessed of solid character that has been forged and polished through faith.

The brilliant light of one's character can overturn malicious criticisms and give eloquent voice to the truth. As the saying goes, "Seeing is believing." For that reason, too, it is vital that leaders do not neglect to meet with many people and engage them in dialogue.

*A*FTER arriving at their hotel, Shin'ichi Yamamoto and the other leaders had almost no time to rest before leaving to attend that evening's discussion meeting. During the short interval they spent at the hotel, Shin'ichi met and interviewed key members in the Los Angeles area for leadership positions in the new chapter that was about to be established.

The venue for the discussion meeting was the Sun Building in Little Tokyo, the center of L.A.'s Japanese-American community.

A young woman stood behind a reception desk that had been set up at the entrance of the building for the occasion. When she saw Shin'ichi, she greeted him with a stiff and nervous expression and said, using a standard polite Japanese expression, "Hello, you must be tired."

"You can say that again! I'm really worn out," replied Shin'ichi, smiling.

A bright smile lit the young woman's face, the warmth of his response putting her at ease.

More than 100 people crowded into the meeting room. A table covered with a white cloth had been placed at the front for the speakers, while on the wall behind it hung a photo of Josei Toda and calligraphy of the Japanese characters for *unity*.

The meeting layout was modeled after the memorable spring general meeting of May 3, 1958, when Shin'ichi announced his vision for the future based on the concept of "Seven Bells,"[2] inspiring the members to overcome their deep sorrow over President Toda's passing and advance with new determination.

In addition, the national flags of the United States and Japan had been hung on either side of the Japanese characters for unity. Even a pine bonsai tree had been placed to one side of the speaker's table. There was also a vertical banner that read in Japanese calligraphy "Los Angeles Kick-off Meeting." Except for the American flag, the meeting could have been taking place in Japan.

There is no need to strive for such uniformity, Shin'ichi thought, to follow the way things are done in Japan right down to the last detail. Rather, he felt, the culture, traditions and character of people in each country should be kept alive and be reflected and expressed in the organization.

However, since almost all of the members who had been working on the preparations for this meeting were originally from Japan, it was perhaps only natural that they should have chosen this way to express their joy and enthusiasm. Shin'ichi appreciated the spirit behind their efforts.

There were many members in the Los Angeles area, the majority of whom were from Japan. These members contacted one another and organized discussion meetings quite regularly. Even though none of the members possessed particularly outstanding leadership skills, through their respective experiences, each had firmly established the conviction that benefit definitely accrues when one earnestly perseveres. Actual experience speaks more eloquently than a million words of theory. The members in Los Angeles encouraged one another in their practice by sharing their experiences of faith.

Here, too, as in the other cities Shin'ichi had visited in the United States, the leading force in activities were Japanese women who had moved to this country as a result of marrying American citizens.

*A*MONG the Los Angeles members was a woman named Kazuko Ellick. She was a nurse who had started to practice Nichiren Daishonin's Buddhism in Japan in August 1954, inspired by her mother's having overcome palsy as a result of this faith.

The following year, an American working for the u.s. military's broadcasting network in Japan asked her to marry him, and she accepted his proposal. However, his mother violently opposed the marriage. Unable to let go of her anger toward Japan, America's enemy during the war, she sent Kazuko a letter in which she had written, "I'm not going to have my son marry a Jap!"

But Kazuko was not going to let the woman get the better of her. When she received this letter, she promptly sent off her reply: "Shut up, Yankee! Don't tell me what to do!"

The war between Japan and the United States was still raging between this would-be Japanese bride and her future American mother-in-law.

Kazuko's husband went ahead and completed all the paperwork for their marriage and then returned to the United States alone to wait until the immigration authorities granted his wife permission to join him there. But then it was discovered that she had tuberculosis, regarded in those days as an incurable disease, and her application to enter the United States was denied.

As a nurse, Kazuko was well aware how serious an illness like tuberculosis could be. She felt as if the world around her had suddenly turned dark, but she refused to admit defeat. "I have faith," she thought. She applied herself to her practice with a vengeance, energetically introducing others to the Daishonin's Buddhism and encouraging her fellow members.

Kazuko and her mother-in-law continued their blistering assaults through the mail for some time, but when the mother-in-law learned that Kazuko was a nurse, her attitude suddenly changed. It turned out that she herself had practiced nursing for many years.

Her mother-in-law now wrote, "Please get well and come to America as soon as possible." She opened her heart and gave her blessing to the marriage. Kazuko wept when she read the letter, as deep gratitude for the great benefit of the Gohonzon welled up within her.

She recovered steadily from her illness, growing healthier each day. Having submitted all the paperwork necessary to move to America, she then checked into the U.S. military hospital in Kanagawa Prefecture for tests. Although her condition had markedly improved, she was not yet completely cured. From Kanagawa, she was flown by military airplane, via Hawaii, to San Francisco, where she was placed in a suburban hospital.

Her recovery here was the final hurdle to beginning her new life in America.

T HE doctor informed Kazuko that she would have to stay in the hospital for a month; the cost would be around $500. All she had, however, was $150. Her husband, who had returned to the United States ahead of her, was struggling financially, and the money she had brought with her was supposed to be a precious nest egg for the start of their new married life together. "I can't afford to stay in the hospital that long," she thought. "With faith, I'm going to recover from this illness in one week, no matter what!"

In her hospital room, Kazuko Ellick chanted with powerful determination. She also resolved to teach people at the hospital about her faith. But she did not speak English. Using a Japanese-English dictionary, she looked up words that would be useful in her propagation efforts and jotted them down on cards. Equipped with these cards, she would boldly step out into the hospital garden and suddenly call out loudly in heavily accented English, "Listen!" With all the people in the garden looking at her in open amazement, she would continue: "Nam-myoho-renge-kyo, number one! If you want go home, speak Nam-myoho-renge-kyo!"

She felt no shame or embarrassment about what people might think. She gave no thought to common sense or the social propriety to which all Soka Gakkai members ought to pay heed.

Her sole concern was to cure her tuberculosis quickly and be released from the hospital. After making her declaration, she would return to her room in high spirits and start chanting frantically.

The content of her prayer was as follows: "Gohonzon, are you listening? I have just sown the seeds of Buddhahood in the lives of forty or fifty people. I'm exerting myself in my Buddhist practice with all my might. You know that, don't you? Therefore, please promise that I can definitely check out of the hospital in one week's time. And, by the way, I only have $150. Please make the hospital bill no more than $125. I need the remaining $25 to rent a room after I'm released."

She was utterly serious. Each day was devoted from morning till night to daimoku and her somewhat unusual style of propagation.

After her first week at the hospital, she received the results of her tests. It was what she had prayed for. She was going to be released. She danced for joy. And the bill for her hospital stay came to exactly $125.

As she left the hospital with her husband, who had come to pick her up, people throughout the hospital leaned out of their windows and called out to her.

Kazuko turned and waved energetically to them, crying out: "Hello! Hello!"

THE clamoring from the hospital ward windows was the shouts of people wanting to know Kazuko Ellick's so-called magic word.

"Okay. Okay," she said cheerfully. She went back inside and wrote down the English spelling for Nam-myoho-renge-kyo on pieces of paper and went around to each ward to hand them out, emphasizing strongly as she did so, "Speak; go home." What she was trying to convey was, "If you chant this phrase, you will be able to go home."

It was anybody's guess, however, whether her message actually got through.

In any event, her prayers had been answered, and Ellick could now walk freely on American soil. With this experience as a source of inspiration, she threw herself into her activities in Los Angeles with equal enthusiasm. Besides Japanese women like herself, there were also a number of adult men, as well as students studying abroad among the membership.

The historic discussion meeting that marked the formation of Los Angeles Chapter began at 6:30 P.M. Here, as on other occasions, Shin'ichi devoted most of the meeting to answering members' questions. As expected, many of the questions concerned illness, financial difficulties and husbands who did not practice.

Interspersing his responses with humor, Shin'ichi answered with embracing gentleness. Though it was a large meeting with more than 100 participants, it was pervaded by an air of warmth and friendliness.

Perhaps because they were so thoroughly at ease, many people who rose to ask questions unconsciously lapsed into the dialects of their native regions in Japan. This drew bursts of good-natured laughter from their fellow members. To these people, exhausted from the struggles of daily life in a foreign country to which they were not yet accustomed, the discussion meeting was an oasis, a tranquil garden.

After bringing the question-and-answer session to a close, Shin'ichi earnestly addressed the audience:

"The United States is a country that enjoys one of the highest levels of material wealth in the world. I would like all of you to enjoy comfortable lives and good health. By the same token, if your hearts — which are most important — are impoverished, you cannot be truly happy. For, as the Gosho states, more precious than the treasures of the storehouse are the treasures of the body, and more precious than the treasures of the body are the treasures of the heart. People here in the United States are at last beginning to recognize this.

"How, then, can people enrich their hearts and culti-vate spiritual wealth? You are the ones who have the answer; it is you, therefore, who shoulder America's future. In that respect, I declare that all the women who are here today are the foremost women in America. Though you may be facing various problems and sufferings right now, I hope you will remember the mission you have and each become a brilliant sun that will illuminate America with the light of happiness."

NEXT, Shin'ichi outlined the guidelines he had stressed consistently throughout his visit to the United States: that Japanese members who had moved to this country should acquire 1) citizenship, 2) a dri-ver's license, and 3) a good command of English.

The members expressed their fresh determination with resounding applause. Finally, it was time to announce the formation of the new chapter. Shin'ichi spoke with still greater energy:

"Los Angeles is an important region that will become the center of the kosen-rufu movement in America. For that reason, I wish to announce the establishment of a chapter here today."

Loud applause and cheers of approval greeted this. The participants were aware that districts had been established in various parts of the United States, but now, to their great surprise, a chapter was being formed right here in Los Angeles. They felt like dancing for joy; everyone sensed that a new age had arrived.

Within the chapter, six districts were also formed: St. Louis, Olympic, First, West, Long Beach and San Diego districts.

The new chapter and district leaders were then announced. "Those whose names are called, please come up to the front. For Los Angeles Chapter chief, I ask Akio Ishibashi to take on this position. Are you agreeable to this?" Shin'ichi asked.

Mr. Ishibashi was a steady and amiable-looking man in his early 40s. He made no move, however, to come up front.

"Mr. Ishibashi, please come on up."

After Shin'ichi repeated this request four or five times, the man finally came out front. When he did so, however, he walked up to where the Soka Gakkai president was sitting, crouched down beside him and, gripping the back of his chair with one hand, said imploringly: "The position of chapter chief is really beyond me. I think it would be better if you asked someone else." This, no doubt, was Ishibashi's honest feeling.

Shin'ichi looked him straight in the eye and said, "You won't do it, even if I ask you as a personal favor?"

Ishibashi stood there looking perplexed.

"Will you, then?" pressed Shin'ichi.

"Yes," replied the man, as if resigning himself to his fate, his tone not reassuring.

Shin'ichi then spoke sternly: "Taking responsibility as a leader in the organization is the quickest way to develop one's life-condition. Rather than deciding it's beyond you before you even try, it's important to accept the position humbly and challenge yourself to the very limit of your ability. Two other men who have a great deal of experience will be there to help you, so I ask that you please make a resolute determination and try your best."

He then read out the names of the two men who would serve as chapter staff.

NEXT, Shin'ichi Yamamoto announced the appointment of the chapter women's division chief: "I ask Kiyoko Kuwano to accept the position of chapter women's division chief. And I would like to appoint Kazuko Ellick, who has been active as a key figure among the women, to serve as the district chief of St. Louis District."

Mrs. Kuwano had only arrived in the United States ten months before and had not yet achieved anything substantial in terms of her faith-related activities. She reluctantly stood up and said to Shin'ichi: "Sensei, I'm sorry, but I don't think I could possibly manage being the chapter women's division chief. I'm really not that capable."

"Don't worry. I will protect and support you. Please have confidence and do your best."

"I will," she said, nodding.

"Well, then, how about saying a few words?" he asked.

Urged by Shin'ichi, the woman addressed the audience: "I have no experience, but I'll try my best. Thank you."

When she heard the announcement of the new chapter women's division chief, Kazuko Ellick's face had clouded over. Her heart burned with jealousy as she watched the exchange between Shin'ichi and Mrs. Kuwano. Tears came to her eyes.

"Why wasn't I appointed women's division chief?!" she raged silently. "Why is she being appointed women's division chief? It's not right. I've worked much harder than she has!"

The district leadership positions were then announced, and Kazuko Ellick's name was now formally called as district chief of St. Louis District. But she refused to answer, turning her head away in a huff.

First, it had been the chapter chief, Akio Ishibashi, then, the new chapter women's division chief, Kiyoko Kuwano, and now Kazuko Ellick: the leadership announcements were turning out in a way that would have been unimaginable in Japan.

The district chiefs appointed that day were all women. In addition, Nagayasu Masaki was appointed as the young men's division leader for North America, while Yuji Nakahara, a student from Japan, became the Los Angeles young men's division leader. Chikako Hayashi, the young woman who had earlier greeted Shin'ichi at the reception desk, was named the district-level leader for the young women's division in Los Angeles.

After all the announcements were made, Shin'ichi said: "Mrs. Ellick, Mrs. Kuwano is older than you. Is it okay with you if we appoint her, as an elder sister, to fulfill the role of chapter women's division chief?"

"No!" she shouted angrily.

*L*OOKING somewhat at a loss, Shin'ichi said: "I can't get you to understand, then? Well, you've got me stumped. All right, Miss Kiyohara, could you explain the situation to her thoroughly later?"

With this, he concluded the leadership announcements.

He then offered some final words before closing the meeting: "President Toda declared that the Soka Gakkai organization was even more precious to him than his own life. This is because our organization is the lifeline of kosen-rufu. We can think of it as a water-supply system. If the system is in perfect working order, then we only have to turn

the tap to get pure, fresh water. We use this water to quench our thirst, cook our food and wash our bodies; it plays an indispensable role in sustaining our lives.

"The Soka Gakkai, organization, therefore, may be called a 'water-supply system of faith' in that it supplies people with the pure energy of faith and nurtures their capabilities. If the leaders who play key roles in the organization lose their seeking spirit, they will be like pipes disconnected from the water source. Also, if the hearts of leaders are impure, then only dirty water will flow through the pipes. If they fail to take action, the water will grow stagnant and eventually rust the pipes. Moreover, when leaders are on bad terms with one another, it's as if the pipes have ruptured. I therefore hope all of you will work together harmoniously to protect and develop this organization, which has appeared in accord with the Buddha's intent. This is my most cherished wish."

After he finished, he presented each person with a souvenir *fukusa* and a copy of *The Soka Gakkai*, the book that had been published to introduce the organization's activities to

English-speaking audiences. He also spoke encouragingly to each person. When he came upon a woman holding a 2- or 3-month-old infant, he picked the child up in his arms.

"What a cute baby!" Shin'ichi said, gently covering the infant with a *fukusa* that he held in his hand. "This *fukusa* is for your baby," he pronounced.

The woman then addressed Shin'ichi, "Sensei, next year, my husband is being transferred to Seattle, so I will have to move there with him." The Japanese woman was married to a U.S. army officer; she sounded forlorn at the thought of having to move to yet another strange new place in this already unfamiliar country.

"Is that so? I've just recently been to Seattle; it's a wonderful city, you know. The climate is pleasant and the scenery is beautiful. It's great that you'll be going there! What good fortune you have to live in such a wonderful place!"

"Really? I had no idea that Seattle was such a nice place. I've never been there, so I've been worried what it would like," said the woman, her eyes now shining brightly.

A DISTRICT has also been formed in Seattle," Shin'ichi commented, "so please do your best when you get there — ride through the beautiful landscape of mountains and rivers as if you were a queen on a white horse."

"Yes, I will," the woman said cheerfully.

Shin'ichi happened to glance down and noticed a book sticking out from the woman's bag on the floor. The Japanese book *The Collected Treatises of Josei Toda* had just been published by the Soka Gakkai at the end of August.

Smiling, Shin'ichi said: "I didn't know this book had already made its way here! Shall I write something inside to commemorate our meeting? May I ask your name?"

"Yes, it's Masako Clarke."

Handing her baby back to her, Shin'ichi then wrote with swift strokes of his pen: "Illuminated by the Mystic Law / may you soar / like a queen."

"Thank you," said the woman, with tears in her eyes. Her expression reflected her deep resolve to continue struggling courageously in her new home.

A person's frame of mind dramatically affects how he or she looks at things. Buddhism causes the sun of courage to rise in people's hearts, leading them to take everything as a source of hope, joy and growth. Guidance is the catalyst that inspires people to transform their state of mind.

Seeing Shin'ichi signing the book, a young man came up to him and said, "Excuse me, would you mind writing something as a memento for me, too?" It was the youth who had taken their photo at the airport. He had just started practicing the Daishonin's Buddhism one month before.

Shin'ichi wrote: "Faith, practice and study."

This prompted other participants, with books and notepads in hand, to gather around Shin'ichi.

The Soka Gakkai president spoke briefly with each person, thanking all of them for their efforts and penning a short message of encouragement for each.

After the meeting, Shin'ichi gathered all the leaders appointed that day in a separate room. Kazuko Ellick sat in the front row, still obstinately refusing to look in Shin'ichi's direction.

Shin'ichi and the other leaders from Japan had deliberated long and hard over the leadership position they had finally assigned to Mrs. Ellick. Everyone recognized she had applied herself energetically and displayed great enthusiasm in her activities. However, if an organization is to grow and develop, it is essential to forge harmony among the members, use the maximum potential of each person, and raise the organization's overall strength.

Leaders also need to have common sense, be calm and rational, and have a head for details. Given these considerations, even though Kazuko Ellick may have outshone Kiyoko Kuwano in terms of experience in activities and energy to take action, Shin'ichi and the other leaders had concluded that the latter would be a more suitable choice for the position of chapter women's division chief.

*T*HE key to the development of the organization in Los Angeles lay in a firm bond between the two women. The organization's effectiveness is determined by the combination of different individuals. When leaders of various backgrounds, personalities and thinking combine their energies, they can nurture people of rich and diverse ability, creating a broad-minded, humanistic organization capable of facing any problem. The organization's true strength lies only in the harmony of its members.

Mrs. Kuwano and Mrs. Ellick had been appointed to their respective positions in the hope that they would become a powerful combination, supporting and complementing one another, each making up for what the other lacked. Shin'ichi and the leaders from Japan also hoped that by appointing Mrs. Ellick, who had so far shown herself to be capable and hard working as a key figure in activities here in Los Angeles, they would raise the awareness of all the other district chiefs.

Shin'ichi continued in a strict tone: "The Soka Gakkai is, first and foremost, an organization for people and faith — an organization advancing just as the Daishonin teaches. Voicing discontent because you're not appointed the central figure is not an action based on faith. It is nothing but vanity; a sign of selfishness. All it does is undermine the unity of the organization that has appeared in accord with the Buddha's decree. Irrespective of the great achievements they may have attained in their past endeavors, those who behave this way have allowed emotionalism to prevail over faith.

"Equally selfish are those who demur from accepting leadership positions. This is laziness masquerading as humility; it is the sign of a self-centered nature. Buddhist practice means being willing to do anything at all for kosen-rufu, to serve and work for the members. Naturally, there may be various circumstances, such as commitments at work, that make it difficult for you to fulfill a leadership responsibility. If this is the case, please feel free to discuss the matter with us so that we can work something out. Nevertheless, if the fundamental spirit of Buddhist practice is lost, then the Soka Gakkai will no longer be an organization of faith.

"The Daishonin urges, 'Become the master of your mind rather than let your mind master you' (WND-I, 486). America is a land of freedom. But freedom doesn't mean that we can do anything we please in the practice of faith. If we lose sight of the essential point of self-discipline, our hearts and minds will grow muddled and confused. And that means unhappiness. Our human revolution only truly begins when we resolutely determine to fight and live for kosen-rufu based on the Buddhist Law, instead of basing ourselves only on our own minds."

Shin'ichi then addressed the two women, "Mrs. Ellick, Mrs. Kuwano, I'm counting on you to work together harmoniously and pool your efforts with the firm resolve to dedicate your lives to kosen-rufu."

SHIN'ICHI'S tone was stern. "If either of you fail," he continued, "it will be the other's fault. Understood?"

"Yes," responded Kiyoko Kuwano, nodding.

Kazuko Ellick, however, remained tight-lipped.

"Come on, please shake hands. It will reassure everyone," urged Shin'ichi.

Mrs. Kuwano extended her hand and looked at the other woman. But the moment their eyes met, Mrs. Ellick swiftly pulled her hand behind her back.

"This is getting us nowhere," said Shin'ichi with a wry smile.

That evening, some of the newly appointed chapter leaders came to the hotel where Shin'ichi was staying. Here, the Soka Gakkai president concentrated on offering guidance to the chapter chief and the two chapter staff members.

"There is a saying that though it may be easy to break a single arrow, three arrows bound firmly together are not so easily broken. The secret to building a strong chapter is unity. It will be up to the three of you to work solidly together and take responsibility for protecting the members. If this proves too much for you, I will move the chapter to New York."

All three men seemed honest and likable, but they lacked the strong awareness and sense of responsibility necessary for those who would serve as mainstays for the other divisions. Because he had high expectations for these men, Shin'ichi's guidance was strict based on a spirit of true compassion.

"Men play a vital role in securing the unity of the entire organization. Ultimately, the full responsibility for the chapter rests with the men's division. Men must have the magnanimity to tell the women and youth, 'Please carry out your activities freely, to your hearts' content!'

"The less ability and confidence a man has, the more likely he is to put on airs and behave in an authoritarian and arrogant manner. Others may outwardly appear to follow such a person, but in their hearts they will despise him. It is also important that men never, under any circumstances, vent their anger on women or shout at them, for it is women who are working the most earnestly for kosen-rufu. It may have been a tradition in Japan in the past for wives to support their husbands and be supported by them in return, but from now on it will probably be just the opposite. I expect this to be even more so since you are living in America, a country that, unlike Japan, follows the etiquette of 'ladies first.' It is important that men discuss things with women and listen to what they have to say."

ONE of the men asked Shin'ichi: "I don't have the experience or ability to teach people about faith. What should I do when they come seeking my advice as a chapter leader?" It was an earnest question.

Shin'ichi smiled and said: "Don't worry, you can gain experience from this position. Guidance in faith is the basis of the Soka Gakkai. This is different from teaching, which means to inform someone about something you have already learned. Guidance means to point out the direction to advance and then join the members in moving ahead along that path. So all you need to do is say: 'This is what it says in the Gosho. This is what the Soka Gakkai teaches.' You can also chant with them and pray for their happiness. Anyone can do this, but it is the most respectable action we can take as human beings. There is nothing more heartening than having like-minded friends who pray for us. This is the greatest source of strength and encouragement.

"I plan to send leaders from Japan to support your activities in the United States in the near future, so if there's anything you don't understand, please don't hesitate to ask them. A seeking spirit is an important quality for leaders." Shin'ichi then went on to patiently outline the basics of leadership.

When the leaders of the new chapter had left, Shin'ichi's companions gathered in his room.

Shin'ichi sat down in a chair and asked Kiyoshi Jujo, "What time is it in Japan now?"

Looking at his watch, Jujo replied: "It's ten minutes to midnight here. Japan's seventeen hours ahead, so it's almost 5:00 in the afternoon, on the 23rd."

"All right, let's send a telegram to Japan announcing that we've formed chapters in Brazil and Los Angeles," said Shin'ichi.

Jujo left the room to send the telegram. Shin'ichi waited until he returned and said quietly: "How we at the Soka Gakkai Headquarters develop the organization in America will be extremely important. Rather than attaching the overseas organizations to some general chapter in Japan, the Gakkai Headquarters should be directly responsible for them and take active steps to ensure their growth. For that reason, I think we should establish an American general chapter, comprising both North and South America. What do you think?"

Shin'ichi had suggested this idea repeatedly throughout their overseas journey and everyone agreed.

"Good, it's decided then," Shin'ichi announced buoyantly.

PRESIDENT Shin'ichi Yamamoto and the other leaders continued their discussion until well after midnight. Shin'ichi dealt with one issue after another.

"We'll have to think about whom to appoint to oversee the new America General Chapter. For the time being, however, the responsibility of providing overall support will fall on the Soka Gakkai Headquarters. So, Mr. Jujo, would you mind if I appoint you as the general chapter chief?"

"Not at all."

"Miss Kiyohara, I'd like you to be the general chapter women's division chief."

"All right."

"We'll ask Masaki and Aota to serve as the general chapter staff. Let's also upgrade the Headquarters' Overseas Affairs Section into a full-fledged division. We'll increase its staff and boost its operational strength. Joji Kanda is probably the only choice for division head. Let's leave the announcement of leadership appointments for the general chapter and the new Overseas Affairs Division until this month's Headquarters leaders meeting. For the time being, though, let's go ahead and inform Japan that we've established the America General Chapter."

With this, the groundwork for future activities in the United States had been laid. Despite his deep fatigue, Shin'ichi's brain continued to bring forth an endless stream of ideas and plans, and he went on to describe his hope-filled vision for kosen-rufu.

On the evening of October 23, two international telegrams arrived one after the other at the Soka Gakkai Headquarters in Japan. Their contents threw everyone into a state of excitement. The first read: "CHAPTERS FORMED IN LOS ANGELES AND BRAZIL STOP JUJO" (Los Angeles, Oct. 23, 12:02 A.M.); the second: "NORTH AND SOUTH AMERICA MADE GENERAL CHAPTER STOP JUJO" (Los Angeles, Oct. 23, 1:28 A.M.).

Those senior leaders and staff members who were still present at the Headquarters when the telegrams arrived could vividly sense the waves of worldwide kosen-rufu surging powerfully across the seas. They were also deeply touched when they pictured President Yamamoto continuing his valiant struggle into the early hours of the morning.

The next day, Shin'ichi and the other leaders set off on a tour of Los Angeles, visiting, among other places, the University of California at Los Angeles. The campus was wrapped in lush greenery, and birds could be heard chirping in the treetops. Shin'ichi recalled how he and his mentor, Josei Toda, had discussed grand plans for establishing a university. Their conversation had taken place at a time when Toda was struggling amid great hardships, his business having run aground.

"Shin'ichi, let's build a university some day," Toda had said. "Mr. Makiguchi also cherished this idea. If I can't realize it in my lifetime, then you do it. Education, after all, is the foundation on which peace is built."

Shin'ichi would never forget the look in his mentor's eyes as he said this.

Strolling through the campus of UCLA, Shin'ichi said softly to himself, "The Soka Gakkai will build a university — Soka University."

Indeed, only eleven years later this dream would become a reality.

*F*INALLY, it was October 24 — time for Shin'ichi and his party to return to Japan. Forty to fifty well-wishers were waiting in the lobby to see them off when they arrived at the airport shortly after 11:00 A.M. The members gathered around Shin'ichi, the air filled with their joyful chatter.

"Sensei, please come to America again!" said one young woman, looking rather wistful.

"I certainly will. And I'll keep coming back until every one of you is happy. In return, I ask that all of you please come to Japan next year. Let's meet again there. And as a souvenir, please let me see how happy you've become. The greatest gift that you can give me is to say that you have received great benefit and become happy."

As the members engaged in bright and lively conversations, Shin'ichi treated everyone to refreshments. Catching sight of Yuji Nakahara, the Japanese student who had been appointed leader of the young men's division in Los Angeles, the Soka Gakkai president raised his glass of juice and proclaimed, smiling: "To the glorious future of the young people of America!" It was a toast to the development of the youth division, whose members he loved so dearly.

At the very back of the crowd encircling Shin'ichi, a woman stood watching this cordial exchange with a mournful expression. It was Kazuko Ellick. After that fateful discussion meeting at which the Los Angeles Chapter was formed, she had gone home weeping bitterly. She was deeply annoyed and disappointed. "I've worked harder than anyone," she thought. "It's not fair that I wasn't appointed chapter women's division chief!"

She was too worked up to do anything when she got home, her mind in utter turmoil. Deciding she would pour out her innermost feelings to the Gohonzon, she began chanting daimoku. At first, tears flowed steadily, but, as she continued chanting, she gradually calmed down, regaining her composure. Shin'ichi's guidance now returned to her with vivid clarity.

Viewing the situation more objectively, she saw that being disheartened merely because she hadn't been appointed chapter women's division chief was certainly not behaving in a manner that accorded with faith. Instead, this attitude was symptomatic of an egoistic desire for honor and recognition.

Realizing this, she was filled with deep shame and regret over her earlier attitude, convinced now that she had made an irreparable error. She was so distraught she couldn't eat the next day.

"What shall I do?" she thought agonizingly. "Will Sensei forgive me if I apologize sincerely for my behavior? But even if he doesn't, I still must apologize to him."

It was with this resolve that Kazuko Ellick had made her way to the airport.

*K*AZUKO Ellick looked for an opening to apologize to Shin'ichi. But she felt so small and so self-conscious that she couldn't find the right moment to tell him.

Shin'ichi sat down on one of the chairs in the lobby and began to write brief words of encouragement for the members who held out books and notepads.

"Oh, dear, what shall I do?" Kazuko Ellick agonized. "I can't get up the nerve to tell him. But if I don't apologize now, I'll probably regret it for the rest of my life."

Summoning all her resolve, she said, "Sensei!"

Shin'ichi looked up at her.

"I'm sorry! Please forgive me for having been so unreasonable." She bowed deeply and then peered at Shin'ichi somewhat apprehensively. He smiled at her kindly.

"Yes," he said. "It's important to be sincere in faith. Those who are pure-hearted in faith will definitely savor victory in the end."

"Yes, I'll do my best from now on." Mrs. Ellick was deeply grateful, tears glistening on her cheeks. It occurred to her to ask him to write a message for her as well. She held out a book and said, "Sensei, please write something for me, too."

"All right, but you're the last one." Shin'ichi wrote swiftly, "Valiant and assiduous practice — Shin'ichi, October 24, Los Angeles Airport."

He then called over Kiyoko Kuwano, the chapter women's division chief.

"Mrs. Kuwano, I would like you and Mrs. Ellick to get along well. The two of you have probably been sisters from the distant past. If you pool your energies, the organization will be solid. I want you to create the world's most harmonious chapter. I have high expectations for you both."

"Yes!" their voices rang out in unison.

Shin'ichi smiled and nodded in satisfaction.

"Sensei, it's almost time for us to board," Eisuke Akizuki informed him.

Shin'ichi stood up and bowed deeply toward the gathered members.

"Thank you for coming to see us off despite your busy schedules. Let's meet again. I'll be waiting for you in Japan. All the best!"

The members sent him off with a round of applause.

Walking briskly, Shin'ichi took his leave. Like a gentle breeze awakening the frozen earth from its slumber and heralding the arrival of spring, he had made the light of hope shine in their hearts.

JAPAN Airlines Flight 811, with Shin'ichi Yamamoto and his party on board, left Los Angeles at 1:45 P.M. After a brief stopover in Hawaii, the plane continued toward its final destination, Tokyo. An announcement had informed the passengers that their flight would be more than an hour late arriving at Tokyo's Haneda Airport — where they were originally scheduled to land at 9:35 P.M.

It was now almost 10:30 P.M. on October 25 in Japan.

Shin'ichi lay back in his seat and closed his eyes. Though the fever and bouts of diarrhea that had plagued him throughout the trip had left, the muscles in his neck were knotted tightly and his back ached. Yet he felt a pleasant sense of fatigue at having fulfilled his mission and given his utmost to its successful completion.

Looking back, he and his party had left Japan on October 2 and followed a punishing schedule that took them to nine cities in three countries in twenty-four days. In that time, they had realized the formation of two chapters and seventeen districts; they had sown the golden seeds of kosen-rufu in North and South America.

Shin'ichi thought that President Toda would surely be pleased with his endeavors. The face of his beloved mentor came vividly to his mind's eye.

"Asia is next," he thought. "We must do our best to bring the brilliant light of peace and happiness to shine on Asia, just as Sensei hoped when he wrote:

To the people of Asia
Who yearn to see
The moon hidden
Behind the vast expanse of cloud —
I vow to send the light of the sun."

Shin'ichi's plans were already in place.

"Pioneers" Notes:

1. Vargas regime: The government of President Getúlio D. Vargas (1883–1954), who was the dictator of Brazil from 1930–45.

2. Seven Bells: At the 18th Spring General Meeting held on May 3, 1958, one month after President Toda's death, Shin'ichi Yamamoto had outlined a 21-year vision for the Soka Gakkai. This was based on observations made by the second Soka Gakkai president, Josei Toda, before his death that the organization's development had been punctuated by momentous events every seven years since its establishment. Toda used the allegory of ringing a bell to mark the start of each new era, and proposed that the Soka Gakkai ring in seven bells as a mid-range goal.

According to Toda, the first bell started ringing in 1930, when the Soka Kyoiku Gakkai (Society for Value-creating Education), the forerunner of the Soka Gakkai, was formed. The second began in 1937, when the organization held its first formal inauguration meeting; the third in 1944, when the first president, Tsunesaburo Makiguchi, died in prison; and the fourth in 1951, when Mr. Toda became the second president.

After Toda's death in 1958, following the accomplishment of a membership of 750,000 households, Shin'ichi declared the start of the fifth bell. During the seven-year period from 1958 to 1965, Shin'ichi pledged to accomplish President Toda's wish for a membership of 3 million households. When the sixth bell began to ring in 1965, the goal would be to achieve 6 million households. In 1972, at the start of the seventh bell, it would be to realize the construction of the Sho-Hondo (Grand Main Temple) at Head Temple Taiseki-ji. During the final seven-year period ending in 1979, the goal would be to form a solid framework for the kosen-rufu movement in Japan, while also beginning a full-fledged era for the kosen-rufu movement around the world.

Index

More on Nichiren Buddhism
and Its Application to Daily Life

*The following titles can be purchased from your local
or on-line bookseller, or go to the Middleway Press Web site
(www.middlewaypress.org).*

**Unlocking the Mysteries of Birth and Death...
and Everything In Between,** by Daisaku Ikeda
(ISBN 0-9723267-0-7; $15.00)

"Strength and wisdom, Buddhism explains, derive from
life force. If we cultivate sufficient life force, we cannot
only withstand life's adversities but transform them into
causes of happiness and empowerment."

This introduction to Nichiren Buddhism explores the philo-
sophical intricacies of life and reveals the wonder inherent in
the phases of birth, aging, and death. Core concepts of
Nichiren Buddhism, such as the Ten Worlds and the nine
consciousnesses, illustrate the profundity of human existence. This book provides Buddhists with the tools they
need to fully appreciate the connectedness of all beings and
to revolutionize their spiritual lives based on this insight.
Ultimately, this is both a work of popular philosophy and a
book of compelling, compassionate inspiration for Buddhist
and non-Buddhists alike that fosters a greater understanding
of Nichiren Buddhism.

On Being Human : Where Ethics, Medicine and Spirituality Converge, by René Simard, Guy Bourgeault and Daisaku Ikeda
(ISBN 0-9674697-1-5; $15.95)

"*On Being Human* is an elegant and timely dialogue. Accessible yet profound, it illustrates the convergence of medical science, bioethics and Buddhist philosophy. Informative and hopeful, it offers wise perspectives on life and death, revealing their deeper meaning and higher purpose. Its three sagacious voices speak as one, to all."

—Lou Marinoffm, author of *Plato Not Prozac* and *The Big Question*

Choose Hope: Your Role in Waging Peace in the Nuclear Age, by David Krieger and Daisaku Ikeda
(ISBN 0-9674697-6-7; $23.95)

"In this nuclear age, when the future of humankind is imperiled by irrational strategies, it is imperative to restore sanity to our policies and hope to our destiny. Only a rational analysis of our problems can lead to their solution. This book is an example par excellence of a rational approach."

—Joseph Rotblat, Nobel Peace Prize laureate

For the Sake of Peace: Seven Paths to Global Harmony, A Buddhist Perspective, by Daisaku Ikeda
Winner of the NAPRA Nautilus Award 2002
for Social Change
(Paperback: ISBN 0-9674697-9-1; $14.00.
Hardcover: ISBN 0-9674697-2-4; $25.95)

"At a time when we squander enormous amounts of human and environmental resources on the study of and preparation

for making war, *For the Sake of Peace* stands as a primary text in the study and practice of making peace.
—NAPRA, Nautilus Award citation

"…a passionate, intelligent plea for mindfulness in both individual and societal action."
—*ForeWord* magazine

Soka Education: A Buddhist Vision for Teachers, Students and Parents, by Daisaku Ikeda
(ISBN 0-9674697-4-0; $23.95)
From the Japanese word meaning "to create value," this book presents a fresh spiritual perspective to question the ultimate purpose of education. Mixing American pragmatism with Buddhist philosophy, the goal of Soka education is the lifelong happiness of the learner.

"[Teachers] will be attracted to Soka and Ikeda's plea that educators bring heart and soul back to education."
—*Teacher* magazine

"Ikeda's practical perscription places students' needs first, empowers teachers, and serves as a framework for global citizenship."
—George David Miller, professor, Lewis University

The Way of Youth: Buddhist Common Sense for Handling Life's Questions, by Daisaku Ikeda
(ISBN 0-9674697-0-8; $14.95)
"[This book] shows the reader how to flourish as a young person in the world today; how to build confidence and character in modern society; learn to live with respect for

oneself and others; how to contribute to a positive, free and peaceful society; and find true personal happiness."
—Midwest Book Review

The Buddha in Your Mirror: Practical Buddhism and the Search for Self, by Woody Hochswender, Greg Martin and Ted Morino
(Paperback: ISBN0-9674697-8-3; $14.00
Hardcover: ISBN 0-9674697-1-6; $23.95)
A bestselling Buddhist primer that reveals the most modern, effective and practical way to achieve what is called enlightenment or Buddhahood. Based on the centuries-old teaching of the Japanese Buddhist master Nichiren, this method has been called the "direct path" to enlightenment.

"Like the Buddha, this book offers practical guidelines to overcome difficulties in everyday life and to be helpful to others. Readers will find these pages are like a helpful and supportive friend. I enthusiastically recommend it."
—Dr. David Chappell, editor of *Buddhist Peacework: Creating Cultures of Peace*

The following titles can be purchased at SGI-USA bookstores nationwide or through the SGI-USA mail order center: call 800-626-1313 or e-mail mailorder@sgi-usa.org.

The Quotable Nichiren: Words for Daily Living
(World Tribune Press, mail order #4281, $12.95)
This easy-to-use, portable reference makes it a snap to find your favorite passage from Nichiren's writings and helps you discover new favorites. With more than 700 passages

arranged under more than 80 topics, *The Quotable Nichiren* gives you a concise introduction to Buddhist philosophy in , Nichiren's own words.

My First Book of Buddhist Treasures,
Illustrated by Peggy Walker
(Treasure Tower Press, mail order #6158, $8.95)
This book, tailored for ages 5-8, presents very short quotes from *The Writings of Nichiren Daishonin* along with a brief explanation and questions for discussion. Arranged by topics suitable for this age group, concepts of our Buddhist practice are highlighted with colorful illustrations and easy-to-understand explanations.

My Dear Friends in America, by Daisaku Ikeda
(World Tribune Press, mail order #4104, $19.95)
This volume brings together for the first time all of the SGI president's speeches to U.S. members in the 1990s.

The Wisdom of the Lotus Sutra, vols. 1–6,
By Daisaku Ikeda, Katsuji Saito, Takanori Endo
and Haruo Suda
Volume 1 (World Tribune Press, mail order #4281, $9.95)
Volume 2 (World Tribune Press, mail order #4282, $9.95)
Volume 3 (World Tribune Press, mail order #4283, $10.95)
Volume 4 (World Tribune Press, mail order #4284, $10.95)
Volume 5 (World Tribune Press, mail order #4285, $10.95)
Volume 6 (World Tribune Press, mail order #4286, $10.95)
A captivating dialogue on the 28-chapter Lotus Sutra that

brings this ancient writing's important messages into practical application for daily life and for realizing a peaceful world.

The Winning Life: An Introduction to Buddhist Practice
(World Tribune Press, mail order #4105 [English], 4106 [Spanish], 4107 [Chinese], 4113 [Korean]; $1.00)
Using plain language, this booklet gives a quick-yet-detailed introduction to a winning way of life based on Nichiren Daishonin's teachings. A perfect tool for introducing other to the benefits of practice.

Faith into Action: Thoughts on Selected Topics,
By Daisaku Ikeda
(World Tribune Press, mail order #4135, $12.95)
A collection of inspirational excerpts arranged by subject. Perfect for finding just the right quote to encourage yourself or a friend or when preparing for a meeting.

For Today and Tomorrow: Daily Encouragement,
By Daisaku Ikeda
(World Tribune Press, mail order #4100, $16.95)
Daily words of encouragement that are sure to inspire, comfort and even challenge you in your practice of faith. Great for the newest member and seasoned practitioners.

A Youthful Diary: One Man's Journey From the Beginning of Faith to Worldwide Leadership for Peace,
By Daisaku Ikeda
(World Tribune Press, mail order #4101, $23.95)
Youthful inspiration for people of all ages. Through the tale of the ever-deepening relationship between the young Daisaku Ikeda and his mentor-in-life, Josei Toda, *A Youthful Diary* is a compelling account of both triumphs and setbacks on the road to establishing the foundation of today's Soka Gakkai.